Sustaining Prosperity

Edited by

Peter Dawkins and Michael Stutchbury

Introduction by

Paul Kelly,
Editor-at-Large,

and Alan Wood,
Economics Editor,
The Australian

MELBOURNE UNIVERSITY PRESS
An imprint of Melbourne University Publishing Ltd
187 Grattan Street, Carlton, Victoria 3053, Australia
mup-info@unimelb.edu.au
www.mup.com.au

First published 2005
Text © The University of Melbourne, 2005, and Nationwide News Limited, 2005
Copyright in the individual pieces remains with the respective authors.
Design and typography © Melbourne University Publishing Ltd 2005

This book is copyright. Apart from any use permitted under the *Copyright Act 1968* and subsequent amendments, no part may be reproduced, stored in a retrieval system or transmitted by any means or process whatsoever without the prior written permission of the publishers.

Cover design by Sandra Nobes
Typeset in Malaysia by Syarikat Seng Teik Sdn. Bhd.
Printed and bound by CPI Group (UK) Ltd, Croydon, CR0 4YY

National Library of Australia Cataloguing-in-Publication entry

Sustaining prosperity.

ISBN 0 522 85206 8.

1. Sustainable development – Australia. 2. Australia—Economic conditions.
3. Australia – Social conditions. I. Dawkins, Peter. II. Stutchbury, Michael, 1957–.

338.994

CONTENTS

ACKNOWLEDGEMENTS

This book is based upon the April 2005 Economic and Social Outlook Conference, *Sustaining Prosperity*, organised jointly by the Melbourne Institute of Applied Economic and Social Research at the University of Melbourne and *The Australian*. Thanks to all the staff at the Melbourne Institute and *The Australian* who made this conference possible. We also gratefully acknowledge the support provided to the conference by The University of Melbourne, The Productivity Commission, Telstra and the Australian Bureau of Statistics.

Thanks to all the speakers at the conference. We have been able to include only a selection of the papers presented. The choice of papers is explained in the Editors' Overview. The other papers and presentations can be downloaded from the Web at www.melbourneinstitute.com.

A special thanks also to Mark Wooden, Deputy Director of the Melbourne Institute and one of the contributors to the book, who provided considerable assistance to us in editing the manuscript.

Finally, many thanks to Louise Adler and Felicity Edge of Melbourne University Publishing for their enthusiastic commitment to this project, and to Heidi McLean of the Melbourne Institute for her administrative assistance.

Peter Dawkins and Michael Stutchbury

CONTRIBUTORS

The Hon. Kim Beazley MP
Leader of the Opposition
Kim Beazley has Masters degrees in Arts and Philosophy, and is a former lecturer in social and political theory at Murdoch University. He has a long and distinguished parliamentary career that commenced in 1980; he served as a Minister throughout much of the period of the Hawke/Keating Labor governments of the 1980s and 1990s. In March 1996 he became Leader of the Opposition and the federal Labor Party, a position he held until just after the 2001 federal election. On 28 January 2005 he was once again elected by his parliamentary colleagues to the leadership of the federal Labor Party.

The Hon. John Brumby MP
Treasurer and Minister for Innovation, State & Regional Development (Victoria)
John Brumby is the senior economic Minister in the Bracks Government. He was elected to the Victorian Parliament in 1993, where he was Leader of the Opposition for almost six years. Prior to that he was a Federal MP in the Hawke Labor government between 1983 and 1990. He has a Commerce degree from the University of Melbourne and is currently the Treasurer of Victoria; Minister for State and Regional Development; and Minister for Innovation.

Mr Michael Chaney AO
Managing Director and Chief Executive Officer, Wesfarmers
Michael Chaney graduated with Bachelor of Science and Master of Business Administration degrees from the University of Western Australia in 1972

and 1980 respectively. He subsequently completed the Advanced Management Program at Harvard Business School in 1992. He joined Wesfarmers in 1983 as Company Secretary and Administration Manager, became Finance Director in 1984 and was appointed Managing Director in July 1992. Michael is also a director of BHP Billiton, National Australia Bank and Gresham Partners Holdings, and holds a number of other appointments with a range of business, community and charitable organisations. He is currently Vice-President of the Business Council of Australia.

Mr Greg Combet
Secretary, Australian Council of Trade Unions
Greg Combet became Secretary of the ACTU in February 2000. He has tertiary qualifications in engineering, economics and labour relations and the law. He worked as a miner and in minerals exploration before being employed by the NSW Tenants' Union as a project officer and then by the Lidcombe Workers' Health Centre. Greg started work with the Waterside Workers' Federation in 1987. He became a Senior Industrial Officer at the ACTU in 1993 and was elected ACTU Assistant Secretary in 1996. During his time at the ACTU, Greg has worked with unions representing employees in a wide variety of industries, has overseen the ACTU's Minimum Wage case for low-paid workers, and has coordinated numerous union campaigns.

The Hon. Peter Costello MP
Treasurer and Deputy Leader of the Liberal Party
Peter Costello was first elected a Member of the House of Representatives for the seat of Higgins in 1990. In 1994 he was elected Deputy Leader of the Liberal Party of Australia and since 1996 he has been the Treasurer of the Commonwealth of Australia. He was also the Chairman of the OECD in 2000. He holds degrees from Monash University where he was, for a time, a part-time teacher in Law and Economics/Politics, as well as a member of the University Council. Prior to entering parliament, he was a barrister, during which time he was counsel in some of Australia's best-known industrial disputes.

Mr David Crawford
Acting President, National Competition Council
David Crawford is Chair of Westralia Airports Corporation, Export Grains Centre Ltd and chair of the Curtin University Graduate School of Business (Board of Advisors). He holds a number of other appointments with a range of business and community organisations. His earlier employment

career included two years with Ranger Minerals NL, seven years with Wesfarmers, of which he was Managing Director of Western Collieries Ltd for four years and Corporate Affairs Director for three years, and 12 years with CSR. He has an Honours degree in Economics from the University of Queensland and a Masters degree in Political Science from the University of Toronto.

Professor Peter Dawkins
Director and Ronald Henderson Professor, Melbourne Institute of Applied Economic and Social Research, University of Melbourne
At the time of the conference, Peter Dawkins was Director of the Melbourne Institute, a position he was appointed to in 1996. Prior to that he was Professor of Economics at Curtin University of Technology. In 1999–2000 he was a member of the federal government's Reference Group on Welfare Reform, and since 2001 has been a member of the Welfare Reform Consultative Forum. He has also been a member of the Australian Statistics Advisory Council (since 1999) and of the Prime Minister's Science Engineering and Innovation Council (since 2003). He was elected a Fellow of the Academy of Social Sciences in Australia in 2001. He has recently taken up the position of Deputy Secretary at the Victorian Department of Treasury and Finance (DTF). Views expressed in the joint editorial with Michael Stutchbury were written prior to his appointment to DTF and should not be regarded as the views of the Victorian government.

The Hon. Peter Dutton MP
Minister for Workforce Participation
Peter Dutton was appointed federal Minister for Workforce Participation after the October 2004 election. As such, he is responsible for the Job Network, Disability Employment Services, Work for the Dole, and improving transition to work opportunities for all unemployed Australians. Prior to entering parliament in November 2001 as the Member for the Queensland seat of Dickson, Mr Dutton was an officer in the Queensland Police Service for nine years and later managed his family's small business. He attended the Queensland University of Technology and holds a degree in Business.

Dr Craig Emerson MP
House of Representatives
Craig Emerson is the federal Member for Rankin, and chair of the Caucus Economic Committee. He was elected to parliament in 1998 and served in the shadow ministry from 2001 to 2004. Previous appointments include Economic Adviser to Prime Minister Bob Hawke, Economic Adviser to

Finance Minister Peter Walsh and Senior Policy Adviser to Premier Wayne Goss. He has also been CEO of the Southeast Queensland Transit Authority, Director-General of the Queensland Department of Environment and Heritage, and Assistant Secretary, Industries, Trade and Resources Division in the Department of the Prime Minister and Cabinet. He holds degrees in Economics from the University of Sydney and a PhD, also in Economics, from the Australian National University.

Professor John Freebairn

Professor of Economics and Director of the Melbourne Institute of Applied Economic and Social Research, University of Melbourne
John Freebairn succeeded Peter Dawkins as the Director of the Melbourne Institute in April 2005. He is also a Professor within the Department of Economics, a position he has held since 1996. Prior to that he held professorial appointments at both Monash and La Trobe Universities. The author of numerous academic publications, he is widely acknowledged as one of Australia's leading applied economic policy analysts. He has a particular interest in the analysis of policy options for taxation reform, labour markets (particularly unemployment), infrastructure pricing and investment, and microeconomic reform.

Professor Ross Garnaut AO

Professor of Economics, Australian National University
Ross Garnaut is Professor of Economics in the Research School of Pacific and Asian Studies at the Australian National University (since 1989). He chairs the ANU's China Economy and Business Program, and the editorial boards of the journals *Asia Pacific Economic Literature* and *Bulletin of Indonesian Economic Studies*. He is a member of the Boards of the Lowy Institute for International Policy (Sydney), Asialink (Melbourne), Centre for Strategic and International Studies (Jakarta), Centre for International Research (Washington) and the China Centre for Economic Research (Beijing). He is also chairman of several companies. His previous positions include Australian Ambassador to China (1985–88), Senior Economic Adviser to Prime Minister Hawke (1983–85) and Chairman of the Australian Centre for International Agricultural Research (1994–2000).

Associate Professor Bruce Headey

Principal Fellow, Melbourne Institute of Applied Economic and Social Research, University of Melbourne
Bruce Headey joined the Melbourne Institute in 2003 as a Principal Fellow. Formerly the Director of the Centre for Public Policy at the University of

Melbourne, he is a specialist in welfare and distributional issues and at the forefront of current international research into the efficacy of social welfare policies in Western Europe and North America. He has published extensively in Australia on this and related issues concerning life satisfaction, subjective wellbeing and income inequality. He is currently Deputy Director of the Household, Income and Labour Dynamics in Australia (HILDA) Survey Project, and is overseeing the Melbourne Institute's longitudinal survey research agenda.

Dr Ken Henry
Secretary, Department of the Treasury
Ken Henry was appointed Secretary to the Treasury in April 2001. He is ex officio member of the Board of the Reserve Bank of Australia and the Board of Taxation, and Australia's Alternate Governor at the IMF. Previous positions include executive director of Treasury's economic group, Head of Treasury's taxation policy division, and minister (economic and financial affairs) in the Australian delegation to the OECD. He was a Senior Adviser in the office of the Treasurer from 1986 to 1991. Ken has a PhD in Economics from the University of Canterbury (NZ), where he lectured for some years before rejoining the APS in 1984.

Mr Paul Kelly
Editor-At-Large, The Australian
Paul Kelly is Editor-at-Large of *The Australian* and was previously Editor-in-Chief (1991–96). He writes on Australian and international issues and is the author of six successful books, including *The Hawke Ascendancy* and *The End of Certainty*. He presented the 2001 five-part television documentary for the ABC on Australian history and character, '100 Years—The Australian Story' and wrote a book with the same title. In 2003 he co-edited *Hard Heads, Soft Hearts*, a new domestic reform agenda for Australia.

A Fellow of the Academy of Social Sciences in Australia, in 2002 he was a visiting fellow at the Kennedy School of Government and a visiting lecturer at the Weatherhead Center for International Affairs at Harvard University.

Mr Andrew McCallum
President, Australian Council of Social Service
Andrew McCallum commenced his working life as a primary school teacher after completing a Diploma of Teaching at Ballarat Teachers' College. After studying in the United Kingdom he moved into the welfare sector, working in a variety of roles before taking up his current position as CEO of St Luke's Anglicare in the Loddon Mallee region of Victoria.

Andrew has held many board positions on state and national bodies, including President of the Children's Welfare Association of Victoria and Chairperson of the Child and Family Welfare Association of Australia. He was the past President of the Victorian Council of Social Service, and during 1999–2001 was a Board and Executive Member of the Australian Council of Social Service (ACOSS), before being elected its President in 2001.

The Hon. Dr Brendan Nelson MP

Minister for Education, Science and Training

Elected to represent the Sydney electorate of Bradfield for the Liberal Party of Australia in 1996, Brendan Nelson was appointed by the Prime Minister to Cabinet as Minister for Education, Science and Training in November 2001. He has been a key contributor on a range of government policy committees including Health, Communications, Treasury, and was Secretary of the Government's Workplace Relations Policy Committee. A general practitioner by training and a graduate of Flinders University in South Australia, Dr Nelson at the age of 35 was the youngest doctor to have ever been elected to the Federal Presidency of the AMA, a position he held from 1993 to 1995. He had previously served as its Federal Vice-President and Tasmanian Branch President.

Mr Tony Nicholson

Executive Director, Brotherhood of St Laurence

Tony Nicholson is the Executive Director of the Brotherhood of St Laurence and has dedicated almost 25 years to improving the conditions of those living on or close to the edges of society. Tony spent 14 years as Chief Executive Officer of Hanover Welfare Services, a Melbourne-based organisation regarded as Australia's leading agency in the field of homelessness. He has brought to the task of leadership at the Brotherhood a strong record of service development and innovation, research and policy analysis, and compelling advocacy on behalf of those disadvantaged in our community.

Mr Michael Stutchbury

Editor, The Australian

Since joining *The Australian* in September 1998, Michael Stutchbury has refashioned the newspaper's business section with a two-pronged emphasis on the new mass shareholder base and the new economy areas of media, telecommunications and the Internet. His appointments included Deputy Editor of *The Weekend Australian*, Deputy Editor (Business) and Business Editor of *The Australian* before his current appointment as Editor. Prior to joining *The Australian*, he worked at *The Australian Financial Review* where he worked his way up from the Canberra Press Gallery to Deputy Editor. Michael has an Honours degree in Economics from the University of Adelaide.

The Hon. Wayne Swan MP
Shadow Treasurer
Wayne Swan is the federal Member for the Brisbane seat of Lilley and Labor's Shadow Treasurer. He was formerly Shadow Minister for Family and Community Services. Between 1993 and 1996 he chaired the Caucus Economics Committee and was involved in the development of the Working Nation reforms. Wayne was previously an adviser to Kim Beazley, Bill Hayden and Mick Young. He was State Secretary of the Queensland Branch of the Labor Party from 1991 to 1993. He has also been a lecturer at the Queensland University of Technology.

Mr Malcolm Turnbull MP
House of Representatives
Malcolm Turnbull was elected as the federal Member for Wentworth at the general election on 9 October 2004. Prior to entering parliament he had enjoyed highly successful careers as a journalist, lawyer and businessman. He is particularly well known for his role in leading the republican case at the Australian Constitutional Convention in 1997 and in the subsequent referendum. He has degrees in law from both the University of Sydney and Oxford (which he attended as a Rhodes Scholar).

Mr Alan Wood
Economics Editor, The Australian
Alan Wood has been Economics Editor of *The Australian* since 1990. He is one of Australia's most experienced and respected economic journalists and has played a key role in the national economic debate. A graduate of the Australian National University, he began his career in the mid 1960s with *The Australian Financial Review.* He has been European Correspondent for *The Financial Review* and Economics Editor of *The Sydney Morning Herald* and *The National Time* and *National Economics* Editor of the Seven Network. Before joining *The Australian,* he was Managing Director of Australia's leading economic consultancy, Syntec Economic Services.

Professor Mark Wooden
Professorial Fellow, Melbourne Institute, University of Melbourne
Mark Wooden is Professorial Fellow and Deputy Director of the Melbourne Institute. He was previously Professor and Acting Director at the National

Institute of Labour Studies, Flinders University, where he had been employed for 19 years. The author of four books and more than 100 journal articles and other academic publications, Mark's main area of research interest has been the operation of labour markets in Australia and, in particular, how these are affected by institutions. He is also Director of the HILDA Survey project, Australia's first large-scale household panel survey.

EDITORS' OVERVIEW

This book contains selected papers and speeches from the *Sustaining Prosperity* conference in April 2005, hosted by the Melbourne Institute and *The Australian*. This was the third conference since 2002 in a series of influential economic and social outlook conferences, with an important focus on the reform agenda. They have become recognised as Australia's most important policy conferences.

The papers in this book were mostly presented at sessions on economic reform, industrial relations, welfare reform, tax reform, competition policy and the wellbeing of Australians. The major theme is about reforms that may be needed to sustain the economic prosperity enjoyed since the early 1990s.

There were a number of other papers and presentations, especially in sessions on the important issues of education policy and health policy. They could fill two more books. In this book we include just one paper on education, the speech by the Federal Minister of Education, Brendan Nelson, and none specifically on health. This should not be interpreted as implying that health and education reform are unimportant ingredients in the reform agenda. The additional papers and presentations, which have not been included in this book, can be obtained from the Melbourne Institute website, www.melbourneinstitute.com. These include speeches by Shadow Minister Jenny Macklin, as well as papers by a number of experts on various aspects of health and education. They are listed at the back of this book.

THE SUSTAINING PROSPERITY CONFERENCE: BACKGROUND AND KEY THEMES

The first of the three economic and social outlook conferences to date, in April 2002, *Towards Opportunity and Prosperity*, highlighted how the economic reforms from the 1980s had made possible the economic success story of the 1990s. But it also highlighted the social problem of about one in six children living in jobless households. Thus, although it was important to maintain pressure on economic reform it was important to achieve a richer blend of economic and social progress. The book *Hard Heads, Soft Hearts: A New Reform Agenda for Australia*, (Dawkins and Kelly, 2003) was the result.

The major theme of the 2003 *Pursuing Opportunity and Prosperity* conference, following the *Intergenerational Report* produced by the Commonwealth Treasury, was the ageing population and rising dependency ratio. The case for raising labour force participation as well as trying to sustain high productivity growth was the central policy agenda discussed. If this could be achieved, the rising fiscal burden due to projected growth in health and other costs would greatly ameliorate the problem and ensure an era of rising prosperity for the next generation. A reform agenda to achieve this was set out in *Reforming Australia* (Dawkins and Steketee (eds), MUP, 2004), following the conference.

With these two conferences behind them, about fifty leading thinkers from academia, politics, public service, business unions and community groups gathered at the April 2005 conference where they presented their research evidence and policy ideas with a central focus on sustaining prosperity.

The thrust of the two previous conferences and associated books was not contested. But a major new concern emerged. Was the economy on as strong a footing? Had we been suffering from a serious problem of reform fatigue over the past few years that threatened continuing prosperity? Were there serious bottlenecks in the economy, which meant that we would have to slow the economy for a period? And after a period of slower growth, would we be in position to return to stronger growth before long, or was the supply side of the economy not going to be responsive because of the lack of a reform program? Ross Garnaut led the charge with this critique.

Before presenting a selection of the papers and speeches from the conference, we present two articles written for *The Weekend Australian* the day after the conference, by Paul Kelly and Alan Wood respectively, to summarise the main themes that emerged. Paul Kelly highlights the evidence that Ann Harding presented to the conference, which suggests that the Howard government has continued the tradition of using taxation revenue to redistribute income from the rich to the poor. Thus it has shown commitment to an egalitarian redistributive role for government and disbursing much of the fiscal dividend from economic growth to low-income families. Questions were arising, however, about whether it has been as committed to an economic reform agenda to achieve a sustained prosperity. It is this topic that Alan Wood develops further.

ECONOMIC REFORM

The economic debate was central to the conference. Will Australia's outstanding productivity performance continue? Should flat export growth ring alarm bells? How big is the ageing threat? What is the answer to reform fatigue? Ross Garnaut's argument and suggested policy implications are reproduced in chapter 4.

Treasury Secretary Ken Henry focused on Australia's international engagement and reform. He emphasised the ongoing importance of international engagement as part of the domestic reform agenda. Productivity Commission Chairman Gary Banks focused on the policy implications of an ageing population, the subject of a report that the Productivity Commission has now completed and which is separately available.

Peter Costello's discussion of economic reform centred mainly on welfare to work. Kim Beazley took the opportunity of the conference to offer the ALP as the party of reform in the tradition of the Hawke-Keating governments of the 1980s. His speech appears in chapter 2, immediately following Peter Costello's chapter 1.

FEDERAL–STATE RELATIONS

Federal–state relations was an important theme. Victorian Treasurer John Brumby made a strong plea for a broad reform agenda to increase productivity and participation, requiring Commonwealth and State governments to cooperate.

David Crawford, the acting Chairman of the National Competition Council, argued for a continuing focus on national competition policy, and regretted the Commonwealth government's announcement that it will cease to make competition payment to the states if they generated reforms in the national interest. Rod Sims presented an overview of his analysis (undertaken for the Business Council of Australia) of the deficiency of investment in infrastructure as well as reforms needed to improve the efficiency of Australia's infrastructure. Rod Sims' presentation can be found at www.melbourneinstitute.com.

THE WELLBEING OF AUSTRALIANS, SOCIAL POLICY, WELFARE TAX AND INDUSTRIAL RELATIONS REFORM

The wellbeing of Australians was explored in the first session of the conference. How prosperous have we become? Is inequality rising or falling? What about the homeless and marginalised? Mark Wooden (chapter 7) from the Melbourne Institute presented evidence from the survey of Household, Income and Labour Dynamics in Australia (HILDA), to complement Ann Harding's evidence discussed by Paul Kelly, with a particular emphasis on the longitudinal nature of the HILDA data. The longitudinal survey has been going long enough now to begin to provide some insights into the persistence of such things as poverty and jobless households. Tony Nicholson of the Brotherhood of St Laurence (chapter 9) also spoke in this session, arguing for a new social policy for the new economy.

On moving people from welfare to work Treasurer Peter Costello used the conference to espouse the case for imposing obligations on lone parents to seek employment, in return for receiving income support. In addition to the Treasurer, the Minister for Workforce Participation, Peter Dutton, provided an overview of the government's approach to welfare reform. The President of ACOSS Andrew McCallum, highlighted welfare reform issues of concern to the welfare sector.

In the area of industrial relations, tax and welfare reform, Michael Chaney of Wesfarmers and the Business Council of Australia argued strongly for further industrial relations reform. One of his arguments, based on advice from Chris Richardson of Access Economics, another speaker at the conference, is that industrial relations does not provide an effective way to achieve equity objectives. If you want to increase the incomes of the low wage earners in low-income families, the tax-transfer system provides better instruments. Greg Combet supported the use of the tax-transfer system to achieve equity objectives but argued that higher minimum wages should also be pursued.

Others at the conference, for example, three of 'the five economists' (Ross Garnaut, Chris Richardson and Peter Dawkins), and the Shadow Treasurer, Wayne Swan, did not contest the idea of increasing obligations on welfare recipients, but argued strongly that the financial incentive to work should also be improved.

John Freebairn from the University of Melbourne joined Malcolm Turnbull in arguing for tax reform with a particular focus on broadening the income tax base and lowering tax rates. Malcolm Turnbull (chapter 17) and Craig Emerson (chapter 16), backbenchers from the Liberal Party and the ALP respectively, spoke in the final session of the conference.

CONCLUSIONS

Since the October 2004 federal election there has been growing doubt about the sustainability of the Australian economic success story and growing calls for more urgency in an economic reform agenda. This reached a crescendo at the *Sustaining Prosperity* conference. It is incumbent upon Commonwealth and state governments to take these calls seriously. By drawing together some of the main contributions to the conference in this volume, the Melbourne Institute and *The Australian* seek to maintain some momentum in this push. In the tradition of the Economic and Social Outlook Conferences, the importance of using economic success for social progress must also be emphasised. This is one of the reasons that welfare reform and education reform, for example, need to be two of the important ingredients of the reform program, along with infrastructure, tax and industrial relations reform.

Peter Dawkins and Michael Stutchbury

Views expressed by Peter Dawkins in this joint editorial with Michael Stutchbury were written prior to his appointment to the Victorian Department of Treasury and Finance and should not be regarded as the views of the Victorian government.

INTRODUCTION: THE HOWARD SURPRISE

'The Prime Minister's true economic performance—perhaps the reason for his electoral success—is only now becoming clear as the Australian economy faces a creeping threat', says The Australian's *Editor-at-Large, Paul Kelly.*

The Howard government suffered a strange fate this week—its record on equity and income distribution has been upheld after years of criticism while its economic management credentials are being called into doubt.

This complete reversal of orthodoxy provided the undercurrent to the third Sustaining Prosperity conference in Melbourne, jointly hosted by *The Australian* and the Melbourne Institute of Applied Economic and Social Research.

Ross Garnaut damned the past five years of the Howard government as the 'great complacency', warned that several further interest rate rises may be required and said that Australia had regressed to the point where short-term politics dictated too much economic policy. He insisted that only a bold reform program would 'break the complacency' suffocating the prosperity cycle and, by implication, threatening the Howard government.

Access Economics director Chris Richardson said: 'Our prosperity is under threat and we've run out of reform juice. Something's got to happen

—this is not just about the federal government, it's about the Opposition and it's about the states.' In short, there is a dangerous gap between economic need and the centre of political gravity across the nation.

In his conference dinner address, Treasurer Peter Costello refused to concede to such pessimism but he did point to the collapse of the 1960s cycle and say that 'without strong economic management and continuing reform, this expansion too could end badly'.

Costello said that down the track Australia will face 'a long-term structural shortage of labour' driven by demography. Nothing can avert this. So solutions to the present supply-side constraints must fold into the long-run challenge and that means 'boosting participation by those who are not presently looking to join the workforce'.

He enunciated a new principle—a welfare system that 'focuses on workforce participation first'. This would be a political revolution if taken seriously. Cabinet, it seems, is moving towards welfare reform along with industrial relations reform.

The mood at the conference was sceptical about whether prosperity could be sustained. This generated, in turn, a greater demand for across-the-board reform and a concern that the Howard government's response was too vapid and narrow.

This mood and the growth slowdown (down to 1.5 per cent) has emboldened Labor Opposition Leader Kim Beazley, who donned the mantle of economic reformer and attacked John Howard for a 'massive squandering of a once-in-a-generation opportunity' to build prosperity. But Beazley will need a credible agenda to sustain himself as a reformer.

The most arresting conference address, however, came on equity issues from Ann Harding, Director of the National Centre for Economic and Social Modelling, whose results, as further developed, may demand a complete re-evaluation of the Howard government.

Summarising her work, Harding told this newspaper: 'From our work we believe that the distribution of final income over the period from the mid-1990s to 2001–02 remained much the same. That is, we don't believe that Australia became more unequal and there may be evidence that it became a little more equal. We were surprised by this.' Harding's research shows that the prosperity of the Howard years has been spread across all income deciles. This is shown by an income breakdown and a postcode analysis. 'The spread of income growth is very positive and there is strong growth at the bottom—the bottom hasn't been left out,' Harding says.

A more critical result comes from the final income analysis that includes the effect of direct and indirect tax, welfare payments and indirect benefits in health, education and welfare.

This shows that the Australian tax and welfare system under Howard is a powerful engine to redistribute substantial cash and resources from the better-off to the lower-income deciles. The extent of this transfer is striking. The top 40 per cent is supporting the bottom 60 per cent.

'Our welfare state has been very successful at redistributing income from the rich to the poor,' Harding says. 'The transfers involved are substantial and when I presented these findings in the US, there was a lot of surprise. This [the Howard government] has actually been a high-taxing government and a large share of the revenue has gone in cash transfers and social services with the net impact being highly positive in terms of redistribution.' This means that the Howard government, judged by results, has operated as a traditional Labor government by imposing hefty taxes, raising revenue efficiently and ensuring that the benefits are redistributed via the tax-transfer mechanism and the welfare state. This is how Labor is supposed to govern. It puts in a new light Howard's penetration of the Labor base vote and the support of the Howard 'battlers'. The battlers are the recipients of significant income transfers. This suggests Howard's success is not just because of economic growth or social conservatism but because of his implementation of an egalitarian and redistributive model.

This is a complete contradiction of the standard critique of the Howard government. It suggests that while individual measures have been attacked as regressive, the overall effect is highly progressive.

The results, in this sense, are startling. The most contentious is Harding's analysis of indirect benefits (Medicare, school funding, welfare services). She finds these are progressive, just as cash payments (the dole, pensions and family support) are progressive. 'There has been a lot of publicity about the private health insurance rebate and the funding of private schools,' Harding says. 'We were surprised to find these indirect benefits are also highly progressive. This applies to the private health insurance rebate that is worth more to a lot of low-income older people.' Central to these results is jobs growth (despite the high level of hidden unemployment). 'The government must be given marks for the fall in unemployment,' Harding says. 'These benefits from lower unemployment have been injected all the way across the entire distribution of income.' That is, creating jobs is one of the best drivers of an egalitarian society.

On the tax front, Harding's research shows the Howard–Costello tax system to be progressive overall when the two contradictory impulses of a regressive GST and progressive income tax system are totalled. In a related analysis, Mark Wooden from the Melbourne Institute offered an update from the first three waves of the Household, Income and Labour Dynamics in Australia (HILDA) Survey, the only such analysis of its type.

He reported that relative poverty rates, while high, declined during the three years 2000–01 to 2002–03 from 14.2 per cent to 12.1 per cent. This was interesting given the recent majority report of the Senate inquiry into poverty that Australia was 'losing the fight for the fair go'.

But HILDA provides a dynamic analysis—looking at movements into and out of poverty—with Wooden reporting that during this period almost one-quarter of the population (24.3 per cent) was in poverty at some stage; but only 7.1 per cent were poor for two of the three years; and only 4.2 per cent for all three years. He concluded that 'although most people who enter poverty soon leave, a more sombre fact is that the longer one remains in poverty, the harder it is to escape'.

While anxious not to 'belittle' the poverty problem, Wooden said the number of people at risk of persistent poverty was clearly less than the numbers in poverty for any single year.

The conference confirmed that the two big headings for reform remain participation and productivity. In his dinner speech Costello said that industrial relations reform was the single most important action to improve productivity, a claim that Labor rejects.

Australia had reached the bedrock philosophical conflict over industrial relations. It was exposed with Wesfarmers chief and Business Council of Australia leader Michael Chaney's statement that the industrial system should be about productivity and prosperity, not fairness—that fairness should be addressed by government through the tax-transfer system (which the Howard government is manifestly doing).

ACTU Secretary Greg Combet dismissed this idea, saying the Australian people wanted a commitment to fairness in the system. Combet said there was 'no genuine process of consultation' and the agenda was being run by 'big business insiders'. The unions and the state governments will fight the reforms in the political marketplace.

The Government–Opposition rift over the welfare agenda (and participation policy) was wide. Costello says that 700,000 people, or 3.5 per cent of the population, have a disability pension (up from 1 per cent 40 years ago) and that 450,000 single parents are on benefits (double the number of 20 years ago). The Treasurer demands a system in which 'people are required to search for work when they are capable of work'.

He insists that a nation facing long-term ageing of the population must confront these reforms to build workforce participation. Costello rejects the option of cutting the effective marginal tax rates to encourage the transition back to work on the 'incentive' side.

This is where Shadow Treasurer Wayne Swan has made his early stand. Attacking as 'astounding' Costello's rejection of this tax reform, Swan pledges Labor will address the interaction of the tax and welfare systems and confront the problem of effective marginal tax rates at the lower end.

Any government adviser in attendance would have drawn three conclusions: the coming budget must be a reform document; the government must signpost its reform agenda for the three-year term; and it needs to incorporate reform more effectively into its political strategy.

Paul Kelly
Weekend Australian
Edition 1—All-round Country
2 April 2005, p. 39

WILL TALK LEAD TO ACTION AT THIS LATE STAGE?

The most remarkable aspect of the Howard government's fourth term is the rapid change in economic atmospherics.

Re-elected largely on its economic credentials, the government now faces serious questions about the immediate sustainability of economic growth and a rapid escalation of pressures across a wide front for a new wave of policy reforms.

A near-term setback to Australia's extraordinary run of economic growth is unwelcome. Yet it may actually help in the difficult task of implementing the longer-term structural reforms that will inevitably create losers as well as winners, by generating a new sense of urgency.

The changing economic climate, combined with the government's unexpected win in the Senate, is also creating a new political dynamic. It is stepping up pressure on John Howard and Treasurer Peter Costello to speed up reform. And it is offering Labor leader Kim Beazley the chance to pull the ALP back from the political abyss.

These shifting economic and political currents were on display at *The Australian's* and the Melbourne Institute's third Economic and Social Outlook conference this week.

The threats to growth were highlighted by prominent economist Ross Garnaut. He said that after a decade of exceptional economic growth, Australians as a community had accepted the excellent economic performance as evidence they had changed enough. They reverted to their traditional preference for having popular politics in command of resource allocation and economic policy making.

Garnaut told the conference that the return to traditional approaches to economic policy making, favouring the ad hoc and expedient over the economically rational, has had broadly based support within the Australian polity and across the organised political spectrum: 'The first step towards restoration of reform and good national economic performance is to break the complacency,' he said. 'This must start with the realisation of the extent of the deterioration in our economic outlook.'

Garnaut's concerns are summed up in Figure 1, which suggests an ominous parallel between the economy now and the recession of the early 1990s. He presented other charts that told a similar story for other economic indicators, such as domestic spending and the current account deficit.

But is recession virtually inevitable, as his chart seems to imply? Garnaut himself notes there are important differences this time. One is that Australia has a much stronger financial system now. To that, one could add more flexible labour markets. He also thinks the Reserve Bank is unlikely to repeat its

Figure 1: Real GDP Growth (1989–92 and 1998–2004)

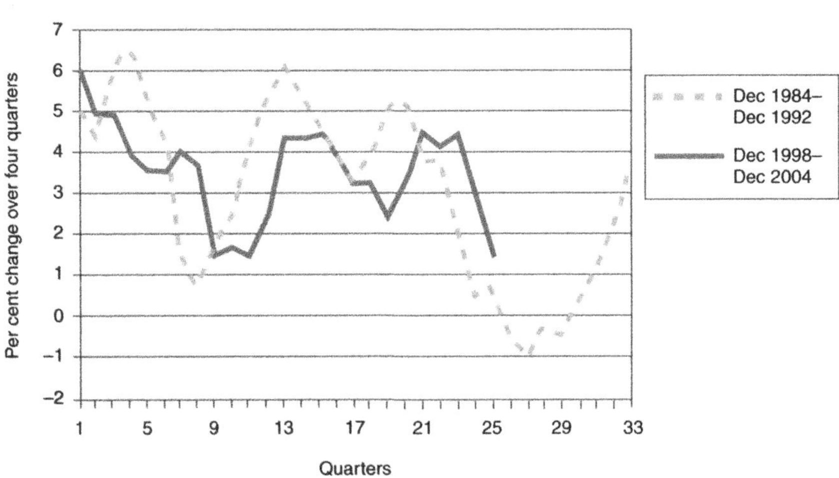

Source: Reserve Bank of Australia Bulletin database

mistake of excessive monetary contraction, which precipitated the early 1990s' recession.

However, he also says that the strength of excess demand in the Australian economy is so strong that several more interest rate increases of twenty-five basis points may be needed. In the absence of further evidence of inflationary pressures, that surely risks hitting the economy too hard— the very risk the Reserve Bank is anxious to avoid.

Its caution is likely to be reinforced by the evidence that the economy is slowing; by how much is the issue. And it is not hard to construct a scenario where a shock from abroad derails growth here.

As Beazley told the conference, our economic fortunes could change abruptly with just one of any number of external events, such as an increase in global interest rates. 'Our prosperity is far more fragile than the government recognises,' he warned.

But Costello and Treasury Secretary Ken Henry reminded the conference of Australia's success in dealing with economic shocks in the 1990s.

Henry made the point this way:

> If, at the start of the 1990s, we had predicted that our largest trading partner would experience average growth of just 1 per cent and suffer four major recessions over the coming decade, that a large part of emerging East Asia would experience a financial crisis and severe recession [1997 and 1998], that US bond markets would effectively grind to a halt for a period [late 1998], that US equity markets would experience the emergence and bursting of a major bubble [2000], that the US economy would experience a not insubstantial recession [2001], that significant acts of terror would occur in New York and elsewhere, that Asia would experience health scares like SARS and avian flu, and that oil prices would rise sharply to levels not seen since 1985, most of us would have thought that the next fifteen years would be pretty miserable ones for Australia. Yet, this has been a period of historic economic prosperity for us.

It's an impressive list and a sound caution against excessive pessimism now. But, as Garnaut warns, that very success can also lead to what he calls the great complacency.

Taking up the theme of the conference, Sustaining Prosperity: New Reform Opportunities for Australia, Costello acknowledged that Australia would not sustain the golden age of prosperity it was enjoying without continuing economic reform.

This has been a theme of all three Economic Opportunity conferences, but at this conference it took on a new edge, partly because of the opportunities offered by government control of the Senate and because of the growing recognition that, after fourteen years of expansion, growth is under threat.

'The prosperity of the 1960s ended in the chaos of the Whitlam government and the high inflation and unemployment of the 1970s,' Costello said. 'Without strong economic management and continuing reform, this expansion could end badly, too.'

What he didn't say was that Australia's current prosperity was built on the reform foundations laid by the Hawke and Keating governments. In his speech to the conference, Beazley strongly embraced Labor's policies of the 1980s and 1990s, a significant about-turn on his earlier attempts to distance himself from them in his first term as Labor leader.

Acknowledging the need to take unpopular decisions if reform was to be successful, he said far-reaching economic reforms such as those of the 1980s and 1990s were urgently needed.

So they are, but will they be delivered? A test for both sides will be the labour market, where the government has talked of significant reforms but has yet to tell us what they will be. And in his speech yesterday, Beazley followed up tough reformist talk by stepping away from any further reform of the labour market.

By the end of the Howard government's fourth term, we will know if we have the political leadership on both sides of the parliamentary divide capable of sustaining prosperity.

Alan Wood
Economics Editor
The Australian
Reprinted from the *Weekend Australian*
2 April 2005

1 NEW REFORM OPPORTUNITIES FOR AUSTRALIA

THE HON. PETER COSTELLO MP
Treasurer and Deputy Leader of the Liberal Party

The theme of this conference—'Sustaining Prosperity: New Reform Opportunities for Australia'—is entirely appropriate on both counts. First, because we are truly living through a period of great prosperity in Australia—a period rivalling the so-called 'Golden Age' of post-war expansion in the late 1960s. Second, we will not sustain this prosperity without continuing economic reform. The prosperity of the 1960s ended in the chaos of the Whitlam government and the high inflation and high unemployment of the 1970s. Without strong economic management and continuing reform this expansion too could end badly. And aside from the cycle we now have much larger structural changes to attend to.

Since 1996 total household disposable income in Australia has increased by a third in real terms. The household balance sheet is stronger than ever. Net household wealth (after allowing for borrowings) has increased 8.6 per cent per annum in real terms. Since 1996 over 1.5 million new jobs have been created. In Australia the unemployment rate has fallen to the lowest level in 30 years.

These achievements are significant in their own right, but are even more remarkable when considered against the challenges that we have faced along the way. These challenges included: the Asian economic and financial crisis; the recession in the United States; the unprecedented terrorist attacks leading to the subsequent War on Terror; the SARS epidemic; the worst drought in 100 years; and now record high oil prices. Our relative success in dealing with these shocks has seen the Australian economy outperform the rest of the developed world, propelling us up international league tables to positions that we have not occupied for several decades.

According to the OECD, Australia's GDP per capita fell to 19th in 1990 but has now recovered to be the 8th highest in the world. More broadly, the United Nations' Human Development Index, which measures a country's average achievement in terms of adult literacy levels, education enrolment, per capita GDP and life expectancy, places Australia 3rd out of 177 countries.

Our economic achievements over recent years have now focused attention away from the demand side of the economy to the supply side. There is a lot of focus now on supply 'bottlenecks'—in physical infrastructure and skilled labour.

I propose to address the issue of labour shortage tonight. As far as problems go, this is a good one to have. If we had been meeting 10 years ago, with unemployment at 8.6 per cent, we would have drooled over this problem. Australia's abiding focus for nearly the last 30 years has been unemployment. And, of course, the 'problem' of labour shortage could be quite easily fixed today by following the recipe that created the high unemployment of the 1990s. As one of my predecessors termed it: 'The recession we had to have'.

SUCCESS IN THE LABOUR MARKET

A lot of the recent commentary has focused specifically on shortages of skilled labour in the traditional trades. Anybody who has built or renovated a house in the past few years will readily confirm that it is hard to get skilled tradespeople and that prices are pretty steep.

But the labour shortage is not just confined to skilled workers. Labour shortages are also present in a range of unskilled occupations. Indeed, of the 87,000 vacancies registered on the Australian Job Search database, the occupation groups recording the most vacancies are: labourers, factory and machine workers (at 14,000); and hospitality and tourism workers (at 7000) —occupations that economists would not normally define as 'skilled'.

In other words, Australia is not in the grip of some unique skills problem. Australia is in the grip of record low unemployment. When unemployment is low, it is hard to find labour. The unemployment rate of 5.1 per cent estimates that 533,000 people are looking for work and can't find it. The Australian Bureau of Statistics Job Vacancies released today estimates there are 148,300 job vacancies at present. The 10-year average of job vacancies in Australia is 99,200. Today's figure of 148,300 is an all-time record.

This is what happens when you have sustained economic expansion. This is the object of economic growth: to produce jobs for people who want to work. And sometimes there are more jobs than people willing or able to fill them.

Is this full employment? Back in the 1960s, unemployment was lower— around 1.9 per cent in November 1969. But participation rates were lower —around 60.9 per cent compared to 64.1 per cent today. This meant a smaller proportion of people wanted to participate in the paid workforce. In particular, married women tended to stay out of the paid workforce to a much higher degree. Also back in the 1960s a lot of employment which was otherwise uncompetitive was subsidised through the tariff system. Without the tariff system, and on today's participation rates, the unemployment rates of the 1960s would have been substantially higher.

Is 5.1 per cent unemployment full employment? I suspect not. But it might be quite close to the cyclical low. How should we respond to it? We could slow the economy to produce fewer jobs. Or we could boost the labour supply to fill those vacancies. It will not surprise you that I favour the latter.

But it is important to think about this issue carefully. We need to respond to our immediate situation. But more than that, what we are seeing now could be an early foretaste of what I believe will become a long-term problem. I do not believe we are yet seeing the beginning of the long-term problem; I think we are just at a favourable point in the economic cycle, a point we should attempt to continue and improve upon. But I do believe in the longer term—in decades' time—Australia will face a long-term structural shortage of labour. Like now but significantly worse.

I would like to respond to our immediate situation by starting some of the long-term structural changes which we will need to cope with the much greater changes that are coming upon us.

THE DEMOGRAPHIC CHALLENGE AND LABOUR SUPPLY

The Intergenerational Report, published in 2002, found that growth in the number of people of working age was expected to fall from around 1.2 per cent per annum over the last decade to almost zero in 40 years' time. This means that the number of working-age people is hardly going to grow in Australia over the next 40 years. But the number of people aged over 65 is expected to double over that period. This means that the ratio of working-age people to support every person aged over 65 is expected to halve within 40 years. Instead of 5 people of working age to support each person over 65 there will be 2.5 people of working age for each person over 65. In the absence of significant policy change, this transition will involve a decline in Australia's trend economic growth rate and put unsustainable pressure on government finances.

When I released the Intergenerational Report in 2002 I described our economic prospects as turning on 3 'Ps'—Population, Participation, Productivity. Put simply, our economic prospects will be governed by the number of people in our country, the rate at which they participate in the labour market, and the productivity of those people who do participate. Our population will be principally determined by our fertility rates—not just the fertility rates of today but the fertility rates of the last 40 years. They have locked in the population structure, in particular the ageing nature of our society over the next 40 years. Demography is destiny.

In broad terms, the participation challenge requires a three-pronged attack:

- preparing children and young adults for a lifetime of productive participation;
- encouraging mature age workers to remain attached to the labour market for longer; and
- encouraging those who currently do not seek to join the labour force to join in.

EDUCATION AND PARTICIPATION

We need high-quality education for children and young adults because education is a powerful driver of labour force participation. Eighty-one per cent of people aged 15 to 64 with a post-school qualification are employed. This compares to a 61 per cent employment rate for those without post-school qualifications—a 20 percentage point gap in employment outcomes.

Education and training are becoming increasingly important to sustaining employment. The rapid pace of technological and structural change means that people often need to up-skill to perform more sophisticated roles in their current job, or to re-skill to enable them to change occupations or industries when their employment becomes vulnerable. Furthermore, while overall employment growth has been strong, the threshold level of skills required to access the labour market is rising as many low-skilled jobs are disappearing from the Australian economy.

For all of these reasons, the Australian government is investing strongly in education, through schools, universities, and the vocational education and training sector.

ENCOURAGING MATURE AGE PARTICIPATION

Life expectancy in Australia is the 7th highest in the world. And it is increasing. Our health standards are among the highest in the world. But the participation of mature Australians, particularly men, in the workforce is comparatively low. For men between 55 and 59 years, Australia's participation rate counts 20th in the OECD. What is significant about age 55 in Australia? Any financial adviser will tell you immediately—age 55 is the superannuation preservation age in Australia.

With life expectancy continuing to rise and with health standards good, we must encourage mature age workers to keep working past the preservation age for superannuation, at least to the retirement age of 65. Mature age workers—who can draw on a wealth of experience and well-developed skills—have a substantial contribution to make to the workforce. And, needless to say, the longer they stay in the workforce the further they will stretch their retirement savings.

This is why the government has introduced a range of incentives to encourage continued workforce participation by mature workers, in the 55–65 age range. Initiatives have included more flexible superannuation access arrangements and the mature age worker tax offset available to those aged 55 and above. This tax offset will encourage mature age workers to choose to stay in the workforce and will provide a maximum annual rebate of $500 on their earned income, payable on assessment (it begins to phase out once earned income reaches $48,000).

More will be done over the coming years to ensure that the retirement income system does not encourage people to prematurely leave the workforce. More will also be done to encourage employers to value and retain mature workers. And our industrial relations system should be open and flexible enough to encourage mature workers to retain a part-time connection with the workforce where they want to slow down but not permanently retire.

WELFARE REFORM AND LABOUR MARKET ASSISTANCE

Increasing labour supply is also about boosting participation by those who are not presently looking to join the workforce.

More than one in five of all adults of working age are on income support. Of these, 7 out of 10 do not have an ongoing obligation to seek work in return for receiving that income support. Most of these people are recipients of either the disability support pension (DSP) or single parenting payment (SPP), previously known as the sole parent pension.

Forty years ago, less than 1 per cent of the population was on an invalid pension. In 2004, we had about 3.5 per cent of the population (around 700,000 people) on DSP, with musculoskeletal conditions such as back pain now registered as the most common complaint. Also in 2004, around 450,000 single parents received parenting payments, almost double the number of 20 years ago. It is true that birth rates to single parents have substantially increased over the last 20 years. It is hard to believe that disability has tripled in the last 40 years.

Let me be very clear. Those people genuinely disabled and unable to work should not be required to seek work. But those people who do have a capacity to work should be encouraged to look for it.

We need to create an income support system that focuses on workforce participation first; a system where work requirements are appropriately set, so that people are required to search for work where they are capable of work. Work can bring so much for people compared to a life on welfare— greater social contact, higher self-esteem, another avenue to contribute to society, and higher income. It is our duty to ensure that these benefits are realised for as many Australians as possible.

Let us now consider those who are eligible for parenting payment. Predominantly these are single parents, mostly mothers. At present they are not required to look for work while they receive this payment because they need to look after their children. But what about when the children go to school? Would it be possible then to look for part-time work? There are a lot of single parents who work. Many work full-time. A system that has no work requirement—not even a part-time work requirement—for a parent of school age children is a very generous one and an inappropriate one in a country with possible labour shortages and long-term ageing of its population. This does not mean that they lose benefits if they cannot find work. It just means that they should be encouraged to look for work in the same way as those who are on an unemployment benefit.

Another element of encouraging participation is facilitating labour market mobility. If people cannot find work in their existing location, they should be encouraged to look for work in areas of labour shortage. Job Network arrangements and other employment services have assisted in this regard, by better matching job seekers with suitable job vacancies. But labour mobility should be encouraged.

WORKPLACE RELATIONS REFORM

A flexible workplace relations system is also a key factor in allowing the labour market to effectively deal with skills shortages. By allowing wages to act as a better signalling mechanism, it provides incentives for workers to move to areas where their skills are most valued. And by more closely aligning wages with productivity in workplaces, wage rises in one area of shortage should not lead to across-the-board wage rises.

Pattern bargaining which attempts to spread wage rises from productive enterprises to less productive ones is the greatest challenge to our climate of low inflation and thereby the greatest challenge to continuing growth.

Until now, the key element of the government's workplace reforms has been the introduction of the *Workplace Relations Act 1996*, which placed the emphasis for determining employment arrangements on employers and employees at the enterprise level. Agreements made directly between employers and employees have delivered greater productivity and flexibility in the workplace than industrial awards. This is partly because there are fewer prescriptions, giving more flexibility and clear incentives for employers and employees to take responsibility for the employment relationship.

But we need a new dose of active wide-reaching and vigorous industrial relations reform in this country. No single reform would boost productivity in the Australian economy to the same extent. The *Workplace Relations Act 1996* was never intended to be the final stage in the reform process. As you know, many of our past attempts to increase flexibility, reduce employment transaction costs and achieve a closer link between wages and productivity were blocked by the Senate. The government remains committed to reforming workplace relations so that more Australians can share in the benefits of productivity and economic growth.

There are currently thousands of federal and state awards that apply to different workplaces in different conditions, in different parts of the country, and create confusion for businesses and workers. The awards carry a great deal of complexity and rigidity in the terms and conditions of employment. While parties can enter agreements to set terms and conditions between themselves, they must be assessed against awards with all of the complexity that they entail.

No one argues with the view that minimum wages are necessary to provide a safety net for employees. However, we must ensure that the way in which minimum wages are set is sustainable and does not unfairly deny people—particularly the low-skilled—from entering the employment market. We must ensure that voluntary agreements are encouraged to operate as widely as possible and that individual workplaces set individual outcomes. Sustaining prosperity is all about rising wages backed by rising productivity. If rising wages are not backed by productivity or if pattern bargaining or award variation take them outside productive areas to unproductive ones, a round of inflation will soon follow and our prosperity will soon falter.

CONCLUSION

While we have been successful in many areas, and improved Australia's prosperity by historical standards and by comparison with like countries, new challenges are now emerging and new threats are apparent. Our greatest long-term challenge is our ageing population, bringing a slower economic growth rate together with a much faster demand for services, particularly health services.

All of our policies should be passed through this test: will it help or will it hinder our response to this challenge? Do our policies promote participation? Do they improve productivity?

An open society characterised by flexible work arrangements, mobility, rapid adjustment to technological change, utilising skills from a strong education and training base is going to be equipped to respond to these challenges. And our institutional arrangements must promote such an economy. This is the reform opportunity to sustain our prosperity into the future.

2 THE ALP AND ECONOMIC REFORM

THE HON. KIM BEAZLEY MP
Leader of the Opposition

This conference is a unique opportunity in our nation's calendar to advance the economic reform debate. Though this is only the third Economic and Social Outlook conference, it is quickly assuming a special place in our national life, so much so that it feels like it's already becoming an Australian tradition.

Today I want to speak about another Australian tradition that I have witnessed during my 25 years in Parliament—the tradition of economic reform. It is a story of how in government in the 1980s and 1990s, Labor rose to the historic challenges it confronted, abandoning its own prejudices to pursue an aggressive program of economic reform. There was urgent work to be done. And though it was often tough, we set aside our own ideological prejudices. In the face of rigid opposition—from our supporters, as well as our opponents—we achieved structural changes that, over two decades, turned our economy around. It was what the times required.

The second half of the story concerns John Howard, a man whom many had hoped would be a champion of economic reform, but who has never delivered on those expectations. He has failed to abandon his own prejudices to make the changes that could have moved Australia forward to its next stage of growth. Instead of embracing a clear-eyed approach to reform, he has spent the balance of his prime ministership distracted by his own personal obsession, a culture war in which he has sought to recreate the imagined Australia of his childhood. And while he has enjoyed the dividends of Labor's past reforms, he has neglected and sometimes even weakened Australia's longer term economic prospects.

Today we need a new reform agenda that deals with the urgent structural challenges that face the Australian economy. Labor's reform agenda will confront these challenges head-on and fireproof this economy against the growing threats to our prosperity.

AUSTRALIA'S URGENT NEED FOR REFORM

One thing must be clear. Australia needs far-reaching economic reforms, and it needs them urgently. Some say that we don't have the urgent need for reform that we did in the 1980s and 1990s. That is wrong. We don't need to wait for the rolling thunder and the lightning strikes to know that the sunshine won't last forever. And, frankly, we should not be waiting for an economic catastrophe before embarking on reform. Even now our economy is flashing warning signs:

- Economic growth is slowing while interest rates are heading up. While John Howard in 1997 promised average annual growth rates of 4 per cent throughout the present decade, we averaged only 2.9 per cent in the first half of this decade.
- Reserve Bank Governor Ian Macfarlane has confirmed that we face a lasting slowdown, that we need to reduce our expectations, with future growth rates starting with 2s and 3s and not 3s and 4s.
- Our long run of strong productivity growth during the 1990s appears to be over.
- We have severe skill shortages in 42 occupations that are constraining economic growth and putting upward pressure on inflation and interest rates. Yet we have more than 2 million people who aren't participating in the workforce as they would like to do.
- Years of under-investment have left us with a creaking infrastructure that is constraining growth and raising inflationary pressures.
- Australia is simply not paying its way in the global economy. We've had the best terms of trade since 1974, and yet the longest run of trade deficits in our history. Since 1996, the rate of export growth has halved, from 10 per cent to 5 per cent per year, and it's been even lower since 2001.
- We also face serious environmental and demographic challenges.

Our economic fortunes could change abruptly with just one of any number of external events: a drop in mineral prices; an increase in global interest rates; financial markets adopting a less permissive attitude to our high foreign debt and current account deficit; a sharp fall in the dollar; or some other external shock.

Our prosperity is far more fragile than the government recognises. We should have used these years of plenty to invest in the next wave of productivity growth and reduce our vulnerability to external threats. But John Howard has been eating the seeds rather than planting them. Our government should be seized with the ambition to build an economy that can give Australian families the highest living standards in the industrialised world, just as we had a century ago.

In the 1990s, we reversed the nation's downward slide in the international league table, and we had climbed to 10th in the world for living standards by 2003. But that momentum is dwindling. We need a government that identifies our reform needs and delivers on them.

REFORM REQUIRES LEADERSHIP

I learned from my years in the Hawke and Keating governments that a comprehensive reform program requires far-sighted leadership. It requires a government that can discern the priorities for reform, and has the maturity to abandon its own prejudices when they stand in the way of what needs to be done; that puts the national interest first, ahead of its short-term political interests; that sticks to its guns even when its own constituencies resist the reforms; and that can work co-operatively and forge alliances, sometimes with old foes, to get results.

We took a broader perspective on economic reform than many other countries. We looked at the economy as a whole: the roles of government, regulation, competition, state enterprises, trade, industry policy, foreign debt, the labour market, taxation and retirement incomes policy. It was all on the table. People on all sides of politics contributed intelligently to that debate, and rigorous scrutiny from the media helped to keep us true to our reform commitments.

That wide-ranging reform debate sets Australia apart from the US and Britain, where policy debate tends to be so much narrower—in Britain, a debate mainly about public services; in America, a debate centred on individualistic issues of personal economic liberty, like tax and personal investment accounts.

Australia's reform tradition is more all-embracing. Sure, it can sometimes get a little technocratic as people quibble over vertical fiscal imbalance and hypothecation. But that wide-ranging debate served us well in the 1980s and 1990s. It lifted economic literacy on both sides of politics, it informed voters, and it resulted in better public policy.

With the challenges we now confront, I believe it is critical that we stoke the fires of the national economic reform debate again. It's one of the reasons why the Melbourne Institute and *The Australian* deserve a slap on the back—because this conference helps to elevate economic reform in public debate. That's a boon for any open-minded government that recognises how important it is to get a clear-eyed and unprejudiced view of what needs to be done.

A REFORMIST GOVERNMENT MUST ABANDON ITS PREJUDICES

In constructing a reform agenda for the next decade, we will not need to repeat the dramatic modernisation program of the Hawke and Keating years. Those reforms changed our economy fundamentally. The economy was restructured from top to bottom—a reform program that affected almost every sector and institution in Australia. After inheriting an economy in long-term decline, with a poor record on living standards, productivity, inflation and unemployment, the Hawke and Keating governments lifted the hood on the economy, reconditioned the engine and flushed out the pipes:

- opening Australia up to a competitive global economy;
- floating the Australian dollar;
- deregulating the financial system;
- deregulating aviation and telecommunications;
- restructuring the tax system, by cracking down on lurks, broadening the tax base and cutting personal and company tax rates;
- ending protectionism;
- privatising government businesses like Qantas, Australian Airlines and the Commonwealth Bank;
- transforming the high-inflation, dispute-plagued industrial relations system into a low-strike, low-inflation system, and then into a decentralised, productivity-based system; and
- introducing the most comprehensive package of microeconomic reforms this nation has ever seen—the national competition policy reforms.

We didn't pretend that we were building a new Jerusalem. We just did the job that needed to be done. And we weren't perfect. We made our mistakes. But we didn't shirk the hard work and the tough decisions. It wasn't the easier path. We forced ourselves to take a clear-eyed, unprejudiced look at the reforms that the Australian economy needed. Just think of how we set aside our own prejudices on industrial relations reforms. Our ideology favoured comparative wage justice, the principle that workers should be paid equally for equal work. In principle, that was fair. But it didn't provide enough incentive to improve work practices.

By the 1990s we had to face the reality that the wages system needed to give individual enterprises more flexibility to reform work practices and reward productivity. That is why we completed the transition to productivity-based enterprise bargaining in 1994, while still underpinning agreements with decent award standards. We achieved 13 years of wage restraint under the Accord. The wage share of GDP came down from 60.1 per cent when we took office to the lowest it had been since 1968. We left office with the wage share of GDP at 55.3 per cent. That allowed corporate profits to rise to record levels in 1984. For every year afterwards, the corporate profit share of GDP was higher than in any recorded year before we had come to office.

By the 1990s, the profit share of GDP was consistently around 23 per cent, a full 5 percentage points higher than when we took office. In other words, we basically slowed wage growth so that we could raise corporate profits by a whopping 5 percentage points of GDP. Convincing our supporters that this was the right thing for a Labor government was not easy, but we believed it was needed to cultivate an investment-friendly, pro-growth climate—a climate that in the long term would benefit all Australians.

We also had to abandon our prejudices in restructuring the tax system. Convincing our own support base of the need in 1985 to cut the top marginal tax rate from 60 cents to 49 cents in the dollar was hard. We knew it was essential, as a trade-off for broadening the tax base and as a means to lift incentive and international competitiveness. When we ended the double taxation of dividends, many of our union colleagues thumped their tables, questioning how a Labor government could ask for wage restraint from workers while rewarding shareholders with this tax cut. But we felt it was necessary and in the nation's long-term interest. Our decision to allow foreign banks into Australia in 1985 was bitterly opposed even by some of our own MPs. We were prepared to put aside our history of distrust of foreign banks in order to foster a more competitive financial sector. And I could go on to talk about other battles we fought, over issues like privatisation, deregulation and industry-based training. These measures weren't vote winners, either. We were opposed by many of our supporters, who thought those reforms were a betrayal of our principles. Some of our supporters still think that way.

We took the fight through the Cabinet room, Caucus, national conferences, branch meetings and public forums throughout the country, because we were convinced that we were doing the right thing for Australia. We were willing to spend our political capital on unpopular decisions that would benefit Australia in the long term. We faced an Opposition that often took the short-cut to easy popularity by opposing our reforms. John Howard now plays a strange game of political amnesia when he says the Liberal Party supported our reforms when they were in opposition. They opposed a great deal of our reform agenda:

- They opposed our tax reforms throughout the 1980s.
- They opposed the fringe benefits tax that cracked down on executives getting up to half their salary tax-free in the form of fringe benefits.
- They opposed the entertainment expenses tax that cracked down on the long boozy business lunches taxpayers were subsidising.
- They opposed the capital gains tax which ended the distortion of taxing earned income while letting speculative gains pile up free of any tax.
- They even opposed the petroleum resource rent tax which returned a share of oil company profits from exploiting Australian resources back to Australians.
- They opposed our targeting of welfare payments, like the assets test on pensions. That was one of the earliest intergenerational reform measures to fireproof the budget, but we almost lost an election on it in 1984.
- They opposed the superannuation guarantee levy in 1992, even though universal superannuation has done more than any other policy to build retirement income security for ordinary Australians. It has also provided a massive pool of funds for investment, and lifted savings levels. While we were introducing the superannuation guarantee levy, the Liberal Party was promising to abolish it the day they came to government.

GETTING TODAY'S REFORM PRIORITIES RIGHT

Today's reform challenge requires the same clear-eyed, far-sighted approach that characterised the Hawke and Keating governments. That starts with getting our reform priorities right. The economic challenges now are different from those we faced in the 1980s and 1990s.

Our greatest economic need is to restore strong productivity growth. Because it is only by doing so that we can simultaneously achieve higher growth rates, low inflation, rising real incomes and improved international competitiveness. As Princeton economist Paul Krugman famously said, productivity isn't everything, but in the long run it's almost everything.

We need to ask ourselves how we'll generate the next wave of productivity reforms. The scope for productivity gains from the old reform agenda of deregulation, privatisation and industrial relations reform is largely exhausted. There's still some unfinished business—in particular, in electricity and water—but with the large-scale structural changes mostly behind us, we won't repeat the windfall productivity gains of the 1990s. The Liberal Party's only answer to the productivity dilemma is to work people harder and longer with their ideological delusions about industrial relations reform.

Labor believes in labour market policies that help people to work smarter. That means investing in the know-how of Australian workers, not returning to a 19th-century world of dog-eat-dog industrial conflict. To improve productivity of capital, we need long-term investment in the nation's infrastructure. I find it extraordinary that, instead of giving priority to new investments in infrastructure and skills, the Howard government has made cutbacks—leaving us with crises in both areas, areas that require a more hands-on approach from government. On these issues, markets functioning alone will fail. Without incentives and public investment in education and training, employers simply will not invest enough in the skills of workers—because with the cost of training, it's easier to poach a skilled worker than pay to train an apprentice who might in turn get poached by another business. Without making infrastructure development a national priority, we just won't get critically needed infrastructure projects on track. Many of these projects are simply too big, and involve too many regulatory issues, for government not to be involved. Public sector investment of some kind will often be required, since not all infrastructure projects can produce commercial returns.

Now some will say, 'Well, isn't this just a typical Labor argument? Labor always wants to expand the public sector. All Labor wants to do is just spend money on training and on infrastructure.' I challenge that. A policy commitment to training Australian workers and building our infrastructure is not a reflex Labor policy. It's the result of a clear-eyed, unprejudiced look at what the nation's economy now needs. The facts don't support the claim that Labor always expands the public sector. Between the 1983 and 1995 budgets, we reduced government spending as a percentage of GDP from 27.4 to 26.1 per cent of GDP. In fact, we cut government spending as a percentage of GDP by 5 percentage points during the 1980s. A Beazley Labor government will only invest in public sector spending if that's the best allocation of those resources. The public sector alone will not solve these problems. The solutions to Australia's skills and infrastructure crises lie in partnerships with the private sector—on issues like funding, construction, service provision, and incentives.

But we now have a crisis in skills and infrastructure, because the Liberal Party has never understood the need for public sector leadership on these issues. It boosts politically popular, short-term public sector consumption spending while public sector investment languishes. The actions most needed to address our economic challenges just don't fit with the Liberal Party's prejudices. This government is too blinded by its own right-wing, American hand-me-down ideology to accept the need for renewed public sector leadership. They are blinded by an obsession with cracking down on unions and weakening collective bargaining. They think that's the only way we can increase productivity growth. They don't want to work with the states on infrastructure, they distrust TAFE colleges and universities, and they want to reserve government spending for political purposes and not the nation's long-term needs. So, instead of letting the facts challenge their prejudices, and putting them to one side, the Howard government has closed its eyes to the skills and infrastructure crises, and ignored the signs of declining productivity.

I find the leaders of our business community far more pragmatic on these issues than this government. That is why a government that I lead will have no problems working with Australia's business community. They just want to see these problems fixed, and they expect the government to lead. But we're not getting leadership from this government, because they're pre-occupied with their narrow ideological obsessions and won't abandon their prejudices. Instead, as the cracks appear in the façade of their economic strategy, they opt for quick fixes, like John Howard's bottlenecks task force. Or they find a distraction—blaming the states, the unions, the Keating government, or whatever.

This is not a mature or consistent approach to economic reform. Instead of blaming the states, the federal government must work with them—just as Labor did in government. Let's not forget that by the end of 1993 we had conservative governments in every state and territory except Queensland. While we had our robust exchanges, we worked together—such as agreeing on the national competition policy reform package, widely regarded as the most comprehensive microeconomic reform measure in Australian history.

I don't pretend that the Howard government's approach has not worked well for them politically. But, in large part, that's because they have been able to coast off the momentum built up from the restructuring of the economy during the 1980s and 1990s. And they've had their share of good fortune, most recently with the soaring prices for mining exports. The enduring payoffs of Labor's reforms, and some good fortune, have meant that their chickens have been slow in coming home to roost. Indeed, the once-in-a-generation windfall from the resources boom might give them a reprieve for a little while yet. But, in the long term, Australia won't be able to escape the effects of this government squandering these years of prosperity.

JOHN HOWARD'S LEGACY: CULTURE WARS, NOT ECONOMIC REFORM

When the historians come to assess John Howard's legacy, I suspect it will tell a surprising story. When he came to office nine years ago, many thought that he could be a great economic reformer. Certainly, a great many of his supporters hoped so.

The great irony of his time in office is that his legacy will not be economic reform but, rather, his true obsession of the last nine years: igniting the culture wars, to turn this country into the imagined place of his childhood and not the confident, independent and outward-looking nation it was becoming in the 1990s. John Howard has turned his back on an Australia that could unselfconsciously celebrate its cultural diversity. He has turned his back on the important work of reconciliation with our Indigenous people. He has turned his back on a humane Australia that respects human rights and works constructively with international bodies like the United Nations. And he has targeted for relentless attack the institutions that he sees as most embodying the cultural values that he hates—institutions like the ABC, universities, unions, and non-government organisations.

Now you can think what you wish about John Howard's culture wars. But one thing is clear: to most Australians, the national economy is far more important than his obsession with his personal culture wars.

But he's neglected the work of shoring up our economy and addressing our long-term challenges—because the only reforms he's been prepared to invest political capital in are those that have been wrapped up in his own cultural obsessions. So, instead of genuine reform, we end up with silly ideological indulgences, like arguments about the price of sausage rolls to justify voluntary student unionism. This is a government that in 2005 is wasting its energy on its inane cultural obsessions, rather than a serious attempt to address the critical need for a skills agenda. These are not reforms, they are crusades. Forcing workers onto unfair Australian Workplace Agreements won't solve the crisis in childcare that stops mums getting back into work. Cutting university funding won't create more skilled workers. Stacking the ABC Board with Liberal Party zealots won't rebuild Australia's run-down infrastructure.

LABOR'S REFORM PRIORITIES

I can assure you that, in contrast, Labor will work hard on an agenda to address Australia's long-term challenges. But our priorities in the areas of skills, infrastructure, participation and export competitiveness are not new themes for us. We have warned about these problems, and the economy would not have its critical problems if the government had been listening.

From the time John Howard started cutting training and education funding in 1996, we warned about the risk of skills shortages and the economic damage that would result from treating education as a cost and not an investment. In each election we've made it very clear that we consider training and education to be the highest priorities of the federal government, and we've had very specific proposals to invest in vocational education and training, apprenticeships and universities.

Our tax and welfare policies have focused on knocking out work disincentives for low- to middle-income earners, such as with the earned income tax credit in 1998, and the tax and family package last year, which would have brought tens of thousands back into the workforce and eased high marginal tax rates.

We have sought to draw attention to national infrastructure needs since the late 1990s, urging the federal government to take on a national leadership role through a national infrastructure advisory council (and before that, a National Development Authority). The Business Council's Infrastructure Action Plan for Future Prosperity released last week has echoed this policy, urging the government to set up a peak intergovernmental body to take the politics out of the infrastructure debate.

CONCLUSION

Today we need a focused government that will take its blinkers off and tackle the problems that put our prosperity at risk. I will lead that kind of government. I have been accused of many things in my time, but I don't think too many people would say I'm an ideologue. I'm not so much into doctrine, whether it's economic ideology or the ideologies of the culture wars. I was warned off ideological excesses as I grew up, by the experience of watching my father denied the opportunity to fulfil his potential in the Labor Party of his day because of petty ideological squabbles. I bring a certain hard-nosed pragmatism to leadership. I'm interested in simply solving problems.

So when I look at Australia today, I see a massive squandering of a once-in-a-generation opportunity to lay the foundations for sustained prosperity in the years ahead. I am distressed by the reckless waste, the $66 billion spending spree between last year's Budget and the election—and the rorting of hundreds of millions of dollars for marginal seat election campaigns by Liberal and National Party MPs. We cannot afford that when we face crises that result from chronic under-investment in education and infrastructure.

I am troubled by the way that spending, imports and debt have soared in recent years, way beyond the growth in what we are producing and what we are selling overseas. I am disturbed by the erosion in our trade performance, especially in manufactured exports and services, and our spiralling foreign debt. I know these trends are not sustainable, despite the blithe responses of Mr Howard to the warning signs. That is why I am committed to leading a government that will initiate a new wave of economic reform, with a far-sighted approach and great ambition for Australia's economic future.

3 AUSTRALIA'S INTERNATIONAL ENGAGEMENT AND REFORM

DR KEN HENRY
Secretary, Department of the Treasury

I want to take the opportunity here to address some aspects of Australia's international engagement. First, I want to look at the connection between domestic reform and openness. Second, I want to consider how we should use international engagement to secure our interests in a substantive and inclusive system of policy dialogue and co-operation. The principal motivation for the second inquiry is that effective international institutions and forums help to secure strong, sustainable and stable economic growth in Australia.

REFORM AND OPENNESS

Let me start with the link between openness and economic reform and growth. There are many reasons for being open to the rest of the world, not just economic. Of the economic reasons, the most powerful is the incentive that engagement with the rest of the world provides for greater internal efficiency and productivity—two enduring sources of higher wealth. The drivers are many: access to cheaper, better and a wider range of inputs and final goods and services; a more efficient allocation of labour and capital, supporting specialisation in areas of comparative advantage; access to international financial markets, enabling the financing of investment, smoothing of consumption, and management of risk; transfer of technology and skills; and enhanced competition in domestic markets, promoting innovation and competitive pricing.

Australia has done a lot over the past couple of decades to liberalise cross-border movement in good and services, capital, and people. The successive reductions in international protection through the removal of quantitative restrictions and tariff cuts have liberalised trade in goods and services (Figure 1), with direct benefits to consumers and businesses. Liberalisation of the financial sector and the earlier removal of capital controls have improved financial intermediation (Figure 2) and made access to finance easier (Figure 3).

These changes have been accompanied by the development of credible medium-term monetary and fiscal policy frameworks, the adoption of a floating exchange rate regime, and greater flexibility in the labour market. Indeed, these latter three changes were introduced in part as a result of pressure exerted on the domestic economy by increasing international openness.

There is scarcely any commercial activity that has not, in some way, been affected by this program of internationalisation, a fact that would have surprised many in the early 1980s. One of the lessons of the last 20 years is that you never really know where the line should be drawn between 'traded' and

Figure 1: Trade Share and Effective Rate of Assistance, 1968–

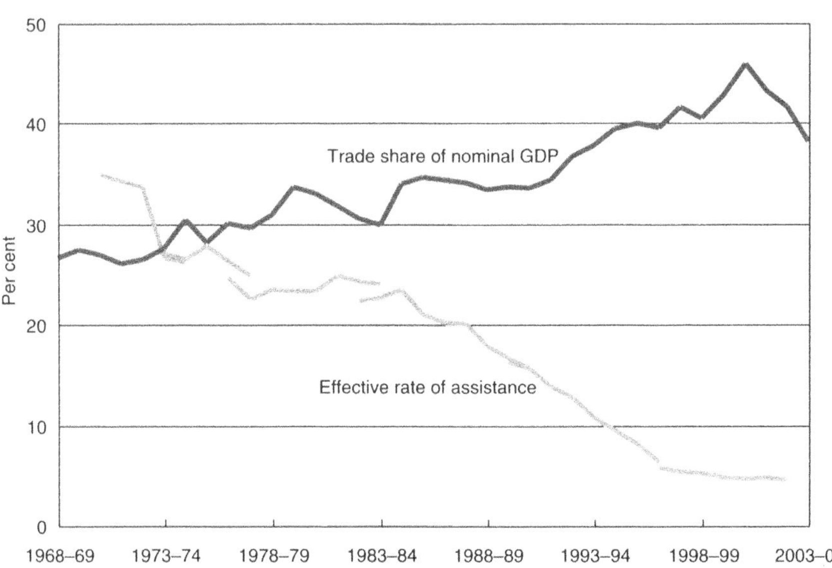

Source: ABS and Productivity Commission.

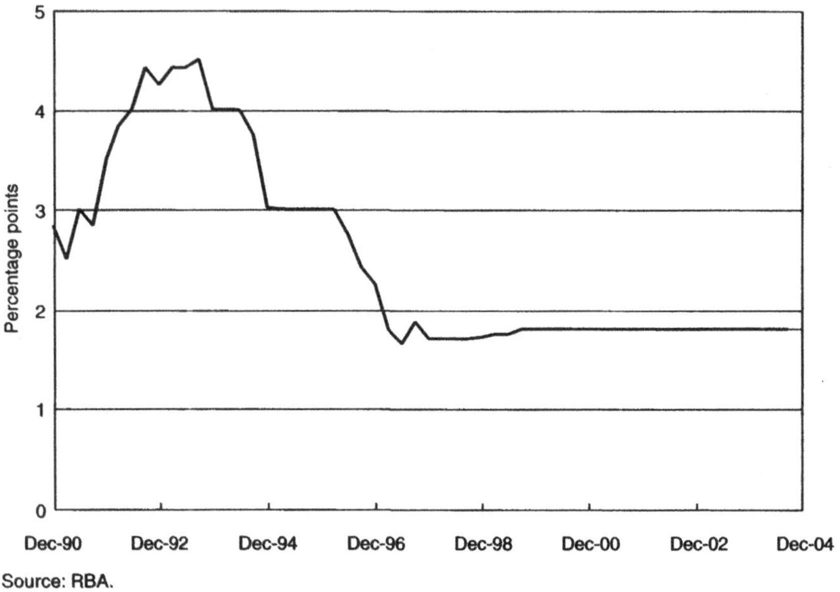

Source: RBA.

Figure 3: Current Account Balance, 1959–2004

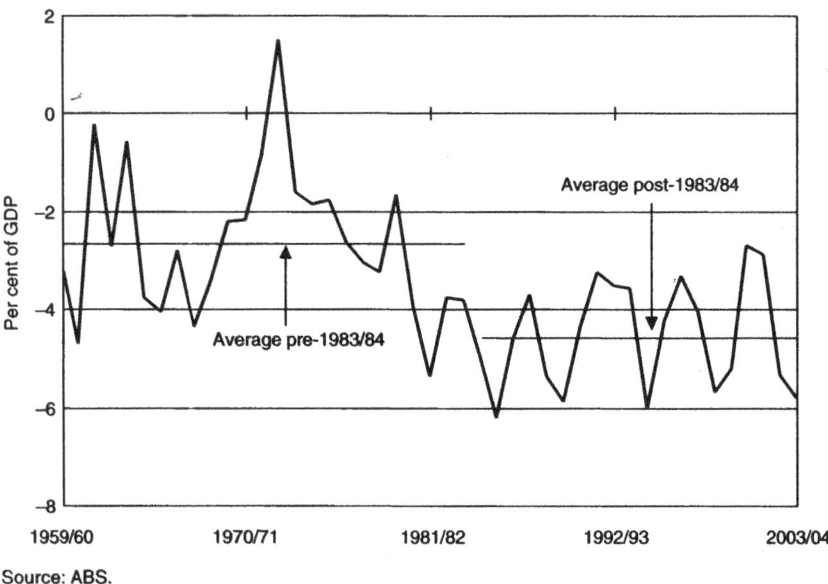

Source: ABS.

'non-traded' activities until you liberalise at the border. Indeed, one might wonder whether the distinction has any real meaning. While openness has been an advantage, it has made us more exposed to the vagaries of events overseas. But the greater economic strength and the reforms to our markets and institutions that have accompanied greater openness have in turn provided us with the means to deal better with international disturbances.

If, at the start of the 1990s, we had predicted that our largest trading partner would experience average growth of just 1 per cent and suffer four recessions over the coming decade, that a large part of emerging East Asia would experience a financial crisis and severe recession (1997 and 1998), that US bond markets would effectively grind to a halt for a period (late 1998), that US equity markets would experience the emergence and bursting of a major bubble (2000), that the US economy would experience a not insubstantial recession (2001), that significant acts of terror would occur in New York and elsewhere, that Asia would experience health scares like SARS and avian flu, and that oil prices would rise sharply to levels not seen since 1985, most of us would have thought that the next 15 years would be pretty miserable ones for Australia. Yet this has been a period of historic economic prosperity for us.

Of course, there have been 'favourable shocks' as well over this period, such as worldwide low inflation and interest rates, and rapid economic development in China, India and parts of Latin America. Internationally, it hasn't been all bad news. But those few bits of good news have not been the reason for our relatively good economic performance. Rather, the basis of our prosperity lies overwhelmingly in having strong institutions, flexible markets, effective and well-targeted macroeconomic policies and credible regulatory frameworks. It is much easier, much less damaging, to take a hit from overseas when the domestic economy is strong: losing one engine of a jumbo jet in flight matters a lot less if the other three engines are working well.

But, despite the successes of the past, we can't now sit still. The rest of the world continues to change. Markets in goods, services and finance are deepening and changing; there is also increasing cross-border movement of people. Domestic deregulation and liberalisation in other parts of the world, combined with the force of ever-changing technology, are affecting the gamut of cross-border economic activity. And economic development, especially in Asia, continues, with far-reaching effects—increasing competition and innovation in markets, and fundamentally changing the global supply and demand of manufactured goods, services and resources. One consequence of comparatively recent international developments is that Australia appears to be experiencing a trend improvement in its terms of trade, another thing that would not have been predicted 20 years ago.

Indeed, it was not predicted, a fact that largely explains much wasted energy in protracted debates about so-called strategic industry policy, even as recently as the year 2000 when a succession of instant experts was wanting to tell us that the world was passing us by because we weren't manufacturing computer chips.

The reforms of the past couple of decades have put us in good shape. We have come a considerable way in improving our international competitiveness; in 2004, Australia was ranked 4th on the IMD (Institute for Management and Development) World Competitiveness Index, up from 15th in 1994 (Figure 4). But without further internal structural reforms and a further deepening of cross-border commerce and people movement, we risk missing out on historic opportunities and failing to deal effectively with significant new challenges. Getting productivity and participation policy settings right is fundamental to our ability to sustain domestic growth and ensure that we can respond to evolving international economic circumstances.

The menu here is a large one. It includes co-ordinated decision making on physical infrastructure such as rail and ports to ensure that they flexibly

Figure 4: International Competitiveness

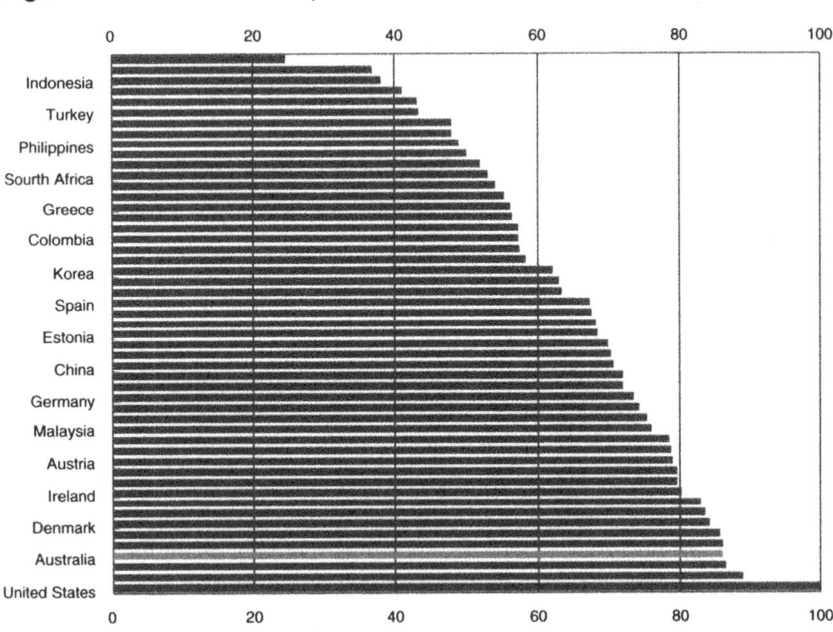

Source: IMD World Competitiveness Yearbook 2004.

meet changing patterns of demand for resources. It means ensuring competitive pricing, adequate provision, and sustainable use of water and energy for both firms and households. It requires that our schools, centres of technical education, universities and firms deliver Australian workers of the future.

Perhaps less obviously, it requires that our institutions and businesses be able to deliver the education and business services that Asian neighbours need to support their further economic transformation as developed market economies. And it means ensuring that our tax, social security and labour market systems provide incentive for economic participation, to boost national income and wealth. I know that reform imperatives in these areas will be much discussed in this year's conference. On a number of occasions I have pointed to the increasingly urgent need to design responses to the looming demographic challenge. Today, my point is that powerful developments in the international environment make domestic reform even more necessary.

INTERNATIONAL ENGAGEMENT

So far, I have spoken about the linkage between changes in the world economy and developments in our own economy. I would like now to change tack somewhat, and look at how these changes in the world economy affect the international policy architecture and the way in which we engage in international decision making. We have a well-established set of institutions and processes for international engagement. These range from 'bricks-and-mortar' institutions like the IMF, World Bank, ADB, OECD, WTO and BIS, to groupings and forums like APEC, G-20, IOSCO, FSF and EMEAP.[1]

These exist to provide practical co-ordination mechanisms for sharing information and supporting co-operation on policy and market issues of economic and strategic substance. Given the extent of cross-border economic activity that now occurs, it is difficult to overstate the importance of an agreed set of 'rules of the game' for international trade, finance and people movement. And as markets develop further, these institutions and forums provide a valuable means of understanding what is going on in the international economy, co-operating in the setting of standards and rules, and facilitating national adjustment in support of well-modulated change in the world economy.

Indeed, the 'rules of international economic engagement' change over time, as circumstances and technology change and as we learn from experience. Active and broad participation by countries in the process by which these rules develop is necessary in order that the rules reflect broad, rather than sectional, interests. The various financial crises of the 1990s, for example, led to a focus on codes and standards for both the public and private sector, as well as mechanisms for garnering international support in a financial crisis (like the New Arrangements to Borrow), all of which could only be realised through co-operative action in some kind of global forum.

Other challenges have emerged in recent years. First, while unilateral trade liberalisation remains a virtual *curiosum*, the multilateral system has played a key role in the post-war period in rationalising border protection and reducing tariffs. But the increasing difficulty in getting multilateral agreement on trade reform and the emergence of regionalism as a potent political force have pushed many countries into seeking bilateral and regional preferential trade and economic agreements. These agreements can play a useful role in international co-operation. But it is a role that is likely to remain limited, and risks being counterproductive if the economic coverage of the agreements is narrow, if their rules and coverage differ substantially between agreements, and if they entrench domestic sectional interests that resist domestic structural reform. This is a substantial risk, given their frequently mercantilist motivation.

Second, we face a substantial threat of violent extremism, and transnational terrorism and crime. These are threats, not just to social and economic stability in the countries most directly affected, but also to international stability, since the spillover effects can be substantial. There is an obvious, if difficult to implement, policy response in the careful monitoring of cross-border movement of people and funds and assisting countries in developing effective internal systems. But the implications for international engagement go much deeper. The threat of transnational terrorism and crime implies a need for countries collectively to address the economic and social conditions that explain these problems, including poor governance, persistent poverty, and a lack of economic engagement.

Economic development has to confront, and deal effectively with, both of these challenges. Given that most of East Asia consists of emerging market and transition economies, addressing these challenges is a particular priority for our region.

Let me now bring these points together. Because we face ongoing change in the global economy—and hence the ongoing challenge of facilitating adjustment to these changes—the need for global institutions and forums remains as strong as ever. To this end, we must remain strongly supportive of the institutions and forums that facilitate international engagement.

But while bricks-and-mortar institutions are essential, the challenges we face will be solved only by the shareholders of the institutions, not by the institutions themselves. Ultimately, the responsibility for international co-operation lies with the countries that need to co-operate.[2] Global institutions and forums are vehicles for international co-operation; they are not the drivers. Vehicles that are not well driven can stall. They can take peculiar detours. They can spend long periods in blind alleys. We need a mix of 'hard' institutions and more informal forums that allow our 'drivers' to sort out what they want their global vehicles to look like and where they want to take them.

To put all of that a little more formally, it is important to have a policy dialogue that is housed outside the 'hard' international institutions, allowing policy makers from different countries to come together to reflect on, and assess, the role of these organisations and the nature of the global architecture in an objective manner.

Many of our international institutions and forums are weighted to the economic influence of the major industrialised economies of the world. The international economic balance is changing but institutions are typically slow to adapt to this. Inclusiveness is particularly important at this stage. Many of the challenges to global economic stability—including in the domains of trade, finance, structural adjustment and the movement of people—involve global adjustment, whether it be imbalances in the US economy; the economic rise and transformation of China, India and other developing economies; or weak governance. The tensions around these developments will not be resolved unless the emergent major players have a seat at the table.

One of the more important international policy initiatives in recent years is the formation of the G-20. At least in the domain of economics and finance, the G-20 is a vital addition to global dialogue. The traditional forum for such discussion, the G-7, lacks the broad membership necessary for it to represent the diversity of global interests. Of course, the G-20 does not have universal coverage, but its mix of industrialised and emerging market economies and broad geographic coverage makes it a workable collection of countries to engage in international economic policy dialogue. And it is the right forum for international discussion on the economic dimensions of key emerging issues for industrial and emerging market economies alike, such as demographic change, people movement, the relative payoffs from multilateral and preferential trade and investment reform, the environment, and the international financial architecture.

As testament to its commitment to effective international co-operation, Australia will host the G-20 meetings next year and will host APEC the year after that, in 2007. These commitments require substantial resources and funds. They are an indication that we take seriously international policy dialogue to improve domestic economic institutions and policy and to catalyse international action to support global economic stability.

CONCLUSION

International engagement is not something that should be pursued for its own sake. It is a means for us to ensure, as best we can, that the rules under which we engage in cross-border activity are effective and sustainable— targeted to domestic economic stability, growth and development. Combined, as it is, with our efforts in regional capacity building, international engagement is also the means we have to work towards economic and social stability globally. It is not something that stands apart from the domestic economy. As an open economy, subject to many and varied international influences, our wellbeing as a nation depends fundamentally on the form and substance of our engagement with the rest of the world. As the last couple of decades have demonstrated, it is a necessary part of the domestic reform program.

---

[1] For the acronym-challenged, these are, respectively, the International Monetary Fund, Asian Development Bank, Organisation for Economic Co-operation and Development, World Trade Organisation, Bank for International Settlements, Asia Pacific Economic Co-operation, International Organisation of Securities Commissions, Financial Stability Forum, and Executives Meeting of East Asia Pacific (central banks).

[2] This theme is explored in my Sir Leslie Melville Lecture: 'Australia and the international financial architecture—60 years on', 16 July 2003.

4   CRACKING OUR COMPLACENCY

PROFESSOR ROSS GARNAUT AO
Professor of Economics, Australian National University

For 14 years following the 1990–91 recession, Australia experienced stronger economic growth than any other advanced nation. Yet today we are in serious danger of getting none of the qualities—economic reform, equitable distribution and strong economic growth—that have defined our favourable economic performance in recent years.

Output growth of 1.5 per cent during the year to the December quarter was close to the lowest among developed countries. Of course, one year's data does not make a new trend, but analysis of the data confirms that there are grounds for concern. The slowdown has been entirely on the side of supply capacity. Domestic demand, led by consumption on the back of the housing boom, is still rising rapidly. An exceptional proportion of the demand growth is being supplied by imports.

The imbalance between growth in domestic demand and supply capacity is being reflected in shortages of labour, goods and services that threaten to re-ignite inflation. It is being reflected in extraordinarily high current account deficits and rapidly increasing net external liabilities as a share of gross domestic product, despite external circumstances that in the past have been associated with lower external deficits—exceptionally favourable export prices and terms of trade.

What went wrong? What is the remedy? And what are the prospects if Australia takes corrective action?

The deterioration had its origin in a great complacency that descended upon the country after a decade of exceptional economic growth. As a community, we accepted the excellent economic performance as evidence that we had changed enough. Our community had never been comfortable with the application of professional economic analysis to policy choice—so-called economic rationalism—but for a while, from 1983 to the turn of the century, had been persuaded of its necessity.

In recent years, Australians have reverted to their traditional preference for having popular politics in command of resource allocation and economic policy making. The links between earlier economic reform and contemporary prosperity have been forgotten. Economic analysis was banished to the periphery of many areas of policy making. Endorsement by business interests and economists hired to argue a case for politically preferred policies again became more important than transparent analysis in trade and industry policy, and to some extent in fiscal policy. The exception was in monetary policy, where the reform era had left a legacy of independence at the Reserve Bank of Australia, which so far has not been endangered by an apparent recent re-politicisation of interest rate policy.

The return to traditional approaches to economic policy making, favouring the ad hoc and expedient over the economically rational, has had broad-based support within the Australian polity and across the organised political spectrum. It is as evident in state as in federal government. The return to populism in economic policy making has had bipartisan support at federal level.

So how to break the complacency? A big step would be to build community confidence in a new program of bold reform that has reasonable prospects of restoring strong economic growth. This requires a return to bold and comprehensive discussion of reform, of the kind that laid the basis for policy change in the 1980s. And it requires recognising the extent of the deterioration in our economic outlook.

The first point worth bearing in mind is that the recent decline in real growth is entirely the result of the economy running into capacity constraints. The capacity constraints in the early 21st century have caused continuing strong domestic demand growth to be manifested in a large, sustained negative contribution of net exports to output. In the late 1980s and early 1990s, the period of extreme negative contributions from net exports was brief, before the reduction in domestic demand and depreciation of the real exchange rate induced rapid correction.

The trade and current account deficits as a share of GDP in the early 21st century have turned more strongly negative for longer than in the late 1980s—indeed, than ever since national accounts have been maintained in a comparable form. In the absence of substantial correction through monetary policy, the deficits continued to grow in the December quarter.

There is debate about the conditions under which deficits on this scale might be sustainable. What is broadly agreed is that Australia now faces risks that would be realised suddenly and with recessionary consequences if there were a significant deterioration in external business conditions while the external accounts remain in their present state.

Capacity constraints and associated competitiveness problems have contributed to a sharp deceleration of export growth since 2000. This weak growth in export volumes since 2000, after 15 years of strong and diversified growth, was an early warning of the emerging imbalances in the Australian economy. That it took so long for the imbalances to become a subject of public concern speaks eloquently of the complacency of recent years.

The growth in the productive capacity of the economy depends on the rates of growth in productivity, the employed labour supply and the capital stock. Each of these contributed to the exceptional growth in the Australian economy through the 1990s to 2003. In the absence of a return to far-reaching reform, labour supply and productivity growth are unlikely to make comparable contributions in the period ahead.

The most important reform task is to improve the trade-off between generous provision for the disadvantaged and economic efficiency. To fail in this task will lead to continued economic underperformance as well as poor outcomes on employment and equitable distribution. The capacity constraints in the economy and the considerable extension of the social security system over the past several years make the issue more important than ever.

The most urgent task is to reduce considerably the effective marginal tax rates for social security recipients, the high levels of which contribute to relatively low labour force participation and high levels of part-time employment. High taxation rates are also significant elements in labour force participation and the attraction and retention of skilled personnel at higher levels—and probably at all but the highest levels of the incomes range.

A reform of taxation rates that established a flat 30 per cent marginal effective tax rate for all corporate and personal income, including capital gains, would be most advantageous for people at the bottom of the income range, and most disadvantageous for Australians on the highest incomes and with the greatest wealth. Contrary to popular perception, it would be progressive and enhance incentives for greater labour force participation. It would have the additional advantage of removing the gains from conversion of personal into corporate income. Raising the rate of taxation on capital gains (it would need to be on real rather than nominal gains) would have the incidental effect of greatly reducing the distortions in capital allocation that have spurred the housing and associated consumption boom.

It would only be possible to establish uniform and moderate effective marginal tax rates throughout the income tax range within a version of a 'negative income tax' arrangement—for which individuals would receive payments related to their objective circumstances and unrelated to income, for participation in the labour force (subject to mutual obligation tests), age, participation in formal education and training (independently of age), disability (calibrated for degree) and responsibility for dependent children. All payments would be subject to an assets test cutting in at considerable wealth, and would be withdrawn when income reached some high threshold.

The biggest beneficiaries, proportionately to current after-tax and after–social-security income, would be those who are now on social security and who had some opportunity to work, and those on low incomes who currently fall outside Australia's extensive social security framework.

The supply constraints on Australian economic growth are tight. The RBA has emphasised that domestic demand is running well ahead of those constraints. Any delay in reducing demand to levels within those constraints will be reflected not in higher growth but in increased inflationary pressure. The greater the increase in government spending or reduction in tax revenue in the period ahead, the larger the requirement further to tighten monetary policy to contain that pressure.

It is always difficult to judge how much fiscal and monetary tightening is required to bring excessive demand expansion back within prudent limits. But the extent of excess demand is so large that several more interest-rate rises may be required. Further, to raise the requirement of monetary tightening through additional fiscal expansion at this time would increase the risk of recession. Recession would be damaging for long-term reform, long-term growth and equity.

It is much better to save the growing Budget surpluses until the growth in demand has fallen back below the growth in productive capacity. By then we will have a clearer view of the extent to which the recent improvements in the terms of trade can be expected to continue for a long period. By then, there will be scope for some fiscal stimulus, helping to finance taxation and social security reform in ways that are beneficial to stable economic growth.

The likeliest economic trajectory suggests there will be room for a decisive step towards fundamental tax and social security reform within the life of this parliament. Or, if this new chance is missed, there will be an opportunity for an alternative government to foreshadow reform early in the life of the next parliament.

5 IN THE NATIONAL INTEREST: A NEW CO-OPERATIVE FEDERALISM

HON. JOHN BRUMBY MP
Treasurer of Victoria

INTRODUCTION

Let me begin this morning with the observation that we need an overhaul of Commonwealth–state relations—and as someone who has served in both state and federal parliaments, I feel better qualified than many to draw that conclusion.

I've seen Commonwealth–state relations from just about every angle— as a federal MP in the 1980s during the Hawke government, as Chief of Staff to a Cabinet Minister in the early years of the Keating government, as Leader of the Victorian Opposition for six years during the Kennett government and as Victoria's 49th Treasurer for the past five years.

There's not much I haven't seen, heard or experienced about the often very volatile relationship between the Commonwealth, states and territories. There always has been—and always will be—tensions between the Commonwealth and the states. But that doesn't mean we should walk away from the task of reforming Commonwealth–state relations, and it doesn't give the federal government of the day a licence to ride roughshod over the interests and rights of the states.

There is clearly plenty of scope for a more co-operative federalism, and there is an urgent need for a co-operative national reform agenda between the Commonwealth and the states to tackle national problems and meet national challenges.

COMMONWEALTH–STATE RELATIONS: THE NEED FOR REFORM

From Victoria's perspective, reform in Commonwealth–state relations is long overdue. But before starting off down the path of reform, we need to address some threshold issues.

For a start, the Commonwealth needs to acknowledge that Australia's federal system generally works very well. It decentralises power and enables local decisions to be made at the local level.

It also has a strong competitive edge that encourages the states to compete for people, jobs and investment. That's a very powerful driver for the states to keep business costs and taxes low, and to become more innovative and efficient—and a much stronger incentive than would apply to a central government.

There's also plenty of evidence about how much can be achieved when the Commonwealth, states and territories work together. Victoria's view is that Australia's federal structure provides ample scope to deliver sensible reforms to meet the challenges ahead.

HORIZONTAL FISCAL EQUALISATION

The Commonwealth also needs to tackle the matter of Victoria and New South Wales continuing to heavily subsidise other states. We need reform of horizontal fiscal equalisation (see Figure 1).

Although Victoria's share of GST grants will rise by $106 million in 2005–06, our subsidy to other states will still be $1.6 billion a year—or $314 for every man, woman and child in Victoria.

To put it another way, this year Victorians will pay $9.4 billion in GST, but Victoria will get back just $7.8 billion. The total annual subsidy is now $3.9 billion, and it's borne entirely by Victoria and NSW.

While there is a reasonable case for a continuing subsidy to Tasmania, South Australia and the Northern Territory, the same cannot be said for Queensland, Western Australia and the ACT.

It's an outmoded, antiquated, clapped out, inefficient and unfair system and it's time the Commonwealth government did something about it.

VERTICAL FISCAL IMBALANCE

This raises the related issue of vertical fiscal imbalance (VFI).

Action to tackle these inequalities is becoming even more urgent because Victoria, like the other states, is now increasingly reliant on revenue from the Commonwealth. As Figure 2 shows, we have been moving to this position over time.

So VFI has clearly been worsening over time and it is not just about the GST. However, the introduction of the GST has worsened VFI.

Figure 1: 2005–06 GST Redistribution

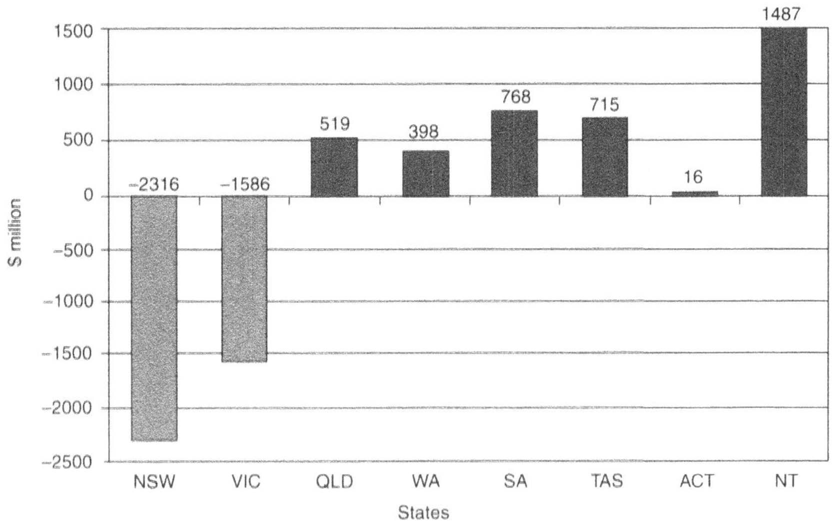

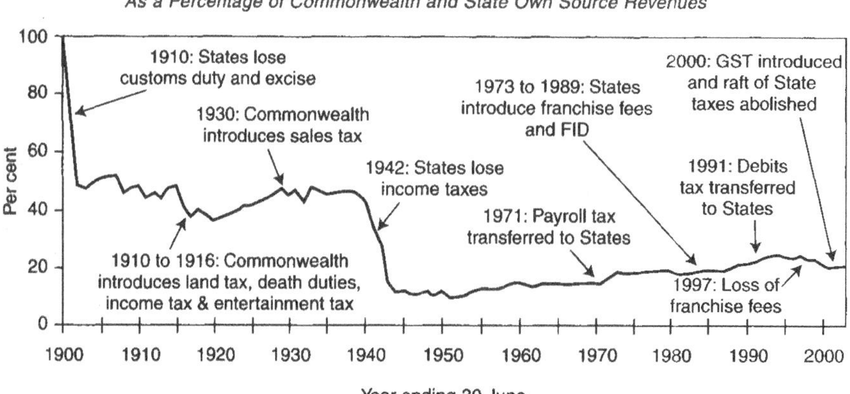

Source: Victorian Department of Treasury and Finance; Revenue Policy Group.

Figure 2: Six State Own Source Revenues

Source: WA Treasury.

As Figure 3 shows, since the introduction of the GST in 1999–2000, grants from the Commonwealth have grown from 35 per cent of Victoria's revenue to an estimated 45 per cent this financial year.

In other words, the states now have much-reduced control over our revenue sources, at the same time as we are experiencing growing demand for services such as health and education—areas where federal ministers are quick to remind us is the responsibility of the states (see Figure 4).

Health funding under the Australian Health Care Agreement is a good case in point. It is meant to be a 50:50 arrangement, but as you can see from Figure 4 Victoria is now footing nearly 60 per cent of the bill for public hospitals, compared to the Commonwealth's share of 41 per cent.

Clearly, health and education are the big ticket areas where the community wants to see investment from state governments, and that means the Commonwealth has an obligation to ensure the states can meet these expectations by distributing revenue in a responsible and fair manner, and by leaving us to determine our own spending priorities.

These are some of the threshold issues that must be part of a constructive dialogue between the Commonwealth and the states. But we need to do a lot more if Victoria and Australia are to meet the challenges that lie ahead—and there are plenty of those on the horizon.

Figure 3: Victorian Own-Source Taxation/Commonwealth Grants

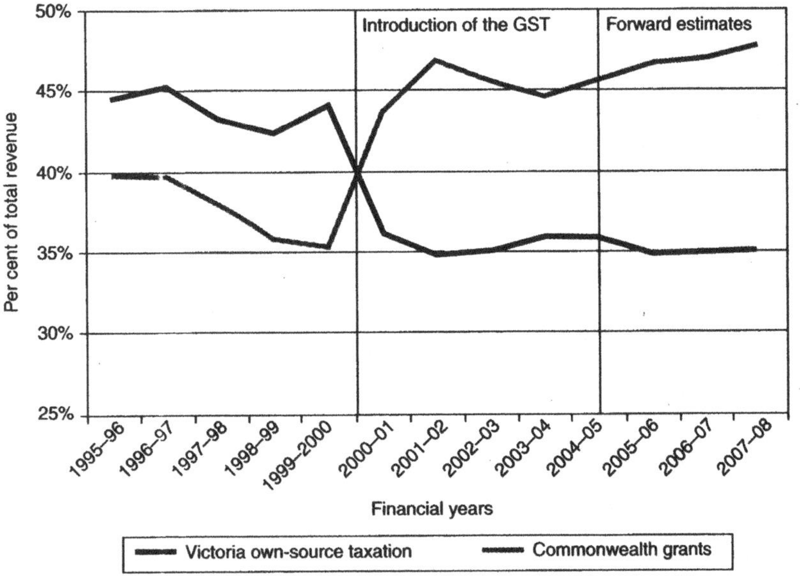

Source: WA Treasury.

Source: Victorian Department of Human Services.

CHALLENGES AHEAD

On the international front, we're facing a new generation of economic superpowers and growing regional economies that will transform the global economic landscape. For example, some forecasters are predicting that, in less than 40 years, the emerging so-called BRIC economies (Brazil, Russia, India and China) could be collectively larger than the G6 economies in US dollar terms (see Figure 5).

We're also facing increasing competition from countries in our region, such as China, India and the Asian Tiger economies, with low labour costs and large workforces.

And just as new economic leaders will emerge, so too will new technologies, such as biotechnology and nanotechnology, create new economic challenges and opportunities.

With these major international shifts on the horizon, it is vital for Victoria and Australia to position ourselves as innovators and reformers or risk falling behind.

On the domestic front, it's becoming clear that Australia is losing the momentum gained from the reforms of the 1980s and 1990s and that we risk moving into an era of slower economic and productivity growth.

Looking longer term, the combination of an ageing population and declining fertility rates will reduce our working-age population and lead to lower levels of labour force participation, falling productivity and rising pressures on the state budgets (see Figure 6).

In short, the coming decades are likely to be testing times for Victoria and Australia. But these problems are not insurmountable: continued strong economic growth is possible if we improve labourforce participation rates and increase productivity, and to do that we must maintain the momentum of the reforms begun in the 1980s and 1990s.

Figure 5: Projected Growth in BRIC and G6 Economies

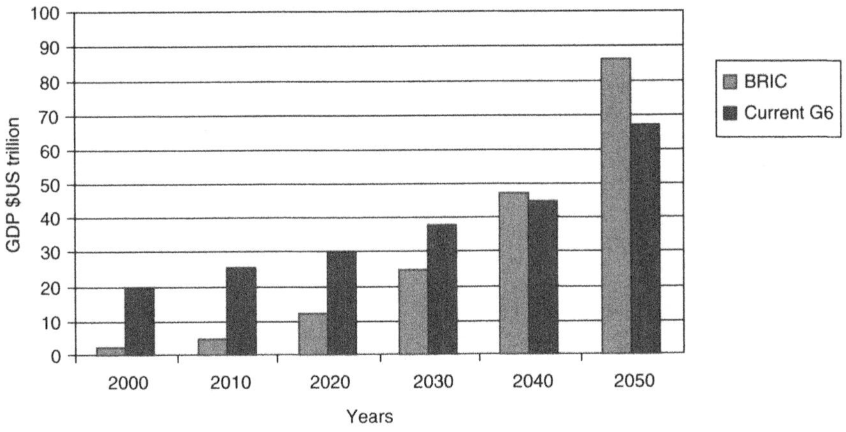

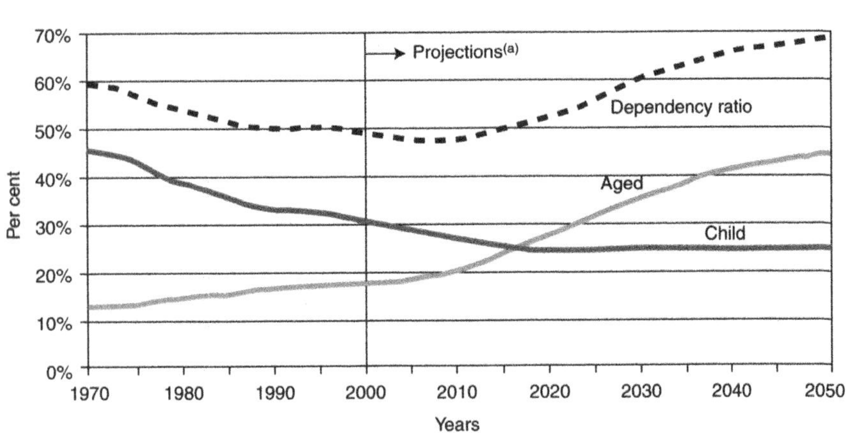

Source: Goldman Sachs, Oct 2003.

Figure 6: Ageing Population Challenges

Chart shows child (<15) and aged (>65) to working age (15–64) ratio.
(a) ABS Series R.

Source: ABS Series.

THE NEED FOR FURTHER REFORM

I remember when the Hawke and Keating governments knuckled down to the task of serious economic reform, and it was not an easy exercise. But tough decisions were made—cutting tariffs, de-regulating financial markets, floating the dollar, enterprise bargaining, competition policy, compulsory superannuation—and a decade down the track, Australia is still benefiting from those reforms.

But the reform picture in 2005 is a very different story.

The Commonwealth government can slice and dice it any way it likes (and create any number of distractions) but I doubt if you will find any independent presenter at this conference who will dispute the fact that the pace of reform has slackened off under the current federal government's watch.

And it has slackened off in the areas we need it most: competition reform, industry policy and investment in infrastructure and skills.

The OECD has also put us on notice, pointing out in its Economic Survey of Australia for 2004 that 'the pace of reform has recently not been as strong as it could have been'.

I am not suggesting the reform task is solely a Commonwealth responsibility: clearly, the states have a major role to play.

But from where Victoria stands, the evidence is pretty compelling: we are well and truly meeting our reform obligations, while the Commonwealth is not.

VICTORIA LEADS ON REFORM

Here in Victoria, we are leading the way on reform.

We are Australia's top competition performer and my department of Treasury and Finance estimate that we account for more than one third of the national gains from implementing the National Competition Policy (NCP).

In 2003 and 2004, the National Competition Council noted that Victoria had out-performed all other Australian jurisdictions and praised Victoria for implementing reforms that have improved productivity and provided a more competitive business environment.

And we're staying ahead of the pack through the creation of the Victorian Competition and Efficiency Commission, which will drive new regulation reform, further reduce business costs and improve Victoria's competitiveness.

In contrast, the Commonwealth's rate of compliance with the NCP is the second lowest in the country—hardly commensurate with national

Figure 7: Contribution to GDP from NCP Reforms

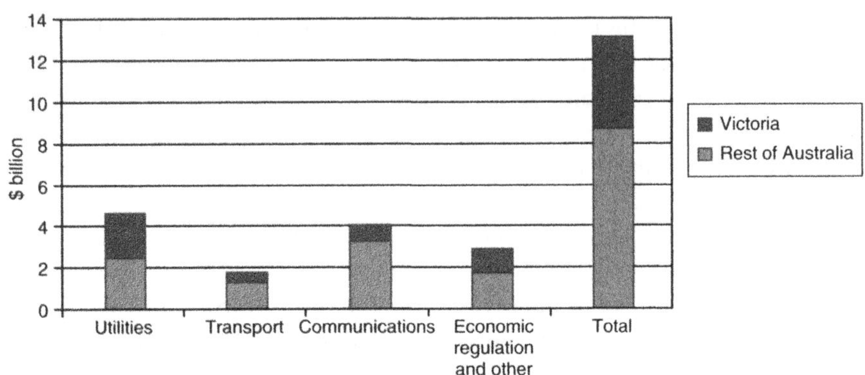

Source: Victorian Department of Treasury and Finance modelling.

leadership on major structural reform. What's more, in 2004 the Commonwealth government unilaterally decided to end competition payments to the states from 2006–07.

In one stroke, that action stripped hundreds of millions of dollars from state budgets, removed incentives for further reform and jeopardised future competition improvements.

That action will cost Victoria around $200 million a year, and it makes a mockery of the Commonwealth's claims that the states aren't doing their bit on reform.

It is undeniable that the federal government has dropped the ball on reform, and that is a serious problem because the states cannot do it alone. We cannot achieve our goals in the areas where it most counts, such as boosting productivity and workforce participation, without a national commitment to reform.

And while the Commonwealth needs to step up and take the leading role in driving reform, it also needs to recognise that a much more co-operative working relationship with the states and territories is essential to addressing the challenges facing the country.

COMMONWEALTH–STATE RELATIONS: A CO-OPERATIVE APPROACH

In this context, last week's impasse at the Treasurers' Council in relation to GST revenues was both regrettable and avoidable.

I say that because in a sense both sides of the argument are right. The states are right when we say we have kept our part of the GST agreement

100 per cent. We have abolished all taxes required to date and future tax reductions were only ever subject to review, on the basis that subsequent abolition would not impede our capacity to deliver vital health, education and community services.

From the Commonwealth's perspective, I can understand why the Federal Treasurer would want some of the future GST revenue flows applied to ongoing tax reductions. We all want to see a more competitive and efficient national economy, but we also have to balance budgets and meet growing demands in health and education.

In terms of Victoria's position, it is worth noting that Victoria has already abolished—or has never had in place—all but two of the taxes listed for review under the Inter-Governmental Agreement (IGA). We've also been very proactive in abolishing or reducing inefficient state taxes, including some not mentioned in the IGA.

Since the Bracks government came to office, we have announced the abolition of six taxes and provided business tax relief of more than $1 billion and land tax relief in excess of $1 billion. So, we're pretty satisfied that we've more than kept our side of the bargain when it comes to both competition and tax reform.

Figure 8: Victorian Taxes Abolished Under the IGA

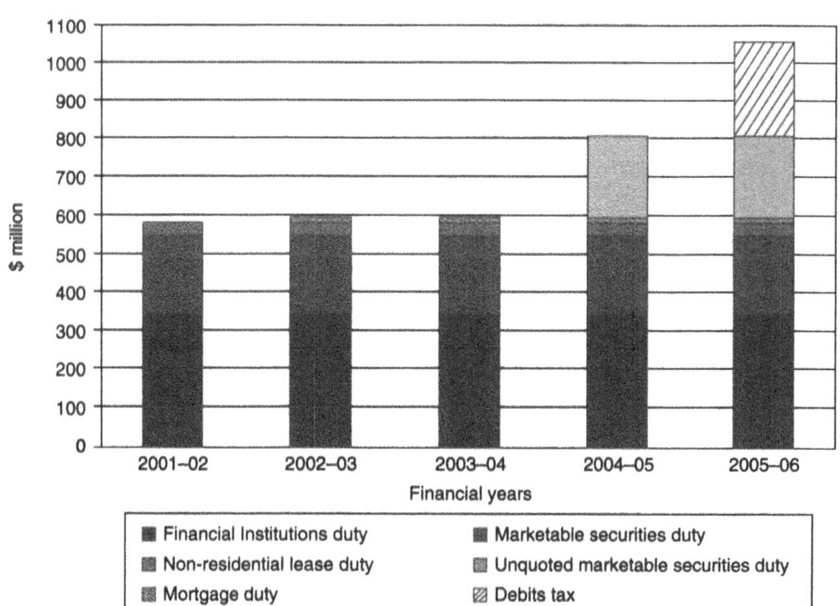

Source: Victorian Department of Treasury and Finance; Economic, Social and Environmental Group.

Because of our strong reform record, Victoria will be the least affected of the states under Mr Costello's proposal.

Over the coming weeks the states and Commonwealth will continue to discuss these issues in an attempt to find a constructive way forward. However, last week's events in Canberra did reinforce the fact that we need a much broader discussion than one centred solely on tax reform.

The Australian economy is running out of steam, and we need a new framework to drive ongoing productivity improvement.

Tax reform is just one factor in the development of a more productive and competitive economy and, instead of trying to bludgeon the states into submission on tax, it would be far more productive to have a much broader discussion about national goals, priorities and responsibilities, especially in services such as education and health.

WE NEED A NATIONAL REFORM AGENDA

Victoria recognises the pressing need for a stronger national effort on reform, and we are pushing for a new agenda that includes:

- a new model of co-operative federalism to address important national priorities, including reform of Commonwealth–state financial relations;
- a nationwide commitment to improving competition and regulation;
- greater investment in world-class infrastructure;
- a new national target for boosting workforce participation; and
- a national approach to growing Australia's population.

These are all critical areas where reform is needed, and where Australia would benefit from improved Commonwealth–state co-operation and a broader national agenda.

For example, we need a national target to achieve the level of workforce participation necessary to maintain economic growth, quality services and standards of living in the face of an ageing population. Over the next fifteen years, we must aim to increase labour force participation by at least five percentage points and nine percentage points over the next thirty-five years.

A recent Victorian study commissioned by my department identified a range of policies to increase participation rates, including:

- improving educational attainment;
- delaying retirement;
- improving childcare services; and
- welfare reforms.

Figure 9: Workforce Participation Target

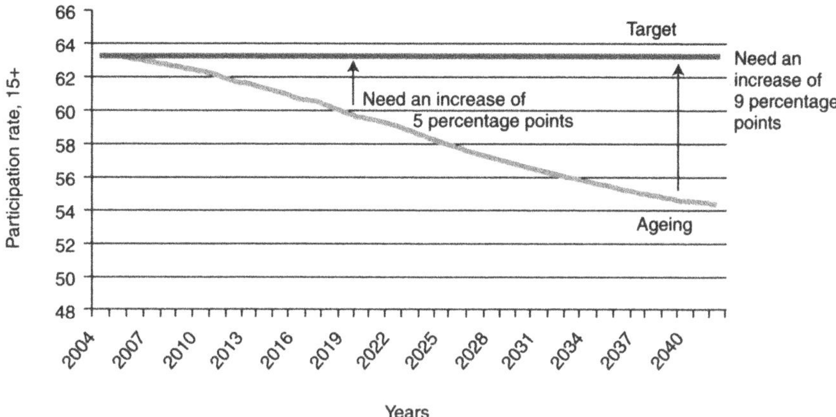

Source: Victorian Department of Treasury and Finance.

Figure 10: Impact of Policy on Participation

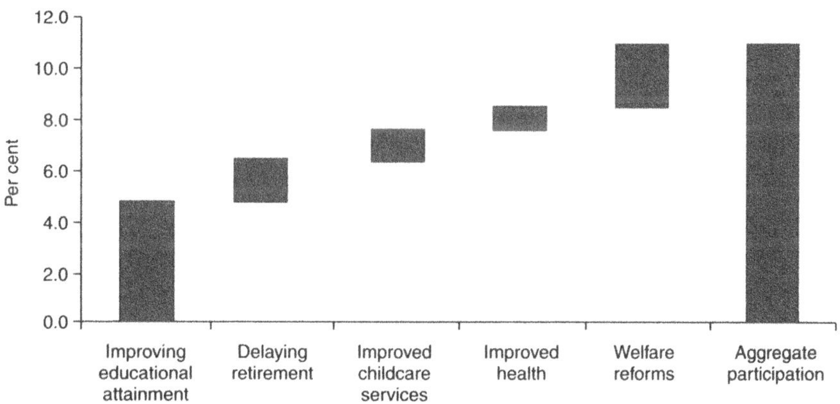

Source: Victorian Department of Treasury and Finance, *Addressing Impacts of Population Ageing on Labour Force Participation (2005)*; Strategic Policy Group.

These are all areas where Commonwealth, state and territory governments have to do much better if we are to avoid a future in which a relatively small workforce ends up supporting a large dependent population.

We've called for national action, financial reforms and planning to follow Victoria's lead in delivering far greater investment in public infrastructure. We're pushing for a strong national approach to address skills shortages and boost skilled migration.

And we've put forward several proposals to get the NCP reform process underway again, including moving ahead with reforms that reflect future challenges, such as population ageing and environmental sustainability.

We can tackle these issues, as we have done in the past, with national strategies, goals and agreements.

And we must tackle them because they are the issues that will affect Australia's international competitiveness and production capacity. They are the issues that will impact upon our ability to sustain growth and prosperity into the future.

CONCLUSION

I say: let's put it all on the table.

Let's acknowledge that Australia needs to pick up the pace of reform and have a mature and robust debate about how the Commonwealth and states can work together to achieve that goal.

I think it's fair to say that there is broad agreement across the country on both the key challenges facing Australia and many of the potential solutions—and that means the Commonwealth has nothing to fear and everything to gain from working with the states to set a new reform agenda.

I mightn't always like the way Canberra is going about it but this isn't about us: this is what is in the national interest. I also see these events as an opportunity for Commonwealth and state governments to consider an improved, more co-operative framework and a new round of much-needed reform.

More than ever before, at this very critical time for Australia, we should not be bickering at the margins: we should be engaged together in the task of reform, recognising that it is a national priority, a national obligation and something that must be undertaken in the long-term national interest.

ACKNOWLEDGEMENTS

Professor Peter Dawkins—Melbourne Institute
David Crawford—Acting President, National Competition Council

6 FEDERAL–STATE RELATIONS AND THE NATIONAL COMPETITION POLICY

MR DAVID CRAWFORD
Acting President, National Competition Council

BENEFITS FROM MICROECONOMIC REFORMS

The effectiveness of the economic reforms embarked on by Australia from the mid 1980s in enhancing productivity and economic growth is now universally recognised, as is the proposition that ongoing reform is needed if Australia is to retain hard-won benefits and maintain adequate growth. Recent assessments of microeconomic reforms in general, and the role of the National Competition Policy (NCP) reforms in particular, indicate that:

- The NCP has delivered substantial net benefits for Australia, but it would be counterproductive to conclude that it is time to sit back and enjoy the dividends.
- Australia has the potential to reap further substantial benefits simply by meeting the productivity benchmarks achieved by other countries.
- Further reform is imperative to lock in the gains achieved over the past two decades and also because Australia confronts an increasingly competitive

global environment, domestic pressures (such as an ageing population), and federal–state arrangements that promote cost shifting and blurred lines of accountability.

A raft of work by domestic institutions such as the Productivity Commission and international bodies such as the OECD supports these interpretations. A recent report by The Allen Consulting Group for the National Competition Council (NCC) indicates that if Australia does no more than complete the remnant aspects of the NCP, then relative to overseas countries, it will be left behind in living standards. All the evidence suggests that we assume at our peril that the reforms to date are sufficient to ensure that the Australian economy is now bullet proof.

NEED FOR RE-INVIGORATED REFORM PROCESS

Last year the Australian government directed the Productivity Commission to report on the effectiveness of the NCP and to outline a renewed reform program. The Commission concluded that further competition-related reforms are needed to improve productivity and raise living standards. Its report will inform deliberations this year by the Council of Australian Governments on how best to proceed. The scene is therefore set for the substantive debate on a new agenda and the institutional arrangements that should underpin it.

The NCC's experience over the last decade of the NCP confirms that institutional arrangements are instrumental to the success of the reform agenda. The success of the NCP is built on three pillars:

1   A formal and binding commitment of governments to an agenda.
2   An independent agency to monitor and assess governments' performance against those commitments.
3   Incentives for governments to progress reforms that, while in the public interest, are sometimes politically difficult to implement.

Had the NCP relied only on the first pillar, the Productivity Commission's draft report would have described the outcomes of the NCP as falling short of those envisaged at the outset. The integrated three-pillar model, which centres on reasonable flexibility and iteration, is a pragmatic recognition of the difficulties in implementing a co-ordinated reform agenda in an Australian federation composed of nine sovereign governments.

THE AGENDA

The NCC supports the Productivity Commission's candidates for a new agenda to promote further productivity growth and, importantly, to maintain the benefits of reform to date, including:

- a review of Australia's health care system, extension of natural resource management reforms, renewed energy and water reform programs, and co-ordinated reform frameworks for freight and passenger transport;
- improving the quality and responsiveness of education and training systems, enhancing the performance of aged care services delivery, extending the scope for workplace flexibility, and removing inefficiencies in the work-incentive effects of taxation and social support programs;
- improving competition and regulatory architecture through a more focused legislation review program, strengthened monitoring and gatekeeping arrangements, improved oversight of infrastructure providers, and continuation of competitive neutrality policies.

While acknowledging the importance of efficient social infrastructure services for productivity, the provision (and regulation) of 'hard' economic infrastructure is likely to remain at the forefront of a new policy agenda.

For a start, there is much unfinished business under the NCP—Australia is yet to achieve a fully competitive national electricity market and there is a need to move beyond the limited road transport reforms to a broader agenda that co-ordinates and integrates road and rail transport services with ports. Moreover, apart from assessing NCP reforms, one of the council's other roles is to recommend on the design and coverage of infrastructure access regimes. This work reinforces that a new agenda must appropriately balance pro-competitive outcomes for users with infrastructure investment. As these important agenda issues will be raised by others, the council has focused on its key area of expertise: institutional arrangements to progress reforms in Australia's federation.

INDEPENDENT ASSESSMENT AND MONITORING

The reality of federal–state relations is that a reform agenda will deliver the greatest benefits by achieving inter-jurisdictional co-operation. But there are enormous challenges, not least of which is implementing welfare-enhancing policies given the practicalities of horizontal (between states and territories) and vertical (between the three tiers of government) co-ordination. As a starting point, it is imperative that the assessment process is sufficiently at arms-length to independently gauge governments' outcomes in meeting the obligations of a reform agenda. An independent assessor can clarify reform commitments and maintain governments' focus on implementing reform.

For example, the NCC has a long history of continual constructive engagement with governments at both the political and official levels to progress reform. Alternatives, such as using agencies within jurisdictions to monitor outcomes, pose serious risks of conflict between the necessarily public interest perspective of the assessor and the political imperatives of governments. Such a decentralised assessment model also cannot properly compare and contrast differences in performance across jurisdictions.

Another alternative would be to have multiple bodies (for example, Ministerial Councils and other CoAG entities) undertaking monitoring and assessment for specific areas (such as transport and energy). While there may well be merit in relevant expert bodies being responsible for policy matters, agenda setting and implementation, the NCC has reservations about such bodies also undertaking assessments. The substantial problem with the multiple assessor model is that, unlike the NCP, it would be a disparate approach unsuited to 'whole of program' assessment.

Similarly, having inter-jurisdictional working groups or committees of the parties assess their own performance (and potentially re-specify targets) would also be problematic. Based on experience, the NCC considers that the prospect of jurisdictions setting, monitoring and reconfiguring their own benchmarks—perhaps in a charged environment of partisan politics— is far less likely to deliver appropriate outcomes. The protracted Ministerial Council process for national reviews, for example, has certainly dissipated the potential benefits through continual re-specification of timelines and shifting targets to meet the desires of particular jurisdictions.

More generally, as the Chamber of Commerce and Industry (WA) told the Productivity Commission inquiry:

> CoAG ... lacks the resources to conduct the detailed and exhaustive analysis necessary to develop good policy on complex, multi-faceted issues. In part, this is because CoAG's activities have tended to be issue-specific, reactive and pragmatic, and not always informed by an in-principle framework for analysing inter-jurisdictional issues and for aligning political incentives with desired outcomes. Perhaps an independent body to research, evaluate and critique cross-jurisdictional policy development is necessary to supplement and critique the work of CoAG ...

A major strength of the current assessment model is its foundation of transparency (involving publicly available assessment reports), adherence to timelines and, most importantly, frank assessments conducted independently of the parties being assessed.

INCENTIVE PAYMENTS

Competition payments, the incentive aspect of the NCP, are based on the view that states and territories should share in the increased government revenues that accrue, especially to the Australian government, from the increased economic activity generated by the NCP reforms.

The Productivity Commission found that competition payments have been instrumental in securing the implementation of NCP reforms. Certainly the NCC can attest that competition payments overcome many of the difficulties of federalism and are pivotal in maintaining reform momentum within the states and territories. Tying performance to financial rewards has also enabled governments to argue that they have had no option other than to meet their NCP commitments, thereby providing a circuit breaker to resist pressure from lobby groups to retain anti-competitive arrangements.

The existence of competition payments has also empowered jurisdictional competition policy units to a far greater extent than otherwise. The benefits of strong competition 'watchdogs' at the coalface should not be under-estimated.

There can be no doubt that governments have had a stronger incentive to pursue outcomes consistent with the public interest because competition payments are available. Conversely, the potential for unwinding, or watering down, reforms would be a real threat without payments.

INTERACTION BETWEEN THE THREE PILLARS

The success of the NCP can be attributed to the interdependencies between the agenda, the assessor, and the incentive payments. These allow for:

- assessments with sufficient flexibility to facilitate reform progress rather than imposing rigid compliance targets. For example, suspensions allow for difficult reforms to be rolled over, thereby raising the potential rewards from compliance and providing time to devise reasonable transitional reform programs;
- different mechanisms to meet different reform agendas rather than recourse to a rigid top-down model that may not be suited to particular jurisdictions; and
- consistent assessment and monitoring of progress across nine governments that are introducing reform measures at different speeds, from different start

points, in highly variable environments (political, geographic, climatic, and so on)—these circumstances can be reflected in payments, suspensions, deductions and provision for transitional reform programs over time.

The evidence of the benefits of the three-pillars approach is clear. For example:

- The legislation review program of the NCP encompasses around 1800 pieces of legislation across nine governments. From 1996 to 2002, the NCC assisted governments to find ways to meet to meet their obligations. As the June 2002 completion date for this element of the NCP approached, the NCC forewarned governments that reductions in incentive payments were likely. The NCC provided a further year's grace period before imposing penalties in 2003. Since the imposition of penalties, compliance rates for priority legislation improved markedly—from 40 per cent in 2001 to nearly 75 per cent in 2004.
- In 2003 the NCC recommended 'pool suspensions' for every state and territory government. (These suspensions related to each government's pool of incomplete legislation review matters.) The following year the NCC recommended that, with the exception of two states, all suspended funds be released to reflect the substantial improvements in compliance.
- Also in 2003, the NCC recommended substantial suspensions be imposed on Queensland for the state's failure to meet electricity reform obligations and on Western Australia for a lack of transparency in water pricing. These obligations were met the following year and both suspensions were lifted.
- Similar positive responses to penalties were evident for many difficult reform areas (e.g. poultry meat, egg marketing and liquor regulation).
- In seeking to progress reforms, many governments used the payments as a tool to leverage compliant outcomes by ameliorating the impact of vested interests.

The judicious use of constructive engagement, and, as a last resort, suspensions and deductions to account for particular circumstances in each jurisdiction, have been critical to the success of the program.

WHERE NOW?

It is the NCC's view that the institutional arrangements for any new reform agenda will be crucial to its success and that the three interlocking institutional pillars that have underpinned the effectiveness of the NCP should continue.

It is one thing to identify what needs to be done: it is another to establish the framework to ensure that reform objectives are carried through to fruition. It would be a tragedy if, in the future, a review of the new reform agenda found that it was a program of meritorious intent unmatched by outcomes because the institutional framework was insufficient to carry it through. Such a missed opportunity would be keenly felt by the Australian community.

Given the practicalities of Australia's brand of federalism, the nation cannot afford to experiment with institutional frameworks and hope that an alternative model will match the goals set by a new reform agenda. The three-pillars model has been shown to work and this should set the benchmark for the new agenda.

Australia is at the crossroads. It has reaped substantial benefits from reform and is poised to embark on a renewed reform program at a time of favourable economic conditions. Australia can go forward with a new workable reform program or it can allow a long history of federal–state tensions to put the nation on a low-growth path.

The NCC considers that, in light of Australia's brand of fiscal federalism, the high-growth path will require effective forms of agenda-setting intergovernmental agreements that reflect:

- independent 'whole of program' monitoring of reform implementation;
- incentives to meet obligations and sanctions for failure to meet obligations;
- overarching principles to ensure desired outcomes are delivered;
- sufficient detail on requirements to benchmark the assessment of performance;
- interim benchmarks (where outcomes are longer term) and mechanisms for priority setting so the reform process does not stall; and
- mechanisms to refine agreements that avoid inappropriately winding back the obligations. This can be avoided by:
  — requiring unanimous CoAG agreement to change the commitments,
  — requiring CoAG to endorse the work of other bodies (e.g. Ministerial Councils) before that work becomes part of the agreements, or
  — providing sufficient detail in the agreements and constraining other bodies to developing approaches consistent with the overarching CoAG agreements.

7 INCOME, WEALTH AND JOBLESSNESS: INSIGHTS FROM THE HILDA SURVEY

Associate Professor Bruce Headey and Professor Mark Wooden
Melbourne Institute of Applied Economic and Social Research,
University of Melbourne

INTRODUCTION

Most of the social statistics we are all familiar with are cross-sectional; that is, they provide snapshots—still photographs—of situations at one moment in time. By repeating cross-sectional studies we can tell whether, at an aggregate level, trends are positive or negative. For example, we can assess whether numbers in poverty or unemployment are increasing or decreasing.

Panel studies are more like movies than still photographs. They can tell us not just whether aggregate trends are improving or declining, but also whether individuals and families have short-term, medium-term or long-term problems. For public policy purposes, this information is crucial, since presumably we would all agree that long- and medium-term problems are more serious, and may need quite different solutions, than short-term problems.

In this paper we use panel data from the first three waves of the Household, Income and Labour Dynamics in Australia (HILDA) Survey to provide new evidence about income mobility and labour force dynamics.[1] We also examine new data on the wealth holdings of Australians. More specifically, after briefly describing the data and providing definitions for key terms used in this paper, we begin by examining data on relative income mobility. We then focus on low-income households and show how our understanding of income poverty can be substantially changed when viewed from a dynamic rather than static perspective. The next section uses the data on wealth collected in wave 2 to examine the composition and distribution of wealth in Australia. Special attention is given to the issue of household debt. While these data do not provide any information about wealth dynamics (detailed information about wealth has only been collected in one wave of the HILDA Survey to date), they nevertheless are of interest because of the absence of such data in Australia prior to the HILDA Survey being administered. We then present information on labour force transitions, with particular focus on episodes of unemployment. In the final substantive section of the paper the focus is on joblessness at the household level, rather than individual level, and in particular on the extent to which household joblessness persists.

DATA

THE HILDA SURVEY SAMPLE

The HILDA Survey is a nation-wide household panel survey with a focus on issues relating to employment, income and the family. It is funded by the Australian government (through the Department of Family and Community Services) but managed by the Melbourne Institute of Applied Economic and Social Research. Described in more detail in Watson and Wooden (2004a), the HILDA Survey began in 2001 with a large national probability sample of Australian households occupying private dwellings. All members of those responding households in wave 1 form the basis of the panel to be pursued in each subsequent wave, with each wave of interviewing being approximately one year apart.

Note that like virtually all sample surveys, the homeless are excluded from the scope of the HILDA Survey. Also excluded from the initial sample were persons living in institutions, though persons who move into institutions in subsequent years remain in the sample.

After adjusting for out-of-scope dwellings (e.g. unoccupied, non-residential) and households (e.g. all occupants were overseas visitors) and for multiple households within dwellings, the total number of households identified as in-scope in wave 1 was 11,693. Interviews were completed with all eligible members at 6872 of these households and with at least one eligible member at a further 810 households. The total household response rate was, therefore, 66 per cent. Within the 7682 households at which interviews were conducted, there were 19,917 people, 4790 of whom were under 15 years of age on the preceding 30 June and hence were ineligible for an interview. This left 15,127 persons of whom 13,969 were successfully interviewed. Of this group, 11,993 were re-interviewed in wave 2 and 11,190 were re-interviewed in wave 3.

The total number of respondents in each wave, however, is greater than this for at least three reasons. First, some non-respondents in wave 1 are successfully interviewed in later waves. Second, interviews are sought in later waves with all persons who turn 15 years of age. Third, additional persons are added to the sample (mostly on a temporary basis)[2] as a result of changes in household composition (interviews are sought with all persons who live with a sample member even if they were not part of the original sample).

DEFINITIONS

Income

The measure of income used throughout this paper is equivalised disposable household income. Following the practice of the Australian Bureau of Statistics (ABS), our income measure does not include income received in the form of goods or services (information on which is not collected in the HILDA Survey). Also in line with ABS practice, we attempt to restrict income to receipts that are of a regular and recurrent nature. Thus income from severance payments, inheritances and bequests, and from other types of lump-sum payments is excluded.[3] The income variable used here is thus best described as total 'regular' after-tax income, which was constructed by summing income from wages and salary, unincorporated businesses, investments, private pensions (i.e. superannuation and workers' compensation), government benefits and pensions, and other regular sources (e.g. child support payments), and deducting Commonwealth taxation payments, which were estimated on the basis of reported incomes, employment and family circumstances (see Headey 2003). Some government payments—Family Tax Payments and Child Care Benefits—were also estimated. Where information on any of the main income components was missing, the value of the component was imputed using a method developed specifically for longitudinal data.[4] The components refer to receipts (or payments) during the financial year preceding interview. Each household's net income is then adjusted using the modified OECD equivalence scale.[5] As is the standard practice in the international literature, the income-receiving unit used here is the 'individual'. That is, all household members (including children) are attributed with the equivalent net income of the household to which they belong.

Income poverty

In developed countries it is generally accepted that poverty is largely a relative concept. That is, a person or household is assumed to live in relative poverty if they are unable to afford the goods and services needed to enjoy a normal or mainstream lifestyle in the country in which they live. We thus follow international convention in defining poverty as having an income level below some pre-specified low-income threshold or 'poverty line'.[6] Further, since the definition of poverty employed here is a relative one, it makes sense to set that poverty line relative to the population median. Thus, we define a household as poor if it has an equivalised disposable income that is less than half that of the median, or typical, income. Clearly, other thresholds could have been chosen. The European Union, for example, has recently adopted a poverty line set at 60 per cent of median income. Very differently, Harding et al. (2000) favoured half the mean income, rather than half the median (but reported both), while in Australia others have continued to rely on the Henderson poverty line, which was central to the 1975 Commission of Inquiry into Poverty chaired by Ronald Henderson (Commission of Inquiry into Poverty 1975). Choice of the poverty threshold clearly matters for the absolute numbers estimated as living in poverty but turns out to have little bearing on the analysis of poverty dynamics.

Wealth

One of the innovations of the HILDA Survey was that it included, in wave 2, questions intended to measure the wealth of Australian households. Specifically, the intention was that the survey would cover all physical and financial assets and debts with the exception of home contents and accounts payable. Many of the questions were asked at the household level and answered by one person on behalf of the entire household. These questions covered housing and property, business assets and liabilities, equity-type investments (e.g. shares, managed funds) and cash-type investments (e.g. bonds, debentures), vehicles and collectibles (e.g. artworks). However, some questions about assets and debts—those that it was felt could not be reported accurately by one person on behalf of all—were asked of individuals. These included questions about superannuation, bank accounts, credit cards, HECS debt and other personal debt. In most cases, respondents were asked to provide exact dollar amounts. Like the income data, where information on any major wealth component was missing, the missing value was replaced with an imputed value.[7]

Labour force activity

The HILDA Survey uses the standard labour force activity framework employed by the ABS to classify the population into employed, unemployed and 'not in the labour force' states. Indeed, for estimates derived at the time of interview, the approach used is close to identical to that employed in the monthly Labour Force Survey.[8] In deriving information about labour force activity in the period preceding (and between) interview dates, the approach used was necessarily much less complicated and based on a self-classification system. That is, respondents were required to determine, for every period between the start of the preceding financial year and the interview, whether they had a paid job, were not employed but looking for work, or were neither employed nor looking for work.

Jobless households

One concept that appears in this paper is that of the jobless household. In its simplest form this is any household where no member is in paid work. The longitudinal nature of the data, however, demands that we specify a time-frame. In the analysis reported here the key time unit is the financial year. We thus could define a household as jobless where no member of the household was employed at any time during that year. We, however, felt this definition was overly restrictive, and opted instead to define a household as jobless (or at least, 'near jobless') when no household member had been in work for more than 25 per cent of the last financial year. Further, for the main analysis we have excluded any household where the household reference person or head was aged 60 years or over or was a full-time student at the date of interview.[9]

WEIGHTS

While the intent was to recruit a randomly selected population that was representative of the Australian population resident in private households, non-response and attrition combine to reduce the representativeness of the sample. Drawing inferences about the wider population thus requires adjusting responses through the application of population weights which account for both non-random response at wave 1 and attrition bias in subsequent waves. All estimates reported in this paper thus use the relevant population weights (both cross-sectional and longitudinal) that are provided with the data.[10]

INCOME MOBILITY

Social science textbooks often present an image of society as being like a layer cake, or a pyramid. Better off and higher status people are pictured on the top layer (or at the top of the pyramid) and the impression is given that they remain there for long periods, perhaps for an entire lifetime (or even longer, given status might be transmitted across generation). Middle income or middle class people are pictured as remaining long-term in the middle layers of society, and the poor or lower status people are shown in the lower layers, or at the bottom of the pyramid. Further, such a static view of society seems, at first glance, to be consistent with conventional analyses of income distribution which show that differences in incomes between those at the top of the distribution and those at the bottom only change slowly over time (e.g. Johnson & Wilkins 2004).

In reality, however, the income distribution is more fluid. That is, the position of households in the income distribution is not fixed, and the relative position of some households will improve over time while others will deteriorate. With longitudinal data, the extent of relative income mobility can be measured. Of course, ideally we would use data over quite a long period (a decade or more), whereas we currently only have three waves of data from the HILDA Survey. Nevertheless, some interesting and perhaps unexpected patterns of change are observable.

Our analysis of income mobility involves classifying individuals into deciles based on their equivalised disposable household income for 2000–01 and then again for 2002–03, and then cross-tabulating to provide a mobility matrix. This is reported in Table 1 and shows how the relative income position of individuals has changed between 2000–01 and 2002–03. Printed in bold italics along the top left to bottom right diagonal are the proportions of persons within each decile group in the starting year whose relative income position did not change at all.

To understand how to interpret this table, consider the first column of numbers. This column shows in what part of the income distribution persons who were in the poorest decile group in 2001–01 are found two years later. Thus 37.5 per cent of this group were still in the poorest decile two years on, while just over another quarter (26.8 per cent) had only moved up to the second poorest decile. Such figures thus suggest a moderate degree of stability, at least at the bottom end of the income distribution. On the other hand, the data also reveal significant upward mobility, with over one-third of persons in the poorest decile moving up by more than one decile group and almost one in ten finding their way into the top half of the income distribution.[11]

Table 1: Relative Income Mobility, 2000–01 to 2002–03 (%)

		Decile income group 2000–01									
		D1	D2	D3	D4	D5	D6	D7	D8	D9	D10
Decile income group 2002–03	D1	**37.5**	22.2	10.0	10.9	5.6	4.0	2.5	2.4	2.9	2.1
	D2	26.8	**37.3**	15.9	7.5	5.8	2.2	2.1	1.2	0.9	0.4
	D3	13.9	19.8	**33.3**	12.1	6.4	4.8	3.8	1.6	3.1	1.2
	D4	7.9	9.7	19.7	**23.8**	19.3	7.0	4.8	4.3	1.5	2.1
	D5	4.1	4.2	8.0	20.9	**24.4**	17.5	9.8	5.1	2.7	3.1
	D6	3.0	2.1	6.2	11.4	18.6	**24.8**	15.7	8.7	5.4	4.2
	D7	2.6	2.1	3.4	6.1	9.5	21.3	**25.4**	17.4	7.6	4.4
	D8	1.8	1.3	1.0	3.6	5.1	10.4	23.5	**27.4**	17.6	8.3
	D9	1.4	1.3	1.1	2.5	3.9	4.8	8.9	21.7	**35.5**	18.8
	D10	1.0	0.1	1.4	1.4	1.4	3.1	3.4	10.2	22.6	**55.3**
		100.0	100.0	100.0	100.0	100.0	100.0	100.0	100.0	100.0	100.0

Note: Unweighted N = 15457.

Overall, we distil four key findings from Table 1. First, there is a moderate degree of stability in the income distribution. This can be seen by looking along the diagonal which shows that the proportion of each income decile group remaining in the same decile varies from 24 to 55 per cent. In total, just under one-third of the population did not change decile group. Second, and reinforcing this picture of stability, most of those persons who had changed their relative income position moved up or down by only one decile. Indeed, a little over another one-third (35.2 per cent) of the population moved up or down by one decile. In other words, most income mobility, at least over this two-year window, is relatively short-range. Third, despite an overall picture of moderate stability, a minority registered large changes in equivalised income. Of those who started in the bottom two deciles in 2001, 8.3 per cent were in the top half of the distribution by 2003. Conversely, among those who started in the top two deciles, 10.1 per cent were in the bottom half of the distribution by 2002–03. Fourth, and directly related to the preceding figures, the asymmetry in the mobility process often found in overseas studies (e.g. Jarvis & Jenkins 1998), where the relative mobility from the top to the bottom is more short-range than from the bottom to the top, is not replicated here. That is, while the rich are very likely to remain rich (55 per cent of the richest decile were still in the richest decile two years later), of those that do move downwards a significant proportion move a long way. So around 20 per cent of the richest decile who move down the income distribution in the following two years, move all the way into the bottom half of the income distribution. Conversely, among those in the bottom decile in 2000–01, the proportion of upward movers who make it into the top half of the distribution is slightly less—16 per cent.

INCOME POVERTY DYNAMICS

We now focus on poverty dynamics and begin by first reporting conventional one-year rates of income poverty. These are given in Part A of Table 2. As can be seen, poverty rates are reported for both the entire population and for the sub-group of children aged under 15 years of age. The first point to note is that these poverty rates are higher than is usually reported from data collected by the ABS, which at first glance should be surprising given analyses of ABS data are concerned with 'income units' and income units are generally smaller than households. Dickens and Wilkins (2005), for example, calculated a poverty rate for 1999–2000 using similar definitions to that used here of 11.9 per cent. In part, the higher rate reported here might reflect the fact that we have not excluded any cases or trimmed any outlying responses. Alternatively, it seems likely that this difference will also reflect differences between the HILDA Survey and the ABS income surveys.[12]

Second, the figures reported in Table 2 suggest that the incidence of poverty in Australia actually declined over the three years covered by the HILDA Survey. Such findings are of some interest in their own right given the emphasis in the recent majority report of the Senate Inquiry into Poverty which concluded that Australia was 'losing the fight for the fair go' (Senate Community Affairs Reference Committee 2004, p. xv). Note that changing the way the poverty threshold is calculated makes little difference to this conclusion. Poverty rates are also found to be falling (though not quite as quickly) when a poverty line set at 60 per cent of median household income is used.[13]

Nevertheless, it is neither the level of poverty (which obviously varies depending on how high or low the poverty line is set) nor the trend in the annual rates which we think is of large importance. Far more important is poverty persistence; that is, how many people remain below the poverty line in each of the three years for which data are available. Summary data on this are provided in Part B of Table 2. Still using the 50 per cent of median income poverty threshold, the table indicates that almost one-quarter of the population—24.3 per cent—were poor in at least one of the three years considered. But only 7.1 per cent were poor in two of the three years, and only 4.2 per cent were poor in all three years. This figure could be regarded as an initial estimate of the rate of medium-term poverty in this country. In other words, the rate of medium-term poverty is a great deal lower than the one-year poverty rate at the centre of most previous poverty discussions. Of course, the corollary of this finding is that quite a large number of Australians are poor at least occasionally.

Table 2: Annual Poverty Rates vs Poverty Persistence

	All persons	Children under 15 years of age
Part A: Annual poverty rates (%)		
2000–01	14.2	15.3
2001–02	13.2	14.5
2002–03	12.1	13.2
Part B: Poverty persistence,		
2000–01 to 2002–03 (% distribution)		
Never poor	75.7	73.0
Poor in only one year	13.0	14.6
Poor in two years	7.1	8.8
Poor in all three years	4.2	3.7

Another way of looking at the issue of poverty dynamics is provided by the tree approach used in Table 3. This table charts transitions in and out of poverty across each of the three waves for the balanced panel (that is, members of households responding in all three waves).[14] Thus we can see that of those measured as being poor in wave 1 (13.9 per cent of the weighted balanced panel), about half were still poor in wave 2, and of this group 60 per cent were still poor in wave 3. Multiplying these three fractions together, we arrive at the three-year poverty rate of 4.2 per cent reported in Table 2. Similarly, at the other end of the spectrum, of the 86 per cent of the population who were not poor in wave 1, almost 93 per cent were not poor at wave 2, and of this group 95 per cent were not poor in wave 3. Again multiplying through, we arrive at the never poor proportion (of around 76 per cent) reported in Table 2.

One problem with the data on poverty persistence reported on in Table 2 (and in Table 3) is that they are left censored. That is, we do not know for how long those people defined as living below the poverty threshold in our first year of data had already been living in poverty. Some

Table 3: Poverty Transitions, 2000–01 to 2002–03

Wave 1 (2000–01)	Wave 2 (2001–02)	Wave 3 (2002–03)
		Poor—60.2%
	Poor—50.4%	
		Not poor—39.8%
Poor—13.9%		
		Poor—28.6%
	Not poor—49.6%	
		Not poor—71.4%
		Poor—37.1%
	Poor—7.4%	
		Not poor—62.9%
Not poor—86.1%		
		Poor—5.1%
	Not poor—92.6%	
		Not poor—94.9%

of our sample members were almost certainly living in poverty for several years prior to 2000–01. Nevertheless, it does seem likely that most people who become poor soon cease to be poor. For example, and as shown in Table 3, of those who were not poor when first interviewed in 2001 but had fallen below the poverty line in the following year, only 37 per cent had not shifted above the poverty threshold a year later.

Although most people who enter poverty soon leave, a more sombre fact is that the longer one remains in poverty, the harder it is to escape. Table 3 demonstrates that the exit rate in 2002–03 for those who had already been poor for two years was considerably lower than the exit rate of those poor for only one year—39.8 per cent as compared with 62.9 per cent. And this exit rate can be expected to decline further as poverty duration lengthens.

Of course, it might still be that these movements in and out of poverty are not all that significant. That is, many of these exits from poverty may involve only small increases in income and/or are only temporary. While it will take more years of data collection before we can reach any definitive conclusion about the permanence of these exits from poverty, it is clear from Table 3 that not all poverty exits in any one year are permanent. Almost 29 per cent of those persons who were poor in wave 1 but were not measured as poor in wave 2 returned to poverty in wave 3. Of course, the flipside of this statistic is that the large majority of people exiting poverty in one year did not return to poverty the next.

With these data we can also examine by how far people escape poverty. In Figure 1 we report, for those persons measured as living in poverty in wave 1 but not in wave 2, the distribution of equivalised household disposable income relative to the population median. Thus we can see that close to half this group (45.4 per cent) had, in wave 2, not left poverty very far—their incomes were still below 60 per cent of the population median which, as noted earlier, is widely used in Europe as the poverty threshold. Further, when we move to wave 3 we can see that almost 29 per cent had returned to poverty while a further 27 per cent were only just above the poverty line (that is, their equivalised disposable income was between 50 and 60 per cent of the population median). On the other hand, it is also true that significant numbers escape poverty by a considerable margin. Most obviously, almost 16 per cent of these poverty exits involved a shift into the top half of the income distribution. Nevertheless, the fact that well over half (55.4 per cent) of those exiting poverty in wave 2 had either returned into poverty in wave 3 or were only slightly above the poverty threshold suggests that the three-year poverty rate highlighted earlier may be misleading. For example, redefining medium-term poverty persistence to include those persons whose income was below half-median in only two of the years, but whose income in the third year was still below 60 per cent of the population median, would almost double the estimated rate to 8.2 per cent.

It is worth reiterating, though, that these results should be treated with a good deal of caution. The HILDA Survey has to date yielded only three

Figure 1: Equivalised Disposable Household Income (Relative to Population Median) of Persons Exiting Poverty in Wave 2 (% distribution)

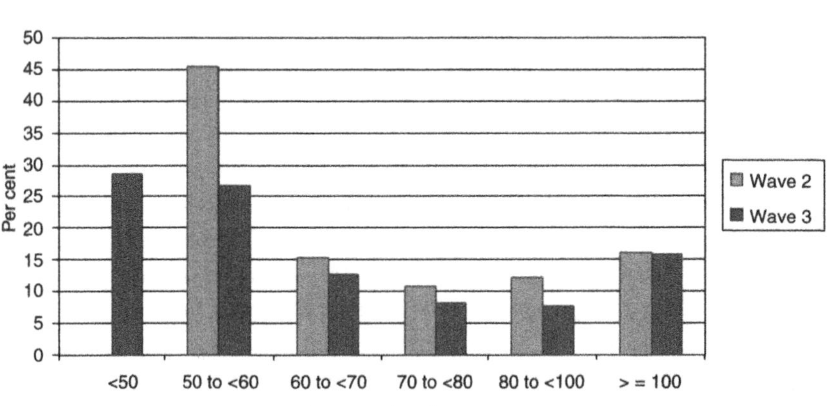

waves of data and it may well be that the data will suggest quite different conclusions once more waves of data come in. In particular, the experience from overseas research suggests that we are likely to find many more people escaping poverty by larger margins once we have even five or six waves of data.

Finally, and returning to Table 2, another significant finding concerns children. Like many other studies, the HILDA Survey data confirm the rather alarming finding that the annual poverty rate for children is typically higher than for the population average—13.2 per cent among children aged under 15 years in 2002–03 compared with an adult rate of 11.8 per cent. The position, however, is reversed when we use longitudinal data to make three-year estimates. The three-year poverty rate for children is 3.7 per cent, which compares with 4.3 per cent for adults. Again, however, we need to take into account how far above the poverty threshold those children leaving poverty in any one year are moving. If we treat short-range movements out of poverty in one year as not constituting a poverty exit, then the medium-term poverty rate for children would rise to 8.9 per cent, which is about one percentage point above the adult rate.

Overall, and unavoidably, it is not entirely clear what conclusions should be drawn from this initial analysis of poverty dynamics. At first cut we were drawn to the conclusion that the majority of Australians living in poverty do not remain there for long. And with additional waves of data from the HILDA Survey this may well be the conclusion that should be drawn. Nevertheless, we have also seen that many of the people who exit poverty in a single year do not move far above the poverty threshold and are clearly at some significant risk of dropping back into poverty.

What is clear, however, is that the number of persons at risk of persistent poverty is less than the numbered measured as living in poverty for a single year; recall that the annual poverty rates calculated from these data ranged between 12 and 14 per cent. Such findings, however, should not be construed as belittling the poverty problem. Rather, it should be used to highlight how serious the financial situation is for those persons and families who are trapped in medium- or long-term poverty, or who experience repeated spells of poverty. Indeed, we would argue that one of the main advantages of longitudinal data is that it can assist in identifying the types of individuals and families who are at greatest risk of poverty persistence and thus most in need of public assistance.

Finally, we conclude this analysis of poverty with a warning. Income measures by themselves do not adequately assess deprivation and disadvantage. It is also essential to assess and remedy those educational, health, social and employment deficits that limit opportunities.

HOUSEHOLD WEALTH

The previous two sections have been entirely concerned with income, but plainly income is not the only or necessarily the best indicator of material standards of living. Indeed, since income is a flow rather than a stock, it is likely to be a second-best proxy for economic wellbeing. What we also need to measure are the wealth holdings of households (and their individual members). Unfortunately, survey data on wealth have only rarely been collected, and as a result estimates of the distribution of wealth in Australia have generally been derived from indirect methods (e.g. based on the size of the income flows generated by selected assets).[15] However, as noted earlier, wave 2 of the HILDA Survey included a detailed series of questions about household assets and debts. Note, though, that these questions have yet to be repeated and so at this stage we can say very little about wealth dynamics. In what follows we present data on both the composition and distribution of household wealth, and then examine the debt holdings of Australian households and their capacity to service that debt.

THE COMPOSITION OF HOUSEHOLD WEALTH

We begin by presenting, in Table 4, the mean and median values of different types of assets and debts, and the percentage contribution each type of asset and debt makes to total holdings.[16] This table reveals that in the last quarter of 2002 the average household had a net worth (assets minus debts) of about $405,000, this being made up of $474,000 of assets and almost $69,000 of debts. However, these figures are skewed upwards by the wealth of a relatively small number of very wealthy households. The 'typical' household had assets of just under $280,000 and a net worth of about $219,000.[17]

As is well known, the asset portfolios of Australians are dominated by housing. The HILDA Survey data confirm this, with housing and other property constituting almost 55 per cent of all household assets and over 70 per cent of the assets of the median household. Indeed, just over two-thirds of all Australian households owned or were buying their own home, while 16.7 per cent had a stake in other property as well (a holiday home or investment property). The latter figure is consistent with Taxation Office data which indicate that some 13 per cent of Australian taxpayers earned rental income in 2000/01 (RBA 2003, p. 19).

The second largest asset of most households is superannuation, but it comes a very distant second—the median household holds superannuation worth only about $18,000, though this rises to $27,000 once we focus on

Table 4: Assets, Debts and Net Worth per Household, 2002

Type of asset/debt	Mean ($000)	Median[a] ($000)	% of assets/ debts
Assets			
Housing and other property	256.7	200.0	54.2
Pensions/superannuation	77.2	27.0	16.3
Businesses and farms	45.2	0	9.5
Equity investments	31.5	0	6.6
Bank accounts	21.6	4.1	4.6
Vehicles	19.0	10.0	4.0
Other assets[b]	17.9	0	3.8
All non-financial assets	324.5	220.0	68.5
All financial assets	149.5	50.5	31.5
Total assets	*474.0*	*279.5*	*100.0[c]*
Debts			
Housing and other property	51.7	55.0	75.1
Businesses and farms	6.9	0	10.0
HECS (student debt)	1.3	0	1.9
Credit cards	1.0	0	1.5
Other debts	7.0	0	10.1
Total debts	*68.9*	*55.0*	*100.0[c]*
Net worth	**405.1**	**219.0**	

Notes:
a. The reported medians are for the median household in the 50th and 51st percentiles of net worth.
b. Other assets include cash investments, trust funds, the cash-in value of life insurance and collectables.
c. The sub-components do not sum to 100 because missing values for some of the sub-components have not been fully imputed.

households in the middle of the wealth distribution. Other holdings of considerable value to some households are business assets and equity investments. The median household holds no equities and, of course, does not own a business. However, the 41 per cent of households that do own equities average about $70,000 worth (median = $15,000), and the average value of businesses, owned by 12.5 per cent of households, was about $291,000 (median = $80,000). It should be noted, however, that equity investments are understated here since, in order to avoid double-counting, respondents were asked not to include superannuation in their calculation of equity holdings, and, of course, some superannuation is held in equities. Moving towards the bottom of the list of assets, the median household has a car worth about $10,000 and just $4500 in the bank.

Household debt is mainly held in the form of mortgages. The average property debt is about $52,000, which is slightly less than the level held by the median household. Most households have very little or nothing in other forms of debt, which will probably surprise many. In part this may reflect some tendency for respondents to under-report debt, perhaps for social desirability reasons. Comparisons between the weighted data from the HILDA Survey and aggregate data from the ABS national financial accounts, for example, suggest that the HILDA Survey may have understated debts by somewhere in the vicinity of 18 per cent (see Headey et al. 2004). It should, however, be emphasised that the HILDA Survey made no serious effort to measure accounts payable (i.e. overdue bills). Further, the low levels of credit card debt may reflect the fact that only what was owed after the last payment made was recorded as debt, and a majority of individuals with credit cards reported paying off their entire balance each month.

Finally, the data in Table 4 indicate that in most households non-financial assets dwarf financial assets. Most households thus lack liquidity. They have relatively little cash and certainly little that they can easily cash up if normal sources of market income are temporarily or permanently cut off, or if emergency expenditures are required. This means that in the absence of usual income sources, many households will be forced to rely primarily on government transfer payments. This is especially clear when one remembers that, until one retires, superannuation is not available and so, while classified as a financial asset, it is not in reality liquid for persons of pre-retirement age.

THE DISTRIBUTION OF WEALTH

As in other Western countries, wealth is much more unequally distributed than income. This is illustrated graphically in Figure 2, which sorts the population of households into 10 equal groups (deciles) based on house-hold net worth and on household disposable income, and then reporting the median value of that decile group relative to the median for the entire population. Thus we can see that among the wealthiest 10 per cent of households, net worth is more than six times the value of the wealth hold-ings of the average household. In contrast, the richest 10 per cent of house-holds only have a net income (based on data for the 2001–02 financial year) which is just under three times that of the average household's income.[18]

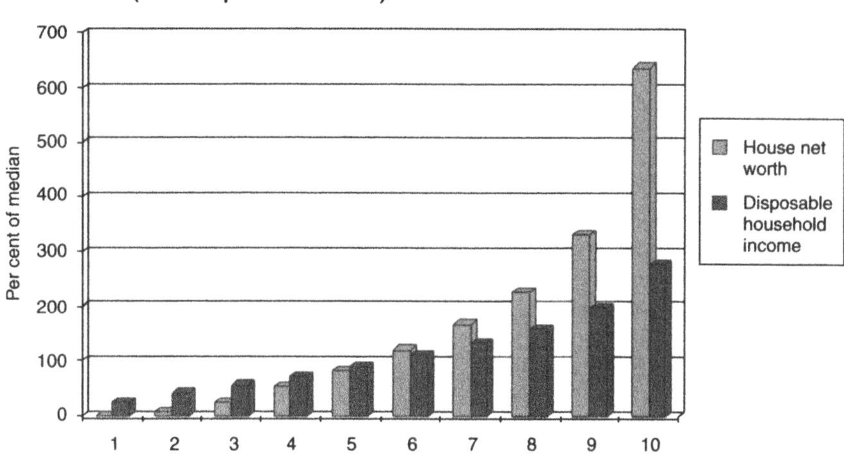

The fact that wealth inequality is greater than income inequality is far from surprising, and reflects the greater dependence of wealth on savings at older ages. Wealth accumulates via both voluntary saving and compulsory superannuation, and these savings grow at compound interest as people age. Income, of course, also increases with age, but the gradient is nothing like as steep as wealth's compound interest gradient.

Further information about the distribution of both household wealth and household disposable income is provided in Table 5. This table, however, distinguishes between assets and debts, and it also sorts wealth and income into decile groups based on both wealth and income ranking. Focusing first on net worth we can see that among the 10 per cent of households that are the least wealthy, average net worth is negative. Further, the bottom half of the distribution own less than 10 per cent of total household wealth. At the other end of the distribution, the wealthiest 10 per cent of households have an average net worth of just over $1.8m (median holdings = $1.4m) and own 45 per cent of all household wealth. The poorest 10 per cent of households in income terms, however, are not bereft of assets. Specifically, assets for this group average $215,000 in value, and this group owns 5 per cent of wealth in Australia. Similarly, at the other end of the income spectrum, the 10 per cent of households that are most income rich have mean net worth of just over $1m and own 25 per cent of total net worth, which while considerable is far less than might have been expected.

Of course, we would expect many older households to be both relatively asset rich and income poor. Nevertheless, restricting the population to households where the 'head' is aged between 25 and 55 years does not fundamentally alter the situation portrayed in Table 5. For example, while the levels of net worth in the top half of the distribution decline, the changes in the percentage distribution are minimal.

Table 5: The Distribution of Household Wealth and Income: Mean Values, $000s (% in parentheses)

Percentile	Sorted by household net worth				Sorted by net household income			
	Assets	Debts	Net worth	Net income	Assets	Debts	Net worth	Net income
1–10	21 (0)	26 (4)	–6 (0)	23 (5)	232 (5)	17 (2)	215 (5)	7 (2)
11–20	29 (1)	14 (2)	15 (0)	31 (7)	240 (5)	13 (2)	227 (6)	16 (3)
21–30	99 (2)	44 (6)	55 (1)	39 (8)	236 (5)	23 (3)	213 (5)	22 (5)
31–40	177 (4)	63 (9)	114 (3)	38 (8)	315 (7)	37 (5)	278 (7)	28 (6)
41–50	247 (5)	66 (10)	181 (5)	42 (9)	319 (7)	50 (7)	270 (7)	35 (7)
51–60	335 (7)	72 (10)	263 (7)	45 (9)	415 (9)	58 (8)	357 (9)	43 (9)
61–70	440 (9)	74 (11)	365 (9)	49 (11)	459 (10)	78 (11)	381 (9)	52 (11)
71–80	588 (12)	84 (12)	503 (13)	54 (11)	595 (13)	111 (16)	484 (12)	63 (13)
81–90	829 (18)	88 (13)	740 (18)	63 (13)	728 (15)	117 (17)	611 (15)	77 (16)
91–100	1973 (42)	156 (23)	1814 (45)	86 (18)	1200 (25)	185 (27)	1016 (25)	127 (27)
Total	474 (100)	69 (100)	404 (100)	47 (100)	474 (100)	69 (100)	404 (100)	47 (100)

HOUSEHOLD DEBT

Perhaps one of the most interesting features of Table 5 is how strongly household debts are correlated with assets ($r = 0.46$). In other words, household debt tends to be held by asset-rich households. The 20 per cent of households that are the least wealthy (the bottom two deciles in terms of net worth) had average debt levels of about $20,000 and accounted for just 6 per cent of all household debt. When we focus on the poorest 20 per cent of households in income terms, the story is even better, with mean debt just $14,000 and this group accounting for only 4 per cent of all debts. The distribution of debt within this group, however, is quite dispersed. Indeed, the median level of debt among the least wealthy 20 per cent of households is just $2000 (and among the lowest income households, it is zero). This implies that there is a sizeable minority of asset- and income-poor households where the level of debt is relatively large.

Whether household debt is a serious problem depends on the ability of households to service that debt. To examine this question we report, in Figure 3, data on the ratio of household debt to annual household disposable income (for the preceding financial year). This figure reveals that about one-third of households have zero levels of debt, and almost another quarter have very modest levels, defined by debts equal to less than half one year's net income. At the other end of the distribution, there are about 9 per cent of households where financial liabilities exceed by more than four times the value of net household disposable income, which is probably around the limit that most financial institutions would set when determining the capacity to borrow (though this varies markedly with individual circumstances).[19] These are obviously the households which are most cash constrained and most likely to be seriously affected by an increase in borrowing costs. Households which are less heavily geared are also exposed, but the main threats they face are from major changes in life circumstances (e.g. job loss, serious illness, unexpected pregnancy). Small and gradual rises in the cost of borrowing will affect the rate at which they can pay off loans but in most cases will not affect their ability to meet scheduled repayments.

Interestingly, we found very little evidence that high debt-to-income ratios were concentrated in any part of the income distribution. Indeed, on the basis of an admittedly crude multivariate analysis, it appears that, with one notable exception, the debt-to-income ratio is not associated in any

Figure 3: Household Debt to Annual Household Disposable Income

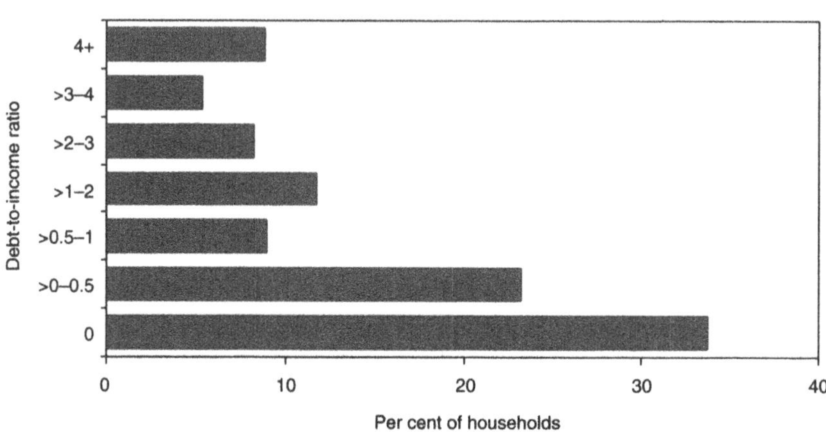

obvious way with observable characteristics of the household or its 'head'. What does appear to matter is home ownership (or more specifically, having a mortgage) and how long ago the home was purchased. Almost two-thirds of those households identified here as having high debt-to-income ratios have a mortgage (compared with less than 28 per cent of all households), and the majority of these (73 per cent) purchased their current home in the preceding five years.

Further, we found almost no evidence that households with these high debt-to-income ratios were reporting higher levels of financial stress. If we restrict the population to just the household head or reference person (thus ensuring only one response per household), we find a mean score on satisfaction with financial situation of 6.1 (scored on a 0–10 scale), almost exactly the same as the population mean. Similarly, when asked whether any stressful financial events had occurred in the past year, the group with the high debt-to-income ratios generally did not stand out as being the most financially vulnerable. Indeed, out of a list of seven stressful events, the only item which this group scored noticeably worse than the population mean was the inability to pay the mortgage or rent on time—11 per cent of this group responded affirmatively to this question in wave 2 compared with a population mean of 9 per cent.[20] And this result is entirely a function of the relatively high rates of home ownership among this group.

Overall, we are drawn to the conclusion that if high debt-to-income poses a serious problem, then the threshold must be a lot higher than a multiple of four. Indeed, scores on the 'satisfaction with financial situation' variable are only significantly lower than the population for households where the debt-to-income ratios exceed, which represent less than 2 per cent of all households. Such conclusions appear to be supported by a recent Reserve Bank report which suggests that the number of at-risk households is relatively small (RBA 2005, pp. 20–2). Also using the HILDA Survey data, that report focused specifically on the property debt held by households with owner-occupier mortgages and reported both debt-servicing ratios (debt-servicing costs as a proportion of after-tax income) and property gearing ratios (property debt to property assets). The report designated debt-servicing ratios in excess of 50 per cent and property gearing ratios in excess of 75 per cent as problematic. The HILDA data suggest that only 2.4 and 4.2 per cent of households were exceeding these thresholds in 2002 and only 0.4 per cent exceeded both.

Overall, the HILDA Survey data suggest that the problem of excessive household debt, which has been much discussed in the media, is concentrated in a relatively small proportion of the population. Further, most households in this group are new home owners who, in most cases, would expect their debt-to-income ratios to decline in the future as incomes rise and debt is retired. That said, it should be borne in mind that wave 2 of the HILDA was conducted in late 2002 and in the following two years aggregate household debt in this country rose by over 30 per cent.[21] It thus follows that the HILDA data will understate the current exposure of some households to deterioration in their financial situation (RBA 2005).

EMPLOYMENT DYNAMICS

LABOUR FORCE TRANSITIONS

We now turn to the issue of employment, the major source of income for most Australian households. Comprehensive employment data are regularly collected and reported on by the ABS, but again the emphasis has always been on cross-sectional comparisons over time. And as with the income example discussed previously, such comparisons will tend to create the misleading impression that change has been relatively modest and gradual. As a simple illustration of this, consider the data presented in Table 6. If we simply focus on the totals for each of the two years presented, we can see that the employment-to-population ratio has increased from 60.7 per cent to 62.3 per cent, the unemployment-to-population ratio has declined from 4.3 to 2.9 per cent and the labour force participation rate has increased only slightly (from 64.9 to 65.2 per cent).[22] Such figures are indicative of an improving labour market over this period, but with net change still being relatively modest (the employment rate rose by only 1.6 percentage points). The extent of true change, however, is understated by this figure. The numbers in Table 6, for example, also reveal that about 15 per cent of the population considered here changed their employment status between 2001 and 2003. Further, not all of the change was towards employment. For example, the employment status of 1 per cent of the sample changed from employed to unemployed, while a further 5.1 per cent exited the labour force after having been employed in 2001. Similarly, while 5.2 per cent of the population moved from outside the labour force into employment, another 1.1 per cent had moved into job search.

For ease of exposition, the data presented in Table 6 are highly aggregated. We could, however, have just as easily distinguished between more varied types of employment outcomes (e.g. between full-time and part-time employment or, among non–labour force participants, between those who want a job and those who do not) and between different sub-groups of the population. More detailed transition matrices are thus reported at the end of this chapter.

Table 6: Employment Status, 2001–03 (% of all persons aged 15 years or older in 2001)

	2003 Employed	2003 Unemployed	2003 Not in the labour force	2001 Total
2001 Employed	54.7	1.0	5.0	60.6
2001 Unemployed	2.4	0.9	1.0	4.3
2001 Not in the l/f	5.2	1.1	28.8	35.1
2003 Total	62.3	2.9	34.8	100.0

UNEMPLOYMENT

The main weakness of Table 6, however, is not the way it aggregates across different groups, but the way it aggregates data over time. We have simply presented information on labour force status at two discrete points of time. Obviously it is relatively straightforward to add a third data point for 2002 when the second wave of interviews was conducted. More importantly, however, the HILDA Survey also collected information about labour market activity between each wave using a calendar approach. Thus, in theory, we can identify every spell of employment and unemployment experienced by each sample member together with the duration of each spell. These calendar data, however, are quite complex, and are still in need of further work, particularly with respect to matching spells across waves.

Nevertheless, Table 7 should provide some indication of the sort of information that can be extracted. In this table we focus specifically on the unemployment experience, reporting the proportions of our (weighted) balanced sample who indicated that they had been out of employment but looking for work at some time during any of the three financial years between 2000–01 and 2002–03 inclusive. The table reveals that approximately 83 per cent of the population never experienced unemployment over this period, implying that 17 per cent were unemployed for at least some time.[23] This proportion varies with age, with close to 40 per cent of young people (persons aged between 15 and 24 years in wave 1) experiencing at least one spell of unemployment, which compares with 18 per cent of persons aged 25 to 54 years and just under 10 per cent of those aged 55 to 64. Table 7, however, also suggests that while many people experience unemployment, relatively few experience persistent or recurring unemployment, with less than 2 per cent of the population unemployed for at least some time during each of three years for which we have data.

Table 7: Unemployment, 2000–01 to 2002–03, by Age (% of persons experiencing unemployment)

	15–24 years	25–54 years	55–64 years	Total (15+ years)
Never	62.0	82.2	90.4	83.3
2000–01	15.2	8.0	5.5	7.4
2001–02	21.6	9.8	5.4	8.3
2002–03	18.4	8.1	4.2	7.7
One year only	24.9	11.5	5.5	10.9
Two years (out of 3)	8.7	4.5	2.7	4.2
All three years	4.3	1.8	*	1.7

* Cell size too small to generate a reliable population estimate.

Of course, to get a better handle on persistence we actually need to know about the amount of time people spend in unemployment. Information on the amount of time spent in unemployment during our three-year window is summarised in Figure 4. This figure reveals a highly skewed distribution, with most people who experience unemployment spending a year or less in unemployment. Nevertheless, there is a sizeable minority who experience lengthy spells in job search. Indeed, around 12 per cent of this group was unemployed for at least 18 months (one-half of the three-year window). The other noticeable feature of this graph is the spikes at 12 and 24 months. These almost certainly reflect reporting problems associated with the 'seams' between waves.

Many of the unemployed can be expected to exit unemployment not by finding a job, but by ceasing to look for work. In Table 8, therefore, we look again at the sub-sample of people who were unemployed at any time during our three-year window and report the proportion of time they spent out of work. As we can clearly see, we find relatively large proportions of this group spending substantial fractions of their time without jobs. Indeed, 15 per cent of this group never manage to find a job, and close to half are jobless for 18 months or more. Not surprisingly, the proportion is especially high among older persons, many of whom effectively retire following job loss and a period of unsuccessful job search. Nevertheless, even among prime-age persons there are considerable numbers spending long periods out of work even though they are or had been looking for work. This should be of large concern to policy makers. While even short-term joblessness can give rise to a variety of social and economic problems, medium- to long-term joblessness is a much more serious policy issue

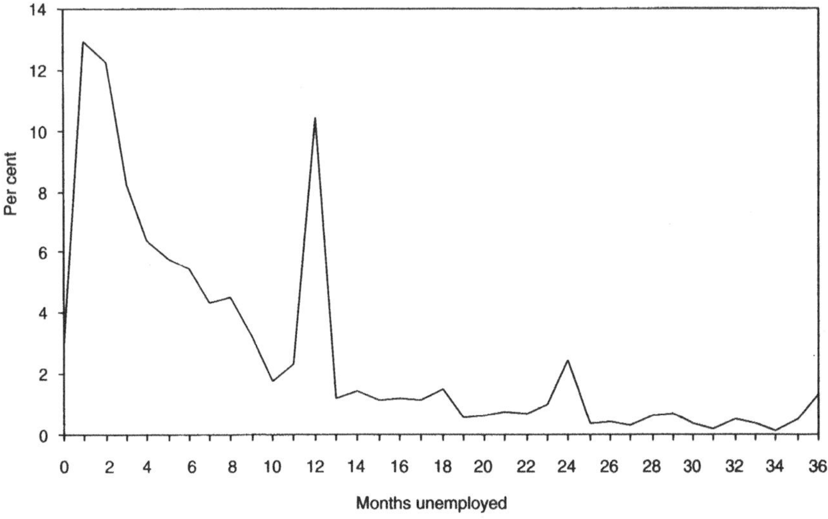

Table 8: Proportion of Time not in Employment: Persons Unemployed at Any Time during 2000–01 to 2002–03

% of three financial years	15–24 years	25–54 years	55–64 years	Total (15+ years)
<5	6.4	9.1	*	8.0
5 to <10	5.0	13.1	*	9.7
10 to <25	16.2	18.6	14.3	17.2
25 to <50	22.6	16.8	13.8	18.1
50 to <100	39.9	28.7	28.5	32.0
100	9.8	13.7	32.7	15.1
Total	100.0	100.0	100.0	100.0

* Cell size too small to generate a reliable population estimate.

because of its implications for long-term income and health outcomes, and because of its potentially damaging impact on the ability to effectively participate in the community.

JOBLESS HOUSEHOLDS

The analysis above was entirely concerned with joblessness from the perspective of the individual, but recent research has identified a growing polarisation in the distribution of employment across households. That is, researchers (e.g. Dawkins 1996; Dawkins et al. 2002; Miller 1997; Scutella & Wooden 2004) have reported evidence of increasing numbers of households in which one or two members work very long hours, as well as increasing numbers of 'jobless households' in which no one has any paid work. All of this evidence, however, has been cross-sectional, which again will typically mean inadequate attention being paid to the dynamics and duration of joblessness.

Here we present some very simple statistics in an attempt to describe persistence. First, however, a brief digression on measurement and definitions is warranted. As noted earlier, the definition of jobless household presented earlier does permit household members to hold a job, but only for a fraction of the year—no more than 25 per cent. Further, we also recommended excluding from the population two groups where joblessness is not of large policy interest: households headed by the retired and those approaching retirement years (i.e. where the head was aged 60 years or over), or by full-time students. Clearly, many other definitions are possible. Table 9 presents a range of alternative estimates for each year of the panel. Our preferred definition produces jobless estimates of 9–10 per cent of the relevant population (which we can roughly think of as members of households headed by a working-age person).[24] It also should be noted that all of these statistics are based on data collected from fully responding households. While information on the employment states at the time of interview of non-responding household members was collected, we know nothing about the labour market activity of these individuals between interviews and so have excluded their households from the analysis.

Turning then to the issue of persistence, we report in Table 10 the proportion of people living in jobless households using our preferred definition cross-classified by the number of years they were in the jobless state. For comparison purposes, we report estimates for the entire population as well as our preferred sub-population. The first column of the table relates to all individuals, and at first glance suggests that the jobless households issue is extremely serious, with 16 per cent of the population living in a jobless household in all three years covered by the data. But as just noted, this estimate includes households headed by retired people and full-time students. Once we exclude these households, the proportion of people living in households that were persistently jobless (i.e. in all three years) is just 4.4 per cent. On the other hand, these same data also show that just over 12 per cent experience at least one year living in a jobless household. Table 10 also suggests that children are somewhat more exposed to household joblessness than are adults, with almost 6 per cent of children under the age of 15 years living in a jobless household in all three years.

Table 9: Cross-section Estimates of % of Persons Living in Jobless Households

Jobless household definition	Wave 1	Wave 2	Wave 3
All persons			
No jobs at date of interview	23.2	21.8	22.5
No jobs during previous FY	19.3	18.6	19.2
No-one worked >25% of previous FY	20.9	20.4	20.8
Excluding households headed by FT students or persons aged 60 years or older			
No jobs at date of interview	11.9	10.7	10.9
No jobs during previous FY	8.3	7.9	8.1
No-one worked >25% of previous FY	9.8	9.6	9.5

Note: Population restricted to fully responding households; FT = full-time; FY = financial year.

Table 10: Proportion of People Living in a Jobless Household, 2000–01 to 2002–03

Years jobless	All persons	Excluding full-time students and households with head aged 60 years or older		
		Persons	Adults	Children (<15 yrs)
None	73.8	87.7	89.1	83.6
One	4.6	3.7	3.3	4.7
Two	5.3	4.2	3.6	6.0
Three	16.3	4.4	4.0	5.7

Note: Population restricted to fully responding households.

Further information about the dynamics of household joblessness is reported in Table 11, which summarises flows in and out of household joblessness over the three-year period. This table confirms that joblessness is relatively persistent (and more so than was the case with income poverty), but also shows that considerable proportions of people from jobless households do move into employed household states—of those persons in jobless households in one wave, around 25–30 per cent will not be in a jobless household the next. The other important feature of Table 11 is how low the inflow rates into joblessness are for people who come from a sustained history of employment. Thus very few of the people represented in the bottom half of the table move into a jobless state in any one year—only 3 per cent of persons from households with jobs moved into a jobless household the next year.

Table 11: The Dynamics of Household Joblessness, 2000–01 to 2002–03

Wave 1 (2000–01)	Wave 2 (2001–02)	Wave 3 (2002–03)
Jobless—8.1%	Jobless—75.2%	Jobless—72.7%
		Not jobless—27.3%
	Not jobless—24.8%	Jobless—31.4%
		Not jobless—68.6%
Not jobless—91.9%	Jobless—3.0%	Jobless—69.0%
		Not jobless—31.0%
	Not jobless—97.0%	Jobless—1.6%
		Not jobless—98.4%

Note: Sample restricted to balanced panel.

Table 12: Household Joblessness, by Household Type, 2000–01 to 2002–03 (% of persons)

Household type[a]	Never in jobless household	In jobless household in at least one year	Jobless in all three years
Lone parent	8.1	38.7	45.8
Couple, no children	27.3	15.4	14.0
Couple with children	53.6	29.0	12.8
Lone person	7.4	11.9	23.5
Other household	3.6	4.9	3.8
Total	100.0	100.0	100.0

Note: a. Determined on the basis of household status in wave 1.

Finally, it is worth pointing out that lone parent households are over-represented among jobless households. As reported in Table 12, members of lone parent households (as defined by their wave 1 characteristics) accounted for 39 per cent of all persons who were in a jobless household during at least one of the three years covered by the data, and 46 per cent of all persons in jobless households for all three years. By comparison, lone parent households account for just 8 per cent of persons in households who never experience life in a jobless household. In contrast, household joblessness is far less prevalent among couple households.

CONCLUSIONS

This paper has summarised new findings about various aspects of income, poverty, wealth and employment in Australia using the first three waves of the HILDA Survey. A panel survey, such data provide an important longitudinal complement to the cross-section snapshot data regularly collected and reported on by the ABS. In addition, the HILDA Survey provides new data on household wealth that have been very lacking in Australia. The key findings can be summarised as follows:

- While there is considerable income mobility from one year to the next, much of that mobility is relatively short range (at least over the three-year window covered by the data).
- The number of persons at risk of persistent poverty is much less than the number measured as living in poverty in a single year. That said, it is also apparent that many of the persons who move above the poverty line in one year fall below it again a year later. Further, many of those leaving poverty have not moved very far above the poverty line.
- Wealth is much more unequally distributed across households than is income.
- The wealthiest households control not only the bulk of household assets, but also the bulk of household debt.
- The problem of excessive household debt appears to be concentrated in a relatively small proportion of households, most of which are new home owners who, in most cases, would expect their debt-to-income ratios to decline in the future as incomes rise and debt is retired.
- Employment states are, over a two-year period, relatively stable. Nevertheless, 15 per cent of the population were in different labour force states two years after wave 1 of the survey was conducted.
- A better guide to labour force mobility is provided by calendar data that document labour market activity between interview dates. According to these data, some 17 per cent of the adult population experienced an

episode of unemployment at some time during the period, 2000–01 to 2002–03. Close to half of this group never succeeded in finding a job at any time during this period.

- Close to one-in-ten persons (from working-age households) in any one year are estimated to be living in jobless households. Further, just over 4 per cent were in jobless households in all three of the years covered by the HILDA Survey data.
- Household joblessness is especially pronounced for persons living in sole parent households.

---

[1] All the data used in the analyses reported here come from the HILDA Survey confidentialised data release version 3.0 issued in January 2005.

[2] All new births become permanent members of the sample. Further, temporary sample members are converted to permanent sample members if they have a child with an original sample member.

[3] For some types of income sources, however, the HILDA Survey does not distinguish between regular and lump-sum payments. As a result, we have had to make assumptions about the form different types of income are more likely to take. For example, all workers' compensation payments have been included as regular income.

[4] For more information about the imputation method that has been used (and other features of the HILDA Survey data), readers should consult the HILDA User Manual (Watson 2005), available on the HILDA Survey website at: <www.melbourneinstitute.com/hilda/doc.html>.

[5] This scale assigns a weight of 1.0 to the first adult in the household, 0.5 to all other adults, and 0.3 to all children. Here we have defined a child as anyone under the age of 15 years.

[6] The income poverty approach is widely used but may be too narrowly focused. There is much to be said for a broader approach which defines poverty in terms of a range of low capabilities, as suggested by the Nobel Laureate, Amartya Sen (1999), or in terms of social exclusion and barriers to participation.

[7] The imputation of wealth data was actually undertaken by staff from the Reserve Bank of Australia. The only missing values not imputed were for those individuals who did not provide an interview but nevertheless were members of responding households. Thus, while total households assets and debts were fully imputed, as were all components collected at the household level, the estimates of superannuation, bank accounts, credit card debt, student debt and other personal debt are based entirely on members of households that completed the personal interview. Again, for details of the imputation procedure used, see Watson (2005).

[8] The most notable difference occurs with respect to the part-time/full-time distinction. Like the ABS, a threshold of 35 hours per week is used to define full-time employment, but unlike the ABS this is determined entirely on the basis of 'usual' hours. In contrast, the ABS system uses a combination of data on both actual and usual hours worked.

[9] Identification of the household 'head' was determined by applying the following criteria, in order, until a unique person was selected. These criteria are: (i) in a

registered or de facto marriage (and still living together); (ii) a lone parent; (iii) the person with the highest financial year income; and (iv) the eldest person.

[10] For an analysis of the impact of attrition on sample representativeness between wave 1 and wave 2, see Watson and Wooden (2004b). Information about how these population weights were constructed can be found in the HILDA User Manual (Watson 2005).

[11] There are good reasons to be concerned about the quality of income data collected in sample surveys, especially at the bottom of the income distribution (see Siminski et al. 2003). Key issues here include non-response bias and under-reporting. While non-response can, in theory, be dealt with through the construction of appropriate population weights, under-reporting is more problematic. In the HILDA Survey, for example, there are a number of households reporting relatively small incomes (the reported or imputed gross annual income was less than $5000 for almost 3 per cent of households in wave 1). While this is entirely possible, particularly for owners of unincorporated businesses, the relatively high proportions involved are of some concern for analyses of income mobility. We thus repeated the analysis reported in Table 1 after omitting all cases where gross private income (that is, exclusive of government benefits and payments) was negative in either wave 1 or wave 3. Essentially, the conclusions remained unaffected, with the notable exception that the proportion of low-income households remaining in the bottom increased (to 42 per cent).

[12] For example, it appears likely that maternity allowance payments have not been adequately reported in the HILDA Survey. Similarly, the HILDA Survey does not deal very well with rent assistance. Very differently, the HILDA Survey has almost certainly not done as good a job as the ABS income distribution surveys in distinguishing lump-sum payments from more regular sources, which may have contributed to the relatively higher median income that is recorded in the HILDA Survey data. Differences in the sample structure may also be partly responsible.

[13] It should be noted that after wave 1 the representativeness of the HILDA Survey sample changes in one important respect—it under-represents new immigrant arrivals.

[14] The balanced panel involves an unweighted sample size of 15,436. The fact that the wave 1 poverty rate reported in Figure 1 is lower than that reported for 2000–01 in Table 2 reflects slightly higher rates of sample attrition by respondents who live in poverty which have not been entirely accounted for by the longitudinal weighting structure.

[15] A survey of wealth was conducted as part of the 1915 War Census. Since that time, the only other survey of household wealth we are aware of is a small study conducted in the 1960s (Podder & Kakwani 1976). For more details about these studies, together with a review of other research imputing wealth estimates using indirect methods, see Headey et al. (2004).

[16] Rather than report the simple median, the medians given here are for the median household in the 50th and 51st percentiles of net worth. This seems a better guide to the typical Australian household.

[17] The numbers reported vary somewhat from those reported in Headey et al. (2004) because we use data from release 3.0 whereas they used data from the previous data release, and the population weights are amended with each data release.

[18] Another way of summarising inequality is through the use of Gini coefficients. The Gini coefficient for household net worth that is derived from the HILDA Survey data

is 0.61, which compares with a Gini of 0.38 for household disposable incomes for the 2001–02 financial year.

[19] Some of these households (especially those which own small businesses) will have reported very low incomes and thus the corresponding debt involved may also be relatively small. Nevertheless, excluding those cases where pre-government income is negative from the population, and ignoring cases where the total household debt is less than $5000, sees the proportion of households with debt-to-income ratios fall only slightly—to 8.7 per cent.

[20] The relevant question asked respondents to indicate whether they did any of the following because of a shortage of money: (i) could not pay electricity, gas or telephone bills on time; (ii) could not pay the mortgage or rent on time; (iii) pawned or sold something; (iv) went without meals; (v) were unable to heat home; (vi) asked for financial help from friends or family; and (vii) asked for financial help from welfare/community organisations.

[21] Based on numbers available on spreadsheet from the ABS, *Australian National Accounts: Financial Accounts* (cat. no. 5232.0), Table 15: Financial Assets and Liabilities of Households ($m).

[22] We are using a sample that only includes cases observable in both waves, thus creating the possibility for attrition bias. In theory, the longitudinal weighting structure is designed to correct for such biases, though that correction is likely to be far from perfect.

[23] Note that very short episodes of unemployment (like a week or less) are unlikely to be recorded given the unit for our calendar was one-third of a month.

[24] While not reported in Table 9, this equates to about 11–12 per cent of households.

REFERENCES

Commission of Inquiry into Poverty 1975, *Poverty in Australia: First Main Report*, AGPS, Canberra [Chair: R.F. Henderson].

Commonwealth Department of Family and Community Services 2003, *Inquiry into Poverty and Financial Hardship: Commonwealth Department of Family and Community Services Submission to the Senate Community Affairs Reference Committee* (FaCS Occasional Paper no. 9), Department of Family and Community Services, Canberra.

Dawkins, P. 1996, 'The Distribution of Work in Australia', *Economic Record* 72, 272–86.

Dawkins, P., Gregg, P. and Scutella, R. 2002, 'The Growth of Jobless Households in Australia', *Australian Economic Review* 35, 133–54.

Dickens, R. and Wilkins, R. 2005, 'Income Poverty in Australia 1981 to 2000', unpublished mimeo, Melbourne Institute of Applied Economic and Social Research, University of Melbourne.

Harding, A., Lloyd, R. and Greenwell, H. 2000, *Financial Disadvantage in Australia, 1990 to 2000*, The Smith Family, Camperdown (Sydney).

Headey, B. 2003, 'How Best To Impute Taxes and Measure Public Transfers?', HILDA Project Discussion Paper Series no. 2/03, October, Melbourne Institute of Applied Economic and Social Research, University of Melbourne.

Headey, B., Marks, G. and Wooden, M. 2004, 'The Structure and Distribution of Household Wealth in Australia', *Melbourne Institute Working Paper Series* no. 12/04, University of Melbourne.

Jarvis, S. and Jenkins, S. 1998, 'Income and Poverty Dynamics in Great Britain', in L. Leisering and R. Walker (eds), *The Dynamics of Modern Society: Poverty, Policy and Welfare*, The Policy Press, Bristol.

Johnson, D. and Wilkins, R. 2004, 'Effects of Changes in Family Composition and Employment Patterns on the Distribution of Income in Australia: 1981–1982 to 1997–1998', *Economic Record* 80, June, 219–38.

Miller, P. 1997, 'The Burden of Unemployment on Family Units: An Overview', *Australian Economic Review* 30, 16–30.

Podder, N. and Kakwani, N. C. 1976, 'Distribution of Wealth in Australia', *Review of Income and Wealth* 22, 75–92.

RBA (Reserve Bank of Australia) 2003, *Productivity Commission Inquiry on First Home Ownership*, Submission by the RBA, September.

—— 2005, *Financial Stability Review, March 2005*, RBA, Canberra.

Scutella, R. and Wooden, M. 2004, 'Jobless Households in Australia: Incidence, Characteristics and Financial Consequences', *Economic and Labour Relations Review* 14, 187–207.

Sen, A. 1999, *Development and Freedom*, Anchor Books, New York.

Senate Community Affairs Reference Committee 2004, *A Hand Up Not a Hand Out: Renewing the Fight Against Poverty* (Report on Poverty and Financial Hardship), Parliament House, Canberra.

Siminski, P., Saunders, P. and Bradbury, B. 2003, 'Reviewing the Intertemporal Consistency of ABS Household Income Data through Comparisons with External Aggregates', *Australian Economic Review* 36, September, 333–49.

Watson, N. (ed.) 2005, *HILDA User Manual—Release 3.0*, Melbourne Institute of Applied Economic and Social Research, University of Melbourne.

Watson, N. and Wooden, M. 2004a, 'The HILDA Survey Four Years On', *Australian Economic Review* 37, September, 343–9.

—— 2004b, 'Sample Attrition in the HILDA Survey', *Australian Journal of Labour Economics* 7, June, 293–308.

ACKNOWLEDGEMENTS

This paper reports on research being conducted as part of the research program, 'The Dynamics of Economic and Social Change: An Analysis of the Household, Income and Labour Dynamics in Australia Survey'. It is supported by an Australian Research Council Discovery Grant (DP0342970).

The paper uses the data in the confidentialised unit record file from the Department of Family and Community Services' (FaCS) Household, Income and Labour Dynamics in Australia Survey, which is managed by the Melbourne Institute of Applied Economic and Social Research. The findings and views reported in the paper, however, are those of the authors and should not be attributed to either FaCS or the Melbourne Institute. The authors also thank Diana Warren for assistance with the preparation of data used in this paper.

APPENDIX: LABOUR FORCE TRANSITIONS, 2001 TO 2003

Table A1: All Persons (%)

2001 labour force status	Wave 3 employment status						2001 total
	Employed FT	Employed PT	Un-employed	NLF—Want job	NLF—Don't want job	Total	
Employed FT	84.9	8.7	1.2	1.8	3.4	100.0	41.6
Employed PT	24.5	58.0	2.4	4.7	10.3	100.0	19.1
Unemployed	31.8	25.1	20.0	12.9	10.2	100.0	4.3
NLF—Want job	11.7	22.4	8.9	26.3	30.8	100.0	7.9
NLF—Don't want job	3.0	6.3	1.3	7.9	81.4	100.0	27.2
2003 total	43.1	19.2	2.9	6.4	28.4	100.0	100.0

Table A2: Males (%)

2001 labour force status	Wave 3 employment status						2001 total
	Employed FT	Employed PT	Un-employed	NLF—Want job	NLF—Don't want job	Total	
Employed FT	89.4	5.4	1.3	1.2	2.8	100.0	56.9
Employed PT	36.2	45.5	5.2	4.9	8.1	100.0	11.5
Unemployed	37.8	20.0	22.1	10.7	9.3	100.0	5.1
NLF—Want job	19.3	17.1	11.0	27.3	25.3	100.0	5.3
NLF—Don't want job	4.4	5.4	*	8.3	80.7	100.0	21.1
2003 total	58.9	11.4	3.3	5.0	21.4	100.0	100.0

* Cell size too small to generate a reliable population estimate.

Table A3: Females (%)

2001 labour force status	Employed FT	Employed PT	Un-employed	NLF—Want job	NLF—Don't want job	Total	2001 total
			Wave 3 employment status				
Employed FT	76.3	15.2	*	3.0	4.6	100.0	27.4
Employed PT	19.7	63.1	1.3	4.7	11.2	100.0	26.1
Unemployed	23.7	31.9	17.1	15.8	11.4	100.0	3.5
NLF—Want job	8.0	25.0	8.0	25.7	33.4	100.0	10.2
NLF—Don't want job	2.2	6.8	1.4	7.7	81.9	100.0	32.9
2003 total	28.4	26.5	2.4	7.8	34.9	100.0	100.0

* Cell size too small to generate a reliable population estimate.

Table A4: Persons under 25 Years of Age in 2001 (%)

2001 labour force status	Employed FT	Employed PT	Un-employed	NLF—Want job	NLF—Don't want job	Total	2001 total
			Wave 3 employment status				
Employed FT	56.7	11.4	*	*	*	100.0	30.0
Employed PT	23.6	52.9	19.0	18.0	19.5	100.0	31.7
Unemployed	8.4	9.6	31.5	10.3	*	100.0	10.5
NLF—Want job	5.5	17.0	28.1	35.7	27.1	100.0	15.3
NLF—Don't want job	5.8	9.1	13.1	26.7	43.6	100.0	12.5
2003 total	43.9	31.7	6.8	8.8	8.8	100.0	100.0

* Cell size too small to generate a reliable population estimate.

Table A5: Persons Aged 25–64 Years in 2001 (%)

2001 labour force status	Wave 3 employment status						2001 total
	Employed FT	Employed PT	Un-employed	NLF—Want job	NLF—Don't want job	Total	
Employed FT	85.3	8.2	1.1	1.7	3.7	100.0	52.7
Employed PT	22.1	60.6	1.9	4.7	10.8	100.0	19.0
Unemployed	29.8	22.4	19.9	15.5	12.5	100.0	3.7
NLF—Want job	10.5	17.2	7.9	29.6	34.8	100.0	7.1
NLF—Don't want job	3.2	8.8	1.7	11.7	74.7	100.0	17.6
2003 total	51.6	19.4	2.5	6.5	20.0	100.0	100.0

Table A6: Persons Aged 65 Years or Older in 2001 (%)

2001 labour force status	Wave 3 employment status						2001 total
	Employed FT	Employed PT	Un-employed	NLF—Want job	NLF—Don't want job	Total	
Employed FT	66.5	*	*	*	*	100.0	2.6
Employed PT	*	49.7	*	*	40.3	100.0	4.7
Unemployed	*	*	*	*	*	*	*
NLF—Want job	*	*	*	*	74.1	100.0	3.0
NLF—Don't want job	*	*	*	2.8	95.8	100.0	89.6
2003 total	2.1	4.1	*	3.4	90.4	100.0	100.0

* Cell size too small to generate a reliable population estimate.

8 HOW CAN WE MOVE MORE PEOPLE FROM WELFARE TO WORK?

THE HON. PETER DUTTON MP
Minister for Workforce Participation

The Howard government is often criticised for being mean-spirited and showing no compassion towards less fortunate Australians. The government's current careful consideration of welfare and workplace reform has been met by hysterical calls that we are slashing and burning and throwing people out of their wheelchairs onto human scrap heaps.

In reality, though, nothing is further from the truth. Our critics would have had a bitter-sweet reaction to Professor Ann Harding's announcement that the poor have done well under the Howard government. Indeed, the bottom 10 per cent of household average weekly private incomes have increased by 165 per cent between 1994–95 and 2002–03. Over the last nine years, economic management has delivered tangible benefits like those that are evidenced in Professor Harding's work.

But, in my view, the bigger challenge for the Howard government is now upon us. Welfare reform has not been legislatively possible over the last nine years. Serious social security reform in this country should have commenced the day the Whitlam government was dismissed in 1975. Certainly the Fraser government failed to implement adequate reform, which has now resulted in a culture of welfare as a starting and finishing point for too many in our country.

I believe the challenge to provide compassionate welfare reform will be met by the government. We will provide ongoing support to those people with a disability who have no capacity to work. Of course we will. We will support parents who have the greatest responsibility of all—to care for, provide for and nurture their children.

But, as a government and as a nation, we must wherever possible help people of working age with work capacity. This must apply equally to all Australians—to fully able Australians, Indigenous Australians, advantaged and disadvantaged Australians alike. Through reform, we must help people with no work ethic understand the benefits a job provides. We must remove disincentives, we must increase incentives, and in doing so we must restore integrity to a system designed as a safety net, not a way of life.

Paid work not only provides the money to live on and raise a family, but also self-esteem and a connection to the community. When people are out of work for long periods, they can lose their skills, self-confidence and even their sense of belonging to a community. If this problem is widespread, it creates problems for families, neighbourhoods and society generally.

The proportion of working-age Australians receiving income support payments has risen from one in twenty in 1974 to one in five today. A key objective of any reform should be to reduce the number of families depending on income support.

WHY WELFARE REFORM?

The welfare system is too passive. The original income support system was designed for a very different world:

- most jobs were full-time;
- most unemployment was short term; and
- mothers and married women didn't work.

Policies that were appropriate then are not well suited to today's Australia. The result is a system that allows too many people to remain on payments for extended periods—a system that doesn't provide people with the assistance, obligations and incentives they need to become self-reliant.

Under this government, employment growth has been outstanding and unemployment has fallen to levels not seen in a generation. Despite this, the number of working-age people on welfare has grown. In June 2004 there were some 2.7 million income support recipients aged 16–64. This is over 20 per cent of all working-age Australians. Most rely on income support for the majority of their incomes. Of this 2.7 million, only 800,000 (30 per cent) actually have a job search requirement or participate in education; 70 per cent of these people (a little under 2 million Australians) receive payments without any obligations to find work or to study. This is particularly a problem for Disability Support Pension (DSP) and Parenting Payment, where the number of recipients now exceeds the number of people on unemployment payments.

The shift in the economic structure away from traditional manufacturing and utilities, towards service-based industries, has seen the displacement of many workers, particularly older males. Too many mature age workers have ended up receiving passive payments such as the Disability Support Pension. Structural change in the economy does not mean people should be written off or exempted from requirements to look for work and not provided with employment assistance. Rather, it highlights the importance of ensuring that all Australians out of work get the best possible chance and incentives to take up jobs. The best way to bring down the amount of time people spend on payments and the cost involved is to help them to actively look for work and provide the right labour market assistance. In this way, they can be ready to take advantage of job opportunities as they come up.

Recent years have seen a strong growth in the number of jobless families, with 826,000 children now living in jobless families. Two-thirds of these households are headed by lone parents. We know that lone parents stay on payment for an average of 10 years. We also know that growing up in a household where no parent is working can affect a child's chances in life. We must ensure that jobless households now don't lead to intergenerational welfare dependency in the future.

Australia's working-age support arrangements are a serious structural impediment to participation and employment growth, and reduce our standard of living. Already our per capita income is 25 per cent less than in the United States, where participation and productivity is higher. While our purchasing power parity is above the OECD average, it is significantly below that of the United States, and below Ireland, the UK, Canada, the Netherlands, Austria and Belgium. If nothing is done, this disparity will continue to grow as the population ages.

Our employment to population ratio (better known as the employment rate) remains below comparable rates for the United States. The most recent comparable data (July 2003) show that in Australia 69.3 per cent of the working-age population were employed compared to 71.2 per cent in the United States. We have lower employment rates than 10 other OECD countries, including Denmark, Sweden, Norway, Canada, New Zealand and the United Kingdom.

INTERGENERATIONAL ISSUES

Workforce participation must rise if Australia is to meet the challenges of an ageing population. In the 2002–03 Budget, Treasurer Peter Costello released the Intergenerational Report. This report considered the substantial challenges faced by Australia's ageing population.

Australians are living longer and having fewer children. This is changing the balance of working-age Australians and retired Australians and is likely to slow the rate of economic growth. The Intergenerational Report projects that economic growth will slow to around 2 per cent by 2020 and beyond, unless steps are taken to increase labour participation and labour productivity. If Australia is to support its ageing population and maintain improving living standards, greater workforce participation is vital.

IMPORTANCE OF ACTIVE PARTICIPATION

The Job Network, introduced in 1998, plays a central role in the government's workforce participation framework. It has been particularly effective in helping unemployed job seekers, including many disadvantaged people, make the most of job opportunities and become financially self-reliant.

The Active Participation Model, introduced in July 2003, represented an important step in the continuing development of individually tailored, publicly funded employment services. Job seekers will be provided with more active, consistent and individualised assistance, with one Job Network member assisting them while they are unemployed. The Model has achieved record levels of performance since implementation. In the last year, around 650,000 job placements were recorded by Job Network members and other Job Placement Organisations, an increase of 50 per cent on the previous 12 months and a new annual record. In the same period, over 174,000 long-term (13-week) jobs were achieved for disadvantaged job seekers and those unemployed for more than three months—again, a new annual record.

NEXT STEPS

I believe that the best form of welfare is a job. There is no doubt that being a parent is the most important job a person can have. Many sole parents now, from all walks of life and backgrounds, are juggling their caring responsibilities with work. It is not an easy balance. The government is mindful of a sole parent's caring responsibilities and any decisions in this area will take that into account. I don't think it is unreasonable to expect some parents to work part-time once their children go to primary school. Parents need to demonstrate to their children the benefits work can provide to their family and stop the welfare cycle.

Similarly, there are many people on a disability pension who could go back to work in some capacity. They may not be able to work full-time or in a job they have previously held and they may need some support. However, this should not preclude them from some form of work tailored to their abilities. I want people with a disability to be able to access services that will help them reach their employment potential. We need to help more people help themselves. This includes making sure the incentives and supports are there to help people 'have a go' by ensuring that services available to job seekers are appropriate and effective; and by encouraging employers to look at people's abilities and be flexible in their working arrangements.

Employers need to seriously consider how they can structure their workplaces to suit the changing labour force. Many people with disabilities are highly educated and motivated. We have to fight entrenched discrimination and realise that many people have a desire to contribute not just to their employer or their family, but to society as well. Parents, the mature aged and people with a disability have valuable attributes that are attractive to employers. They are highly motivated. Employers who give them a go say they are reliable and dedicated employees.

It makes good business sense for employers to work with government to increase participation of all these groups to address skills shortages. We have a suite of employment services, such as Job Network and Disability Open Employment Services, that are well placed to assist these groups back into work. We are now looking at how we can get more people to the right service and not just onto income support for life. We need to reassess what having a capacity to work while having a disability or being a lone parent means in terms of work and ensure that income support payments remain a safety net and not a way of life.

When the media report on welfare reform, they use old school language such as cost-cutting and slashing. The reality is that there will be no short-term savings in getting people back into work. Every assistance must be provided to help those who want work to find it and this is expensive. If the government wanted to save money it would not be investing in assisting people, it would be doing nothing. The government is showing its commitment to improving the lives of Australians and their families.

PILOTING NEW APPROACHES

The government is already piloting innovative ways of engaging more parents and people with a disability. These pilots aim to increase voluntary participation in the Job Network and to improve the services that parents and people with disabilities receive in Job Network.

DISABILITY SUPPORT PENSION PILOT

The Disability Support Pension Pilot, conducted between December 2003 and June 2004, explored the best way to help work-able DSP recipients into a job through the Job Network. It took a pro-active approach and asked Job Network members to actively reach out and ask people on the DSP if they would like help to find work. The results are very encouraging—half of those who commenced have been placed in employment and I expect this figure to continue to rise. This pilot shows that the DSP need not be the 'end of the road' in a person's working life.

EARLY INTERVENTION AND ENGAGEMENT PILOT

I have found in discussions around the country that people with disabilities want to be seen first and foremost for their ability to participate and contribute rather than their disability. Current assessment processes mean many people are not being connected with available rehabilitation and jobs assistance early enough. For many, this sense of being left alone is a source of frustration and despair rather than a pathway towards a more positive and optimistic future.

I am pleased to announce that the Australian government will be funding a pilot study to improve assessment of the work capacity of people with disabilities and to link them more quickly with appropriate rehabilitation and employment assistance services. The Early Intervention and Engagement Pilot, which will be conducted over the next couple of months, will ensure that those people with a disability who wish to seek work are referred quickly for a work capacity assessment. They will then be referred directly to an appropriate rehabilitation or employment assistance program.

This will cut down the number of assessment hoops people have to go through, ensure that they are encouraged to have faith in their ability to work, even part time, and connect them to appropriate forms of rehabilitation and employment assistance earlier. I want people with disabilities to be given encouragement, practical support and hope rather than be told the pension is the only option.

The pilot will be conducted across three states, involve 1000 people with disabilities, and involve four organisations: Health Services Australia, Advanced Personnel Management, CRS Australia, and Centrelink. I hope it will be the basis of a new assessment tool as our modernisation of the welfare system takes place.

PARENTING PAYMENT WORK FOR THE DOLE PILOT

Over the last eight years, Work for the Dole has been successful in helping prepare mainly young job seekers for employment. It is a compliance mechanism, highlighting the government's strong commitment to mutual obligation, and it is an important tool in developing a work ethic, the value of teamwork, investment in our local communities and valuable work experience. It has proven very effective in re-engaging those who receive income support with their community.

Last month, I announced the Work for the Dole Parenting Pilot to encourage recipients of parenting payments to participate in local Work for the Dole projects. We know that many parents would like to return to the workforce but lack the skills and confidence to make that transition. This voluntary pilot is about improving self-esteem and ensuring participants gain confidence from greater interaction with their peers. It aims to provide parents with additional support that will help them into paying jobs to ensure more Australians are available to work so that our economic prosperity can be maintained.

The government remains committed to Work for the Dole. In the coming months, I will be announcing ways in which it can be further enhanced to build on the experiences of participants who have achieved positive outcomes through the program.

CONCLUSION

As I said earlier, the easy option for the government would be to do nothing. But I, for one, do not want to give up on anyone in this country. The time is right to assist those people who have been discounted or excluded from participation in the past. We have built a strong and stable economy. It is important that all Australians benefit from this.

Everyone must be given the opportunity to reach their full potential and to do this, where possible, without the need for income support, because we all know it is better for individuals, it is better for their families, but most importantly it is better for their children's future. If we are to sustain prosperity, increased workforce participation across all generations is essential.

9   A NEW SOCIAL POLICY FOR THE NEW ECONOMY

Mr Tony Nicholson
Executive Director, Brotherhood of St Laurence

Thank you for this invitation and its implicit recognition that the Brotherhood of St Laurence—and indeed the welfare sector in general—has a crucial role to play in the economic reforms that lie ahead.

I want to start by saying that I believe there is cause to be optimistic about reducing poverty and disadvantage in this still wonderfully fair-minded country of ours. In the last two decades, after a shaky start, we have gained a better understanding about how to effectively manage a deregulated economy. Central banks and other policy makers are now better placed to keep interest rates, unemployment and inflation down. While we are not yet as advanced in dealing with the social consequences of a deregulated economy we are beginning to see more clearly, today, how to prevent people from being excluded from participating in wealth creation.

How to include more people in mainstream economic and social life of the country—*this* is the debate we need to have, not the sterile argument that has raged over recent years, about how we measure poverty. Sustained economic growth has the potential to convince us that poverty—defined in a one-dimensional way—is no longer significant. But I know, from my work among the disadvantaged and homeless over the past two decades, it not to be the reality.

I don't agree with all of Mark Wooden's earlier published conclusions from the HILDA data that poverty in Australia is a short experience for most. For instance, it should involve housing data and its poverty line seems arbitrarily low. And like other measures it doesn't include the homeless. At the last census the ABS counted over one hundred thousand homeless. Most were in the first third of their working lives. About half were actively in the labour market. I challenge anyone to suggest they are not experiencing persistent poverty.

Most importantly, the HILDA data are too short in duration. While I agree that short-term poverty is far preferable to long-term poverty, the HILDA data fail to measure the extent to which short-term poverty is intermittent. International evidence shows that although the proportion of the population that is continuously poor is low, the population with low average incomes over the long term is significantly higher. This is explained by repeat spells of poverty, suggesting that those in poverty may move into low-paid work but then lose their job and move back into poverty again. The international evidence also suggests that the proportion going onto higher paid jobs is small. So perhaps all that's being measured by the HILDA data is 'churn', leading us to ignore the key policy issue: how successful or otherwise we are in lifting people out of the poverty cycle altogether.

That said, Mark's research highlights one important fact: our society is still producing a hard core of people in persistent poverty, and we need to direct much of our effort to helping them lift themselves out of it. I want to propose a way of thinking about poverty that all of us—hands-on welfare practitioners, policy makers, economists and commentators from all orientations—can agree with.

The debate on all sides has lagged seriously behind the changed nature of the economy, our patterns of work and family life, and the new types of inequalities that can result. I believe the new economy demands a new approach to social policy. I call it 'the new social policy'. If we get it right we can not only reduce poverty but also give a powerful boost to wealth creation. It requires all of us, particularly governments, to do things differently.

SOCIAL EXCLUSION

We can start by adopting a new understanding of the nature of poverty— one that is already practised around the world—'social exclusion'. This is, of course, the dominant policy approach in much of Western Europe, and I can see straightaway that its adoption by 'social democratic' countries and the EU possibly provokes misgivings among some more free-market-inclined policy makers. This is mistaken. And not just because governments like Tony Blair's are active economic reformers with a sound record of strict financial management.

At the core of 'social exclusion' are the ideas of someone who passionately believes in the liberating possibilities of the free market—the Cambridge economist, Amartya Sen. Sen's basic point is that by giving people more 'capacity' to participate in the market economy we can give the market greater moral legitimacy. Tackling 'social exclusion' should therefore be seen as a means of increasing the capabilities of people to participate in a meaningful way in the market and the community. It is essential to boosting productivity and economic reform.

If this approach sounds familiar and attractive to many of you, it's because in essence it's the same approach employed by Noel Pearson and others. There is no reason to believe that the approach proposed by Noel for Indigenous communities and cultures wouldn't work equally well for Australians from other communities and cultures. We all saw the violence at the Glenquarie Estate in Macquarie Fields a few weeks ago. Perhaps the best way to understand and deal with it is to focus on the similarities between the behaviour of the Glenquarie Estate rioters and those in Redfern and on Palm Island recently.

The point is not to excuse violence by saying that 'society is to blame' but to recognise that when similarly excluded from society and the economy, young, unskilled, bored and often substance-abusing young people tend to act the same way, whether they're from Indigenous or European backgrounds. And as a result, we're seeing something we hoped never to see in Australia—people hurling missiles at riot-shielded police.

A 'social exclusion' approach says, 'rather than give people passive welfare or churn them through bouts of short-term poverty by reducing wages and carrying a big stick, we should give them the skills to become active members of the new economy, producing even more wealth for all of us to enjoy'. There are millions of Australians who want to be part of the new economy, and we're holding them back.

This isn't just a theory; it comes from real experience. I have spent a lot of time in the front line of welfare service delivery, and I can tell you that whenever I ask people who have lost everything and are living in crisis accommodation, when I ask them about their aspirations, they don't answer: 'To get more welfare'. They almost invariably say: 'To get skills that will get them a job, to get decent accommodation, to get back with their families'—in that order. They don't aspire to be part of an underclass. They have modest mainstream aspirations.

I like to think of it this way: every Australian wants to be part of the big event in our national life—building prosperity and creating a better place—

yet we've got too few seats in the stadium and we're locking millions out. Let's add that extra capacity, those extra seats.

As Director of the Brotherhood of St Laurence, the last thing I want is to allow people to remain on social security for long periods when there are other options. Good welfare programs have an honoured and highly important place in our economy and society. But the idea is to lift people out of welfare. At the Brotherhood our interest will continue to be primarily with the prevention of disadvantage rather than alleviating its symptoms. Tackling 'social exclusion' is the best way to do that.

NEW ECONOMY + NEW WELFARE = A 'MOBILITY GUARANTEE'

This brings me to my second major point. The welfarist models currently employed by many participants on both sides of the debate about poverty are based on an outdated ideal of the Australian economy—a post-war model of full-time permanent employment and single-income 'nuclear' families. They concentrate too much on one dimension of poverty—income.

That's why we at the Brotherhood are working with the Melbourne Institute and Ken Henry and others to produce a new set of social indicators. We currently measure joblessness inaccurately—leaving out the under-employed and those on non-activity tested benefits. ABS estimates of 'extended labour force under-utilisation' conclude that there are 1.2 million people who would work more if they could find it. At the Brotherhood we reckon the figure closer to 1.5 million.

I think all of us here today can agree that welfare policies must now be brought into line with the realities of the new economy. In short, this means giving those who are unemployed, under-employed, receiving non-activity tested benefits, or suffering chronic poverty due to substance abuse, disabilities or mental illness the 'capacities'—as Sen would say—to cope with the new economy, the capacities to cope with a more flexible employment market, which demands higher skills and in which people have different family responsibilities. And the capacities to contribute to the nation's economic growth.

I don't think the answer lies in reducing wages to create low-paid jobs, even if mitigated by a system of earned income tax credits. For one thing there is serious doubt about whether even large wage cuts would produce many jobs. Empirical evidence fails to show an unambiguous relationship between minimum wage changes and employment. The second is that there is a crying need already for skilled workers, and with our workforce ageing as it is, we should aim to meet this need now and into the future.

In concrete terms, I'm arguing for giving people more access to the big passport for success in the employment market—education and life skills. We want people to move from welfare to a job and then on to an even better job—not from welfare to a succession of low-paid, low-skilled, short-term jobs (as some interpreting the HILDA data have wrongly suggested is sufficient to tackle poverty). Our own analysis of that data shows that people in low-paid casual work are much more likely to spend time out of work and on benefits.

We should call these skills a 'mobility guarantee' to allow the poor to succeed in a more flexible, skilled and mobile economy. Let me suggest three ideas to make this happen.

FIRSTLY, FOR YOUNG PEOPLE

The Dusseldorp Skills Forum estimates that each year we produce over 200,000 people aged between 15 and 19 who are 'at risk', being neither in full-time work nor full-time study. We have to do something to prevent these potential contributors to our nation from becoming long-term unemployed or entrenched in the low-skill, low-wage segment of the economy.

Rather than re-invent the wheel, we believe the answer lies with guaranteeing all young people a Year 12 or an equivalent qualification and providing intensive, case-managed support for early school leavers to either re-engage with education or to gain employment.

SECONDLY, FOR OLDER WORKERS

Retrenched workers face serious risks of long-term unemployment. Given the right skills and opportunities, retrenched older workers can go on to successful and fulfilling careers—like a second chance at life. That's what we want for all of them. Unfortunately for many, the impact of retrenchment —in unemployment, under-employment and depression—can still be measured more than a decade later.

We need to take lifelong learning seriously—and this means giving employed workers, especially those most at-risk of future unemployment, paid time out of the workforce to gain skills that are in demand.

The Brotherhood proposes the creation of 'Lifelong Learning Accounts' with the aim of building enough funds to pay for extended periods of study, possibly one or two years. Funds would be contributed by employees, employers and government, with the largest government contribution going to those at most risk of retrenchment, or the lowest paid.

While governments could subsidise half the cost for low-paid workers, with subsidies tapering off as income increased, employers and employees could share the other half, perhaps as part of a one-off deal around wage adjustment as occurred with superannuation contributions. Employees could contribute their notional wage increase to the learning account, on the condition that employers made a matching contribution. Alternatively, existing entitlements such as long-service leave could be folded into the accounts.

THIRDLY, FOR THE LONG-TERM UNEMPLOYED

The Brotherhood has developed an innovative employment program to assist long-term unemployed public housing tenants into employment. Many of these people have multiple problems that prevent them from taking part in the economy—low skills, poor self-esteem, health problems and family responsibilities. They need intensive help. The Brotherhood already does this. Through a combination of case management, intensive personal support, pre-vocational and vocational education and work experience, we help people gain the skills necessary to get and hold onto a good job.

Our program has many similarities to the principles proposed for the Neighbourhood Renewal program in the UK. Importantly, it works. Once again, let me point out that all three of these policy ideas should have strong appeal to proponents of the free market and economic reform. They unleash skills, involve personal financial commitment from the unemployed and 'at-risk workers' themselves, and emphasise the virtues of hard work, employment routine and self-sufficiency.

I suspect I won't be the first or last person at this conference to say this, but I can't think of a more effective long-term way for the federal government to invest some of the current proceeds of growth and the projected $10 billion Budget surplus than in some of the ideas I've just outlined.

SPATIAL DISADVANTAGE NEEDS A 'NEW REGIONALISM'

There's one last major point I want to make, and that's the need to build the capacities not just of individuals but also of whole communities. This means recognising the spatial dimension of poverty—which has been the subject of some fine research by people like Boyd Hunter, Bob Gregory, Robert Stimson and, most recently, Tony Vinson. I think we should all be disturbed by Tony Vinson's finding that in New South Wales and Victoria

5 per cent of postcodes accounted for a quarter of all unemployment, child abuse and imprisonment. Such communities are not only a moral indictment, they are also acting as a drag on wealth creation. Let's do something about them.

The factors that lead to social exclusion—such as low income, ill health and unemployment—are interrelated, and therefore need the complementary resources and skills of a number of people and agencies. We cannot simply 'wait' for spontaneous market solutions to emerge. My experience has been that all too often the public assistance that is delivered to individuals and groups in these communities is so lacking in integration, and so out of touch with the realities of those communities, as to be rendered largely ineffective and wasted.

We need to radically change the way in which governments relate to these disadvantaged communities and to the community organisations working in them. We need a 'new regionalism' that builds the capacities of communities by engaging their citizens in a partnership with all levels of government. We need to give these communities a greater say in the governance of public monies expended in their midst. This will, of course, involve new and innovative forms of accountability, but it can't be beyond our know-how to create them.

Initiatives like the community strengthening and Neighbourhood Renewal programs of the Victorian government, which the Brotherhood participates in, have made a good start. But they need to go a lot further, particularly in the way they are integrated into regional economic development plans. Again, let me emphasise that there's an important element of this that even the most conservative of us can agree on: the idea that governments can't solve everything; that communities, businesses and individuals have to take up their share of responsibility for finding the way out of poverty.

CONCLUSION

It is time the welfare sector, business leaders, economists, policy makers and governments recognised we could all potentially be heading in the same direction. The 'new social policy' approach to poverty and disadvantage I have outlined here has something for everyone. It builds the capacities of people to take advantage of a new, reformed economy. It is not about 'something for nothing', because it requires everyone to take personal responsibility and invest in themselves. And it is not about leaving everything to government to sort out. Ultimately it helps to legitimate economic reform and will make the economy work even better. It is essential to the economic reform agenda.

That said, we believe it has a powerful moral case, regardless of the economic benefits. Because together we can make economic reform work for everyone and address that nagging misgiving in the back of our minds —that, as we've got more prosperous, we've left too many of our fellow Australians behind.

10 SIGNPOSTS TO WELFARE REFORM

MR ANDREW McCALLUM
President, Australian Council of Social Service

In this federal Budget the government is likely to announce major changes in our systems of social security and employment assistance for jobless people. In responding to these proposals, ACOSS will ask five questions:

1   Will jobless people be better off or worse off financially?
2   Will the changes improve their future job prospects?
3   Will they strengthen or weaken the fairness and security of the safety net?
4   Will they strike a reasonable balance between the obligations of jobless people, government and employers?
5   Will it help make Australia a fairer and more inclusive society?

The government's main argument for change is that too many people are dependent on social security. The media has picked up this theme. A recent media report was headlined 'Jobless crisis costs $4.7 billion'.[1] The irony is that the official unemployment figures are at 30-year lows—close to 5 per cent. How can reliance on social security be rising when unemployment is falling? The short answer is that reliance on social security has *fallen* over the last seven years as full-time jobs have grown. *There is no welfare dependency crisis.* But as unemployment falls, it is the people facing the greatest obstacles to employment who still rely on income support. Helping them find secure jobs is the real challenge.

The basic facts are these. Reliance on social security is below the OECD average (Figure 1), and it has been falling as full-time job growth has picked up over the past seven years. Reliance on disability pensions is about average.[2] Social security spending is well below the average. The Productivity Commission acknowledges that social security is affordable, even as the population ages.[3] ABS and FACS data show that reliance on social security has fallen with strong growth in full-time jobs over the past seven years (Figure 2). But for most of the 1990s we enjoyed strong growth

Figure 1: Proportion of People of Workplace Age Reliant on Social Security, 1999

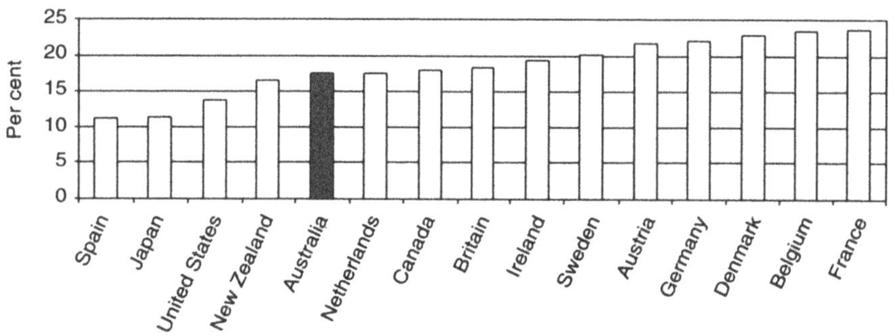

Source: OECD 2003, *Employment Outlook.*

Figure 2: Social Security Recipients and Growth in Full-time Jobs, 1990–2002

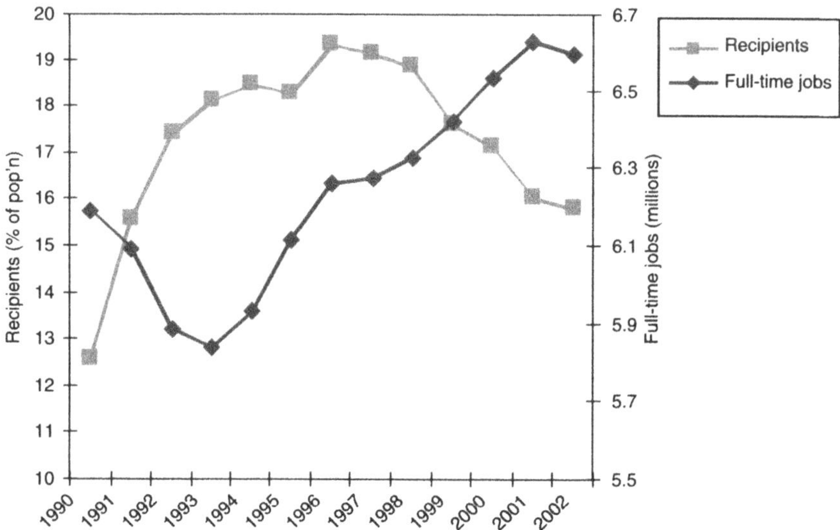

Source: FACS data on receipt of social security payments (excluding age pension and student payments); ABS data on full-time employment.

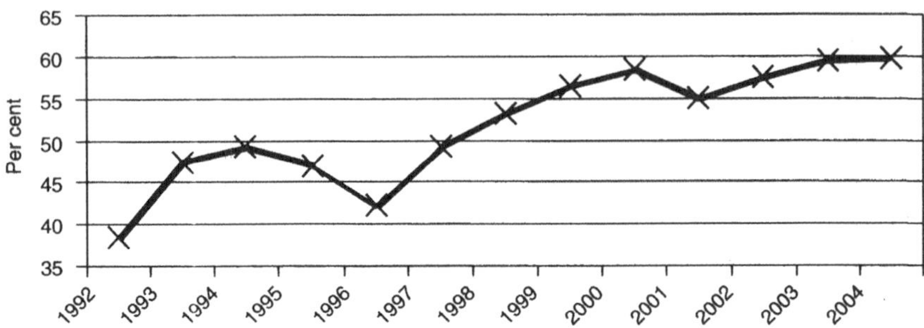

Source: OECD 2003, *Employment Outlook.*

only in part-time jobs. Many social security recipients got part-time work, but their income wasn't enough to take them off income support. In the recession of the early 1990s many full-time jobs were lost. That led to the sharp rise in reliance on social security in the early 1990s.

At this stage of the business cycle, people facing the greatest barriers to employment form a growing proportion of social security recipients. Getting them into work becomes harder. For example, the proportion of unemployment payment recipients on benefits for more than a year has risen from under 40 per cent after the last recession to over 60 per cent today (Figure 3).

BARRIERS TO WORK

- 60 per cent of people with disabilities have no post-school qualifications.
- 350,000 Newstart and Youth Allowance recipients have been on payments for over 12 months.
- 25 per cent of sole parents on Parenting Payment suffer from depression.
- DSP recipients are medically assessed and must be unable to work full-time for at least two years.
- At least 50,000 Newstart recipients are assessed as having disabilities or illnesses.

The barriers to work include limited education, lack of recent work experience, disabilities, poor physical and mental health, and lack of affordable childcare. These facts provide no grounds for 'moral panic' over 'welfare dependency'. But we do have an historic opportunity to assist the most disadvantaged jobless people into work. In the short term, employment is still booming. Over the next 30 years, labour shortages will emerge as the population ages.

ACOSS enthusiastically supports efforts to assist people off social security into employment, where this is a reasonable and realistic expectation. We have consistently supported positive policies to that end from Working Nation in the mid 1990s to the Australians Working Together changes in 2000. I emphasise this because this support is often forgotten, or taken for granted, in the heat of debate.

Over the past five years there has been a broad consensus over welfare reform, in favour of the broad directions advocated by the government's Reference Group on Welfare Reform in 2000 (the McClure Report). The key elements of that report, and the 'Building a Simpler System' paper released by Ministers Vanstone and Abbott in 2002, are as follows.[4]

THE MCCLURE REPORT'S FRAMEWORK FOR WELFARE REFORM

- Encourage participation in the labour market, subject to people's capacities and caring responsibilities.
- Employment assistance, advice and support based on individual needs.
- A simpler and fairer social security system in which distinctions between 'pensions' and 'allowances' are removed.
- Improve work incentives by easing income tests and assisting with the direct costs of work and further education and training.
- Use penalties as a last resort only.

If the government builds on this framework, it will announce five things in the Budget.

First, a substantial improvement in employment assistance, especially the Job Network. Those who remain out of work long term today are among the most disadvantaged people in the labour market. Many have been out of work for two years or more. It would be misleading to argue that simply imposing greater obligations will turn this problem around.

The Job Network must now focus on the individual needs of the most disadvantaged job seekers, and both the Job Network and specialist providers must be available for sole parents and people with disabilities. The government should give Job Network providers the resources they need to invest in wage subsidies and substantial training. They can now use a Job Seeker Account to help overcome work barriers. But the average sum available is around $1000—enough to buy a few weeks' training. That won't overcome years of educational disadvantage and exclusion from mainstream employment. It would be a mistake to burden the Job Network with social security administration, for example, work testing. The Job Network would start to look less like an employment service and more like a privatised Centrelink. There is already too much emphasis on benefit compliance, and too little scope to offer people the individual help they need to get them into work.

The government is planning changes to the CDEP (Community Development Employment Projects) for Indigenous communities. The key to reducing the very high levels of Indigenous joblessness is a partnership between the government, Indigenous communities and employers. Change should not be imposed from above. On the employer side, a national strategy to encourage and support employers to take on people with disabilities, mature age workers and other disadvantaged job seekers is needed.

Second, the unfair and counterproductive anomalies between pension and allowance payments should be removed without making anyone worse off. For example, if a disability pensioner undergoes rehabilitation and is able to work again they are likely to be transferred to Newstart Allowance. This means a drop in income from $235 per week to $197, a fall of around $40 per week. If they then undertake full-time study to improve their job prospects they go onto Austudy, which is at least another $30 per week less. People are penalised for trying.

The old distinction between 'allowances for people able to work' and 'pensions for those who aren't' is the worst work disincentive in the social security system. Pensions have become 'dead-end payments'. But people are discouraged from leaving them because they would be even poorer on the Newstart Allowance. This is what would happen if the government proceeds with proposals to shift people with disabilities who can work part-time from the Disability Support Pension to Newstart Allowance. We urge the government not to go down this track. There is no evidence to suggest that the people affected could easily get full-time work if compelled to do so. Most would simply end up on Newstart Allowance, and at least $20 to $40 a week worse off. The DSP would become even more of a dead-end payment because people would be reluctant to try part-time work in case they lose it.

The solution is to close the gap between pension and allowance payments, not to shift people to the cheaper payment. This was proposed by the McClure Report five years ago and raised by Ministers Vanstone and Abbott in their discussion paper three years ago. This is the direction New Zealand is taking. We hope Helen Clark convinced Prime Minister Howard to follow suit.

Third, work incentives should be improved by offering more help with the costs of job search, training and employment and by easing the most severe income tests. An unemployed person living on around $200 a week can't afford to look for work. They don't get the same public transport concessions and telephone allowances pensioners receive. Nor do they get the pensioner education supplement to help with the cost of fees and books for their TAFE course. And if they earn more than $71 per week, they lose 70 cents of their allowance for every additional dollar earned, together with income tax. People with disabilities face much higher work-related costs—for example transport—but receive too little help with those costs.

Fourth, obligations for recipients must be realistic, grounded in individual circumstances, and balanced by a substantial government investment in employment and support services. For example, the government imposed new activity requirements on Parenting Payment recipients in 2001—to participate in part-time employment training or voluntary work once their youngest child reached 13 years. Those requirements were balanced by investment in personal advisers at Centrelink and an expansion of childcare subsidies. Efforts were made to keep breaches and penalties down to a minimum. Parents unable to meet the new requirements (for example those who are subject to domestic violence or whose children are ill or have a disability) were exempted. Breach and penalty arrangements were changed.

If activity requirements for parents are increased without maintaining and improving these protections and supports, the wellbeing of poor children would be jeopardised. The McClure Report argued that governments must invest up-front to reap benefits later on. If the forthcoming welfare reform package saves money, or even if it is revenue-neutral, that means there will be a large number of losers. It will be a cost-cutting exercise, not welfare reform.

Fifth, the harsh, counterproductive breach regime should be eased and the review and appeals systems strengthened. The present system imposes penalties of up to two months' loss of payment where people fail to meet requirements that are often unrealistic and badly administered. For example, many people with mental illnesses are in breach because their illnesses are not properly identified and they fail to attend an interview, or to declare earnings, when they have an 'episode'.

The Social Security Appeals Tribunal and other protections against arbitrary and unfair decisions should be strengthened, not removed. These protections are all the more important if the government is considering extending activity requirements to vulnerable groups like sole parents and people with disabilities.

CONCLUSION

The government says it will not use its control of the Senate in a harsh or pre-emptive way and that they won't impose American-style welfare reform on Australians. There are indications that the Minister (Kevin Andrews) understands the barriers that confront jobless people in their efforts to raise themselves out of poverty.[5] The government has been talking with community organisations about these issues, but has only formally consulted over about the last four weeks.

It took two years to develop the McClure Report and the directions for reform in that report are broadly supported. We urge the government to stick with the balanced approach, the consensus approach to welfare reform. This requires an investment of public funds now to reap benefits in future years. It requires a careful balancing of requirements and legislative protections for vulnerable Australians. It requires much more substantial consultation than four weeks to get it right.

We urge the government to build on the work already done, not force welfare recipients to take a leap in the dark in the name of welfare reform.

---

[1] *Herald Sun*, 29 March 2005.

[2] ACOSS 2005, *Disability Support Pension: Myths and Realities*, at <www.acoss.org.au>.

[3] Productivity Commission, 'Economic Effects of Population Ageing', draft report, 2004.

[4] Reference Group on Welfare Reform 2000, *Participation Support for an Equitable Society*; Abbott and Vanstone 2002, 'Building a Simpler System'.

[5] Hon. K. Andrews, speech to Sydney Institute, March 2005.

11 · PUTTING INCENTIVE BACK IN THE SYSTEM: TAX REFORM FOR GROWTH AND PROSPERITY

THE HON. WAYNE SWAN MP

Shadow Treasurer

As they say, there are two things that are certain in life: death and taxes. While there is no avoiding death there are plenty of people who would like to avoid tax or at least pay less of it. Whether we like it or not, paying tax is part and parcel of living in a prosperous and civilised society. Having accessible and high-quality health and education systems—which themselves are a driver of prosperity and opportunity—requires a sound revenue base.

Being a politician often involves a delicate balancing act, because it is necessary to try and balance the long-held aversion of many to paying tax with the general desire for quality services. For too long the debate about tax has been hung up on whether we should have lower or higher taxes.

What I would argue is that we need a more internationally competitive tax system that maximises wealth creation while being fair and efficient. A competitive tax system, with a lower tax burden, is not cheap government as some would claim, it is good government. It's an investment in increased purchasing power for families and a down payment on higher living standards into the future.

The design of our tax system should allow the economy to grow, maximising both participation and productivity. An intelligent tax system that places the economy on a higher growth path with the dividend of growing revenues is a much preferable option to ever higher burdens of taxation on a flat lining economy. If we are to avoid the latter of these two outcomes, reform is desperately needed. It would be charitable to say that our current tax system and structures are an inefficient mess that punish hard work and sap incentive.

I do not propose here to perform a complete post-mortem on the entire system. While not diminishing the urgency of reform in other areas, I believe reform of personal income tax and transfer arrangements is the most pressing to address. Such are the appalling disincentives, the current system is a ball and chain shackling our aspirations and wearing down our will to work.

INTERNATIONAL COMPETITIVENESS

Australia's economic fortunes are, more than ever, hitched on our ability to compete in a globalised economy. Greater international mobility of capital and skilled labour means we must continually reassess the competitiveness of our microeconomic structures. We simply cannot afford to recline back and return to the days of the lucky country, content to be a farm and quarry to the world. Despite record commodity prices, the present state of the nation's external accounts and the prospect of below-average growth over the years ahead suggest we have much work to do to improve our economy's competitiveness.

Tax reform is an essential element for us to improve our international competitiveness. At an aggregate level, Australia's tax burden, at 31.5 per cent of GDP, is relatively low among OECD nations. But in comparison to our major trading partners, located in the Asia–Pacific region (29.1 per cent) and the United States (26.4 per cent), it is somewhat higher. While these aggregate measures make useful comparisons they really don't tell the whole story.

With regard to the tax burdens for individual workers and families, the latest estimates from the OECD in its annual *Taxing Wages* report make interesting reading. The net burden of tax and transfers for a person on average earnings at 24.3 per cent is only enough to rank us 13th lowest in the OECD. For a single-income family on average earnings the burden falls to 12.8 per cent but our ranking slips to 15th. These average tax rates show we are in the middle of the pack but a long way off the world's lowest.

Perhaps more telling are our marginal tax rates. Regardless of our average tax rates, what really matters is the level of our marginal rates—the tax we pay on additional income. By this I don't just mean the nominal marginal tax rate structure but the effective marginal tax rates that apply once the withdrawal of transfer payments are also taken into account.

High marginal tax rates are an insidious disease that have for years been taking a toll on the aspirations of hardworking Australians. High marginal rates are important. They are likely to discourage workers from seeking promotion, continuing their education or working overtime because of the poor marginal returns involved. They are also likely to discourage saving, as the returns on their investment are diminished by high marginal rates of tax.

Almost two years ago I spoke at this conference of the need to address high effective marginal tax rates. At that time it was hard to raise any interest in the topic—I'm glad now we are beginning to have a serious debate. It is this aspect of the OECD's report that the Treasurer has been so keen to avoid by attempting to distort its other findings.

While the marginal tax rate for a single worker on average earnings seems reasonably competitive at 31.5 per cent, it is only good enough to rank us 13th lowest in the OECD. But when we look at a single-income family at the same earnings, the withdrawal rate on family tax benefits sees them plummet to near the bottom with an effective marginal rate of 51.5 per cent—the second worst work incentives in the OECD. For a typical two-income family the OECD found Australia had the worst work incentives with a marginal tax rate of 61.5 per cent. In three out of four scenarios of families with children, our marginal tax rates are ranked worst to fourth worst in the OECD.

But this disastrous outcome could have been much worse if the OECD were to examine some other family types. While it found the highest marginal tax rate of 61.5 per cent was experienced by a primary income earner in a two-income family, the secondary income earner in such families may face a marginal tax rate of 68.5 per cent. In a testament to the regressive incentives in our tax system, the situation gets worse at lower incomes. Here secondary income earners may face marginal tax rates of 83.5 per cent if they also have a dependent child on Youth Allowance. For a single person moving off unemployment benefits, marginal tax rates are as high as 87 per cent, and for a sole parent they may top 91.5 per cent excluding childcare. There are even worse scenarios but I'll deal with them later.

As the debate on marginal tax rates has progressed I'm pleased to see at last recognition by those who are relatively comfortable that the worst disincentives are found not on the top marginal rate, but for those struggling

on lower incomes. With such poor work incentives it is no wonder
Australia has below-average participation rates and flagging productivity.
Why would you work harder if you stood to gain little or nothing from
your extra efforts? I'm sure many are asking why even work at all. In the
face of these problems I find the government's indifference to high marginal tax rates astounding.

WHY WE HAVE SUCH POOR WORK INCENTIVES

The Howard government is keen to downplay the problem of high effective marginal tax rates for two reasons: the first is its abject failure over nine
years in office to address them, and the second is its role in contributing
directly to the problem.

The Treasurer asserts that high effective marginal tax rates are the price
we must pay for targeted social security and family benefits. There is no
doubt that higher marginal rates are a consequence of a targeted transfer
payment system. At this point we need to ask who has broadened the
transfer payment system.

Close analysis of the OECD report shows the personal tax burden
increased in Australia between 1996 and 2004. This increase was offset in
most instances by an expansion in transfer payments. But this expansion has
resulted in more widespread interactions with marginal tax rates, causing
poor workforce incentives.

According to the OECD a single-income family in 1995 on average
earnings faced a marginal tax rate of 35.7 per cent. By 1999 the same family
faced a rate of 44.5 per cent. With the introduction of the New Tax System
in 2000 the same family's marginal tax rate leapt to 61.5 per cent. This
increase, along with those created with the introduction of Youth Allowance
in 1998, more than offset the new system's worthwhile reductions for other
lower income families by reducing the overlap between family benefits and
parenting payment. Only after the latest changes in the 2004 Budget has this
average-income family's marginal tax rate fallen, albeit to 51.5 per cent—a
level which is still the second worst in the OECD.

Lower income families were not so lucky. Before the Budget, a single-
income family on the minimum wage faced a marginal rate of 83 per cent.
You would think that this family would be especially worthy of relief from
these crippling effective marginal tax rates. But after the Budget, their marginal tax rate leapt to 104 per cent.

In a revealing Senate Estimates hearing following the Budget, Treasury
officials coyly admitted no modelling was done of the Budget's impact on

marginal tax rates until after it was signed, sealed and delivered. What a disaster—and precisely why the Melbourne Institute's modelling of the Family Benefit changes in last year's Budget suggested 22,000 individuals would withdraw from the labour market.

Despite inheriting a growing economy and ample opportunity to undertake lasting reform, the Coalition's approach has been short-sighted in the extreme. Fiscal policy has been stuck on a three-year timer switch. Every three years, the spigots get opened, and the entire country just about drowns in cash. The time has come to ask the serious question: where did this money come from, and what has it been spent on?

In engaging in its three-yearly spending sprees the government has missed the opportunity to pursue lasting reform to lower marginal tax rates, particularly where they are at their worst. The Coalition has completely ignored the appalling disincentives faced by those seeking to move from welfare to work. For a period they made matters worse due to the abolition of the earnings credit scheme in 1997—a system of temporary relief from high marginal tax rates that was only reintroduced in 2002.

Just imagine what the unemployment rate could be today if the unemployed could keep more than the paltry 13 cents of each extra dollar they earned.

DEFINING THE PROBLEM

Despite the importance of addressing high marginal tax rates there has, to date, been only a muted debate about the options available to reduce them. This is despite Labor's efforts in the 1998 and 2004 elections to propose positive options. The difficulties these policies faced were in part due to a lack of understanding of what they were trying to address. Without effectively defining the problem there has been depressingly little interest in possible solutions.

That is now changing, with high-profile interventions from the IMF, OECD and even our own RBA Governor that have shone a spotlight on the reason why so many see so little reward from their extra efforts.

While the interactions that cause high marginal tax rates may be complex, the underlying reasons are relatively straightforward. As we here all know, high marginal rates are caused by the simultaneous withdrawal of transfer payments or tax offsets at the same time as tax is being paid. The problems are worse when there is a high rate of withdrawal on a transfer payment or when several transfer payments or tax offsets are being withdrawn at the same time. Some of these interactions are brief, leading to high marginal rates over short income ranges—others are not. Evidently, removing or minimising the potential for these interactions is the only way to deal with them.

OPTIONS FOR REFORM

In beginning the task of lasting reform there are a number of approaches on offer. There is reform of the marginal tax rate structure. There is reform of the transfer payment system. And a more altogether ambitious approach would seek to integrate the two. Regardless of the approach, reform should aim to simplify the existing system, lower the highest work disincentives, and not create unintended disincentives elsewhere.

My firm belief is that we should, as a point of principle, aim where possible to address high effective marginal tax rates through the marginal tax rate structure, rather than further liberalising means tests on income support payments.

We have relied too much on the social security system to redistribute income rather than on our primary redistributive mechanism, the tax system. The welfare bill is already a staggering $80 billion and drawing more people into the net will inevitably snare more people in the high marginal tax rate trap.

MARGINAL TAX RATES

Advocates of reductions in marginal tax rates have primarily concentrated on the two ends of spectrum. At the bottom, the 17 and 30 per cent marginal tax rates give rise to negative interactions with social security payments. At the top, the 47 per cent rate has been criticised because it cuts in at a relatively low multiple of average earnings, interacts with family payments, and encourages the use of mechanisms to avoid paying it.

There are valid arguments for reform of both, but in the first instance our priority should be dealing with the interactions at the bottom of the marginal tax rate spectrum. In terms of dealing with the worst effective marginal tax rates most attention has been given to increasing the income level where the 17 per cent rate cuts in by lifting the tax-free threshold.

Proponents of this approach suggest that the tax-free threshold ought to be lifted substantially so that a single person does not have to pay tax while income support is being withdrawn. This in itself is not an unreasonable suggestion. Currently, the 17 per cent marginal rate combined with the 70 per cent withdrawal of social security allowances gives rise to marginal tax rates of up to 87 per cent. However, the increases to the tax-free threshold would need to be significant—for example, the taper range for Newstart Allowance is currently $15,500 to $17,000 whether you are a single or couple, compared to the existing tax-free threshold of just $6000.

The sort of increases required would come at a considerable cost, primarily because the benefit would flow to all taxpayers, not just those on low incomes for whom we are seeking to reduce effective marginal tax rates. The approach would also provide new incentives for high-income couples to artificially split income through trust structures. On its own it is a very inefficient mechanism for reducing effective marginal tax rates.

As an alternative, others advocate a targeted increase in the tax-free threshold by utilising a tax credit. However, if it were simply bolted onto the existing system, it would give rise to higher marginal tax rates as it is withdrawn—a potentially undesirable outcome.

In yet another alternative that seeks to address these deficiencies, others have argued that the general tax-free threshold be abolished and replaced with a targeted tax-free threshold for low-income earners via a tax credit. For middle- and higher income earners, the loss of the tax-free threshold would provide considerable scope for a trade-off where marginal tax rates are cut.

The other key problem with the marginal tax rate structure is where the 30 per cent rate cuts in—just $21,600. For a single-income couple this 30 per cent rate may be combined with a 70 per cent withdrawal of their spouse's parenting payment, and a 4 per cent reduction in the low-income tax offset, giving rise to a marginal tax rate of 104 per cent. Lifting the threshold for the 30 per cent rate would diminish this interaction by extending the coverage of the 17 per cent rate—a 13 percentage point improvement. Reforms that further sought to rationalise the low-income tax offset would reduce the marginal tax rate by a further 4 percentage points. Although lifting the 30 per cent rate from $21,600 to $30,000 is also a costly proposition, it would be a cheaper option than an equivalent increase in the general tax-free threshold.

These are just a few examples of possible reforms. There are many others, including those recently advocated by the Australian Industry Group which proposes abolishing the 42 cent rate to significantly extend the income range where the 30 per cent rate applies. Professor Peter McDonald has also recently presented three reform scenarios which seek to boost the tax-free threshold as well as alter marginal rates to increase the income level where a maximum 35 per cent average tax rate would apply or move to a flat 35 per cent marginal rate.

All of these approaches have their strengths and weaknesses. But whatever their relative merits, the time has come for the government to stop stonewalling on reforms. None of these reforms are especially cheap, but significant reforms introduced in a staged approach would be affordable over time. In this context there is no reason why the government should not be able to point the way forward. The ball is now clearly in the Howard government's court—we should let the debate begin.

UNTANGLING TRANSFER PAYMENTS

In tandem with marginal tax rate reform, the worst interactions between transfer payments need to be addressed. Currently, payments like Youth Allowance, Parenting Payment Single, Child Care Benefit and Family Tax Benefit B have income tests that may operate over the same income ranges as Family Tax Benefit A. Seeking to restructure or even rationalise payments holds out the potential to reduce the opportunity for income tests to overlap. In cases where payments cannot be rationalised, changes can be made to free areas so that income tests operate over different income ranges, reducing the capacity for benefits to be withdrawn at the same time.

While some have quibbled about Labor's 2004 election policy, it embraced targeted marginal tax rate and transfer payment reforms. At the heart of the changes was an overriding objective to boost participation, particularly among jobless families. A transferable tax-free threshold for couples enabled a tax-free area of up to $12,000 for one parent. Combined with a new working tax bonus, incentives for a jobless parent to move off benefits and into work were dramatically improved by almost completely removing the need to pay tax while Newstart was withdrawn—slashing effective marginal tax rates by 17 per cent.

Family Tax Benefits A and B were combined into a single payment ensuring the two family benefits could not be withdrawn at the same time. The income threshold before family payments were withdrawn was lifted substantially from just over $30,000 to $50,000 per year—greatly improving rewards for work for middle-income families by significantly reducing the overlaps with Youth Allowance and Child Care Benefit.

The Melbourne Institute assessed the impact of Labor's package on participation and concluded that up to 71,000 extra persons would be drawn into the labour market, including 49,000 jobless parents, with the potential savings in social security outlays and extra tax revenues rising to more than $1 billion per year. Further analysis by the National Centre for Social and Economic Modelling found the package in net terms reduced effective marginal tax rates for over one million persons. And it did all this while delivering larger Budget surpluses than the Coalition.

NEGATIVE INCOME TAX

A combination of reform of marginal tax rates and transfer payments will only go so far to improve workforce incentives. The most comprehensive approach to deal with the interactions with tax and transfer payments is to adopt a negative income tax type model where tax and transfer benefits operate in a single unified system.

There are different variations on a negative income tax approach. Tax and transfer payments may be effectively netted out resulting in either a positive credit or a tax liability, or the transfer component may be fixed as a guaranteed minimum income, leaving tax as the only variable. In either case there is no potential for tax to be paid while transfer payments are being means tested away.

The two key advantages advanced for such a system are that it can be designed to ensure marginal tax rates never exceed a particular level, and significant efficiencies are gained because churning of tax only to be handed back as a cash transfer payment is minimised.

In theory it sounds promising; however, there are significant administrative hurdles to overcome, not least of which is the fact that government currently administers transfer payments while employers generally administer tax withholdings. A negative income tax model would require these two systems to be drawn together—not an impossible task, but one with daunting information technology and privacy challenges. I don't advocate that such a system is achievable in the short to medium term, but I believe it is worthy of long-term consideration.

SETTING A TIMETABLE FOR REFORM

The most important aspect of reform as I see it is that we must get started. We simply cannot waste any more time pretending there isn't a problem and pursuing further short-sighted reform that either ignores the problems or makes them worse. To this end a very useful contribution has recently been made to the debate by ANU academic Peter McDonald.

In his paper, 'Reform of Income Tax in Australia—A Long Term Agenda', he outlines how significant programs for reform may be achieved over time if an objective is set and the plan executed to a predetermined timetable. His contribution is important because it shows how important reforms can be achieved over time without placing significant pressures on fiscal policy.

In the context of the current macroeconomic climate it would be most unwise to significantly loosen fiscal policy. But well thought out and executed reform in combination with offsetting savings means we can make significant changes over time without adding undue fiscal stimulus to the economy —an aspect which is crucially important to keeping downward pressure on inflation and interest rates.

CONCLUSION

This tax debate we're just beginning is long overdue. It's a debate that starts from broad agreement, right across the political spectrum, that Australia's tax system is broken. It's been given new impetus by helpful contributions from both sides of politics, from industry, universities, the OECD and, of course, *The Australian* newspaper and the Melbourne Institute.

The tax system is broken because it does little to encourage productivity and participation and it's not internationally competitive. The government's preference for election handouts, instead of carefully considered tax reform, has created appalling work disincentives that must be fixed if we are to increase participation and productivity.

Our most pressing priority, above all else, should be to address those crippling effective marginal tax rates that fail to reward those who work hard to make our economy strong. Because, by untangling the mess that is the interaction between income tax and transfer payments, and putting incentive back into the system, we stand the best chance of encouraging participation, productivity and international competitiveness and sustaining Australia's prosperity into the future.

As Shadow Treasurer, with an ambition one day to be Treasurer, I do not under-estimate how daunting tax reform is for my party or the country. But we have now reached the point where it must now be done to secure our future prosperity.

12 INCOME TAX REFORM: BASE BROADENING TO FUND LOWER RATES

PROFESSOR JOHN FREEBAIRN

Professor of Economics and Director, Melbourne Institute of Applied Economic and Social Research; University of Melbourne

Broadening the income tax base, or taxable sum, by removing special exemptions and deductions has been a characteristic of many tax reform programs in Australia and overseas. Usually the stick of a larger tax base is matched by the carrot of lower tax rates that can be funded in a roughly revenue-neutral package. In addition, such a tax reform package contributes to greater tax neutrality and then increased economy-wide productivity, it simplifies the tax system and lowers costs of tax administration and compliance, and arguably the package contributes to greater horizontal tax equity. Introduction of the fringe benefits tax, capital gains tax and some other base broadening measures in Australia in 1985 helped fund large tax rate reductions, including a drop in the top rate from 60 per cent to 49 per cent. Replacing accelerated depreciation with depreciation over the economic life of plant, equipment and buildings in 2001 funded most of the drop in the Australian corporate tax rate from 39 per cent to 30 per cent. The very significant income tax reforms in the 1980s in New Zealand and the US involved removing many special exemptions and deductions, a larger tax base, and lower tax rates.

This chapter explores options to remove a number of special exemptions and deductions which reduce the current Australian income tax base and which have little or no justification on economic efficiency grounds, add to complexity and are very uneven in their incidence. The efficiency and equity effects of using the up to $10 billion a year gain in revenue to fund lower tax rates, particularly to bring the top rates down towards the 30 per cent corporate tax rate, are explored. The first section of the chapter provides a list of potential current deductions and exemptions which lower taxable income and which have dubious, if any, good efficiency reasons. Some data are provided also on the likely first-round revenue implications of broadening the tax base and on the incidence of the deductions and exemptions if they were to be removed. A reform option in which the extra revenue from such base broadening measures was used primarily to fund lowering the top personal income tax rate towards the corporate 30 per cent tax rate is sketched in the next section. The final part evaluates some of the efficiency implications of the base broadening and lower top personal tax rate reform package in terms of reduced distortions to business organisation, financing and funding decisions, to the choice of mix of savings and investment choice options, and to the attraction of Australia for internationally mobile skilled labour and capital.

SOME OPTIONS TO BROADEN THE INCOME TAX BASE

Information from the Australian Taxation Office (2004) and the Australian Treasury (2005) provides a fruitful list of current exemptions and deductions which might be removed as part of an income tax base broadening component of a tax reform policy package. This section discusses the economic efficiency arguments for removing the exemption and deduction, the revenue effect, and the first-round distributional incidence of the current deduction or exemption.

WORK-RELATED EXPENSES

Data from the ATO show that, in 2001–02, 74 per cent of individual taxpayers claimed a total of $9.325 billion in work-related expenses. The largest claims were for work-related car expenses ($3.7 billion), work-related travel expenses ($0.75 billion), work-related uniform/clothing expenses ($1.079 billion) and work-related self-education expenses ($0.679 billion). It is difficult on efficiency grounds to justify a deduction for travel costs from one place of work to another but not the costs of travel from home to work, to give some workers in some industries a deduction for uniform/clothing expenses but not in others, and to give a deduction for work-related self-education expenses once employed but not prior to employment.

One option would be to eliminate all deductions for work-related expenses. This would level the playing field, or not add to distortions with the current fairly ad hoc incomplete list of allowable deductions. It also would greatly reduce the number of people seeking professional tax advice, which in 2001–02 was sought by 52 per cent of individual taxpayers who claimed an additional $0.9 billion in deductions for the cost of managing tax affairs.

As shown in Table 1, deductions for work-related expenses are skewed in favour of those on higher taxable incomes. Taxpayers at all income levels make claims for work-related expenses, with nearly three-quarters making a claim. However, while those with taxable incomes of $50,000 a year or more represent 22 per cent of taxpayers, they made 37 per cent of the dollar sum claims.

Table 1: The Distribution of Claims for Work-related Expenses, 2001–02

Taxable income ($ per year)	Number of taxpayers (million)	Percentage who claimed work-related expenses (%)	Expenses claimed ($ million)
6,000–20,000	1.914	62.3	1,112
20,001–50,000	4.655	76.2	4,791
50,001–60,000	0.731	83.2	1,188
>60,000	1.096	75.4	2,234
Total	**8.396**	**73.5**	**9,325**

Source: Compiled from ATO (2004), Table 5, Part C.

The revenue gained by deleting deductions for work-related expenses in 2001–02 would be in the range of $3–$3.5 billion. The estimate is based on the marginal tax rates of taxpayers shown in Table 1, with some reduction in claims for costs of professional assistance in filling-in much simpler tax forms, and with some increase in claims by businesses either in additional business expenses or in higher compensating wage increases. The latter term clearly is difficult to quantify.

FRINGE BENEFITS CONCESSIONS

The under-valuation of the value of vehicles for private use is estimated by Treasury (2005) to reduce the tax burden by $1.1 billion in 2003–04, compared with paying employees a salary and then purchasing a vehicle from after-tax disposable income. This tax expenditure distorts the choice of form of remuneration and the mix of expenditure. It seems likely the benefits are skewed in favour of middle- and high-income earners, and they involve an element of horizontal inequity as between people who take all their remuneration as wages and salaries versus those who take a portion as a fringe benefit vehicle.

Other remaining elements of concessionary taxation of fringe benefits counted as tax expenditures by the Treasury (2005), but not listed for removal in Table 2, include fringe benefits provided to many employees in the not-for-profit sector of the economy.

CAPITAL GAINS TAX CONCESSIONS

Concessions shown in Table 2 with the taxation of capital gains exceed $3 billion a year. The largest concession is the halving of the tax rate for assets held for more than 12 months, costing $2.5 billion a year. Small businesses receive additional concessions worth nearly $0.5 billion a year in the form of roll-over relief, a 50 per cent exemption for so-called 'active sales', and an exemption for capital gains destined for retirement income. In addition, and not counted as a tax expenditure by the Treasury, capital gains tax is levied only on realised gains and not accrued gains, with this treatment representing a form of deferred tax or interest-free loan to taxpayers with capital gains but not available to taxpayers with some other forms of capital income or to wage and salary earners.

The efficiency arguments for concessional taxation of capital gains in terms of effects on both the aggregate levels of saving and investment and on the compositions of aggregate saving and investment are ambiguous in theory and as yet not resolved by empirical evaluation. To a large extent the uncertainties about the inefficiencies of capital gains taxation arise because of the hybrid or mongrel system of taxation of different forms of capital income in Australia, and also internationally, whereby different forms of investment and saving face different tax systems and different effective tax rates.

Investment and saving in owner-occupied housing is accorded a consumption tax system tax treatment (no tax on the capital income earnings whether taken as imputed rent or as capital gains). By contrast, saving and investment through financial deposits, debentures and distributed corporate and unincorporated business income are given a nominal income tax treatment (with the annual earnings effectively taxed at the personal rate). Retained corporate earnings face a flat 30 per cent corporate tax rate, versus rates for income subject to a progressive personal tax rate schedule. Again, the taxation of superannuation is a mixed system and even varies as between employer versus employee contributions and between lump sum versus

Table 2: Some Special Deductions and Exemptions Measured as Tax Expenditures, Revenue Cost 2003–04

Expenditure item deducted	Treasury tax expenditure code	Annual cost in $ million
Fringe benefit		
Concessional statutory formula for deductible cost of vehicles	D25	1,100
Capital gains		
CGT exemption on sale of small business for retirement income	C6	90
Venture capital exemption	E12	20
50% exemption for small business active asset sale	E13	240
Roll-over relief for small business	E14	75
50% CGT rate	E15	2,530
Lump sums		
Concessional treatment of non-super termination funds	C3	850
Capped tax rates for lump-sum payments for unused leave	C4	190
Tax of 5% on unused leave accumulated before 1978	C5	85
Income averaging		
Authors, inventors, artists, etc	A48	8
Primary producers	B81	190
Primary producers		
Three-year depreciation of water capital expenses	B26	25
Accelerated depreciation of horticultural plants	B32	6
Farm management deposit scheme	B82	250
Cost valuation of livestock	B86	105
Remote area concessions		
Remote zone tax offsets	A46	185
Remote area housing allowance	D15	80

Source: Drawn from Australian Treasury (2005).

annuity withdrawals. As a result of these different tax systems, different forms of saving and investment face different effective tax rates. The effective tax rate on options returning capital gains is towards the lower end of the spectrum, but not as low as, for example, owner-occupied housing. At a minimum, the very different effective tax rates on the different saving and investment choice options distort the composition of aggregate investment and saving.

More controversial are the net effects of current income taxation on the aggregate levels of saving and investment. Income taxation, including that on capital gains at concessional rates, distorts decisions against saving relative to current consumption. However, an aggregate revenue-neutral tax package with a decrease in taxation of capital income means an offsetting increase in taxation of labour income which results in aggravated distortions to work versus leisure and other decisions in the labour market. Resolving the net effects of the different effective tax rates on distortions to economic decisions in the capital and labour markets, and the associated loss of national productivity, is a non-trivial empirical exercise which has not been undertaken to date for Australia.

Individuals in 2001–02 declared $6.4 billion in net capital gains and paid $2.5 billion in capital gains taxes for an average tax rate of 40 per cent. Companies paid $1 billion on $4.8 billion of net capital gains, and funds paid $0.4 billon on $2.9 billion of net capital gains. While there are individuals at all income levels who report capital gains, 66 per cent of the net capital gains were in the hands of the top tax bracket taxpayers even though they represent only 13 per cent of all taxpayers (Table 3). That is, the benefits of special exemptions and deductions for capital gains taxation are highly skewed in favour of those with high taxable incomes.

Table 3: Distribution of Personal Capital Gains, by Taxable Income, 2001–02

Taxable income ($ per year)	Taxpayers with capital gains (%)	Net capital gains ($ million)	Share of total capital gains (%)
<20,000	7.2	313	5.2
20,001–50,000	9.5	1,293	21.5
50,001–60,000	13.3	426	7.1
>60,000	18.9	3,990	66.2
Total	**10.4**	**6,025**	**100.0**

Source: Data from ATO (2004), Table 2: Capital gains tax.

LUMP SUMS

Some lump sum payments to employees, other than superannuation, are given a concessional tax treatment relative to the income taxation of wages and salaries. On efficiency grounds there is no logical argument to treat one form of labour remuneration differently from another form of remuneration. The Treasury tax expenditure statement estimates the revenue cost for 2003–04 of three of these items shown in Table 2 at over $1.1 billion.

While there will be some low-income people who benefit from the concessional tax treatment of lump sum payments, the majority of payments in dollars are received by people at the end of their career and on higher income levels.

INCOME AVERAGING

The choice of an annual accounting period in assessing taxable income is an arbitrary, if not a long-established convention. Against a progressive income tax schedule, those with more variable incomes and the same average over many years will pay more tax than those with a more stable income. On both efficiency and equity grounds, a case therefore can be made for some form of general income averaging. Australian taxation allows primary producers to average over a five-year interval, and averaging is allowed for some artists, inventors and sportspersons. However, averaging is not generally available, including for unincorporated businesses tied to agriculture, other businesses with fluctuating incomes, and many employees have fluctuating incomes, including part-time employees and women with career interruptions. The efficiency and equity arguments for providing averaging for a small subset of taxpayers, and not generally for all taxpayers, are weak at best. Then, removal of the current selective concessions seems a viable alternative tax simplification strategy.

The Treasury (2005) tax expenditure statement estimates for 2003–04 the revenue loss of the current selective availability of income averaging at $198 million, with almost all going to primary producers (see Table 2).

PRIMARY PRODUCERS

While the 2001 reforms of business income taxation of 2001 removed most of the special exemptions and deductions in the measurement of taxable business income, a number of costly concessions for primary producers were not removed as a part of this more comprehensive income tax base reform package. Some of the remaining concessions shown in Table 2, which are drawn from the Treasury (2005) estimates of tax expenditures, are accelerated depreciation allowances for some water investments and horticultural plants, the cost valuation of livestock, and the system of deferred taxation of income invested in farm management deposits. For 2003–04 the concessions are estimated to have cost $280 million. These special concessions favour some forms of primary production activity over other avenues of agricultural production, and they favour over-investment in the agricultural sector relative to other sectors of the economy.

REMOTE AREA CONCESSIONS

Over the years political lobbyists have sought and locked in special tax concessions as an offset for the higher costs of living in remote Australia. In general, higher living costs in remote Australia, or in any other tagged region for that matter, reflect social opportunity costs. An efficient economy would locate businesses and households in such areas only if the returns matched the opportunity costs, and employees would seek appropriate compensating pay differentials. In effect, the remote zone tax offset and remote area housing allowance, estimated to have cost $265 million in 2003–04, is a subsidy to businesses and individuals who choose to locate in remote Australia. In the majority of cases the recipients of these subsidies are among the higher paid members of Australian taxpayers. Therefore, neither efficiency nor equity arguments support retention of special allowances for remote Australia in computing taxable income.

POSSIBLE REFORM PACKAGES

If, as in the past, political and other restrictions on acceptable tax reform are to include approximate aggregate revenue neutrality and to result in a small number of net large losers, both relative to the status quo, close links have to be drawn between the revenue gains from base broadening and the tax rate reductions they fund. In this restrictive context some observations on the funding and distributional effects of some general rate reduction options are noted.

The base broadening measures discussed in the preceding section were estimated to raise between $9 and $10 billion a year in current dollars, the savings would come from all levels of taxable income, but most of the base broadening measures would fall on those with higher incomes. Clearly the aggregate sum could be increased further if other base broadening measures were pursued, including reducing or ending the 30 per cent private health insurance subsidy, the first home owners scheme subsidy, and other tax expenditures identified by Treasury (2005). Since the base broadening measures were justified in part to reduce current tax distortions which reduce productivity and national income and in part to reduce tax complexity and associated taxpayer and tax collector operating costs, some efficiency dividend in terms of a more productive economy and larger tax base will itself generate extra funds. Further, the lower tax rates funded by the base broadening measures also will reduce taxation distortions and provide incentives for a larger and more productive economy. Compiling estimates of the magnitude of the fiscal dividend from tax reform is inevitably a challenging and controversial exercise, but neither should such efficiency gains be ignored and arbitrarily set to zero.

In the current environment of non-indexation of the tax brackets, because of fiscal creep, income tax revenue as a share of GDP rises with increases in both nominal and real incomes over time. Arguably, some of the revenue gains from fiscal creep could be used as a component of a package to fund lower tax rates.

An idea of the order of magnitude of fundable personal tax reductions, assuming no changes in the current tax thresholds, is provided in Table 4 for 2003–04. Reducing all rates by one percentage point would cost about $3.2 billion. Cost reductions for the different brackets as a result of the bracket changes in July 2004 and planned for July 2005 will cost more in the case of the current 30 per cent bracket (which will be widened) and reduced for the top two brackets (which come in at higher and higher income levels). The top two rates could be reduced to the corporate 30 per cent rate for a total annual outlay of between $10 and $12 billion.

Table 4: Estimated Revenue Costs of Reducing Personal Income Tax Rates, 2003–04

Rate reduction	Revenue cost in $ million
17% to 16%	1,245
30% to 29%	1,330
42% to 41%	185
47% to 46%	560
Reduce all rates by 1 percentage point	3,240

Source: Computed from Melbourne Institute Tax and Social Security Simulation Model.

Revenue neutrality and maintaining a broad sense of equity across taxpayers on average across the different tax brackets suggests a small reduction of no more than two percentage points for the bottom brackets, and more substantial reductions in the top two brackets, in excess of five percentage points but not enough to go all the way to a 30 per cent rate in the first instance. Clearly there will be some redistribution among taxpayers within each tax bracket. Those who now are not beneficiaries of the exemptions and deductions to be removed will be clear winners with the lower tax rates. Up to 40 per cent of taxpayers with incomes less than $50,000 are likely to be winners in this category, but less than 20 per cent of those with higher incomes would not lose some exemptions and deductions. Those who currently are large beneficiaries of the to-be-removed deductions and expenses will not be fully offset by the lower tax rates. For many, the loss of foregone deductions and exemptions will approximate the gains from lower tax rates. Behavioural responses to the new set of incentives, and the national efficiency gains and a resulting larger economy driven by the more efficient tax system, will in time further reduce the numbers of losers and the magnitudes of any losses.

ARGUMENTS TO LOWER THE TOP TAX RATES

A number of arguments for greater efficiency and greater simplicity in income taxation by bringing the top 42 per cent and 47 per cent tax rates down towards the 30 per cent corporate tax rate can be made. An ambitious base broadening package might fund a top personal tax rate of 30 per cent, a capital gains tax rate of 30 per cent, being a small increase on the present 23.5 per cent, and the current 30 per cent corporate rate.

Lower top income tax rates will lead not only to lower rates per se and hence lower incentives to reorganise economic decisions to reduce tax paid, but also they will result in more comparable effective tax rates across different forms of business organisation and across different options for saving and investment. With lower incentives and rewards for changing decisions to utilise different tax rates on different choice options to minimise tax, national productivity can be expected to rise with both the reduction of the distortion or deadweight costs of taxation and with less wasteful diversion of scarce resources to tax administration and compliance.

Examples of reductions in differences in effective tax rates and in the distortions to business organisation and funding decisions include: incorporation versus unincorporated and the formation of trusts; contractors versus employees; the payment of dividends versus retained earnings; and debt versus equity financing. Even with the continuation of the different tax systems for different investment and savings options, including consumption base (e.g. on housing), nominal income tax base (e.g. on financial loans and borrowings, and on distributed corporate income), and mixed systems (e.g. on superannuation), both lower rates and more comparable tax rates across the different choice options reduce tax distortions to choices among the different savings and investment options. That is, the quality or society-wide productivity of a given quantum of aggregate saving and investment would increase.

In the context of Australia as a small player in the global economy, lower tax rates on the incomes of the internationally mobile capital and skilled labour inputs are likely to entice more of these resources, both those with an Australian initial location as well as those with an initial overseas location, to locate in Australia. The owners of most skilled labour and capital resources in choosing an Australian or an international location place considerable weight on the after-tax return to be gained from the alternative locations. Clearly there is uncertainty and legitimate argument about the magnitude of the elasticity of supply of skilled labour and of capital to an Australian location if the after-tax return from location in Australia were to be increased with a reduction of the present 46 per cent and 42 per cent rates towards the 30 per cent corporate rate; but there is no doubt that the elasticity exceeds zero and also that it is less than the small country infinity extreme. Importantly, an increased inflow of skilled labour and of capital will increase the mix of these resources in production with the internationally immobile unskilled labour input. In turn, productivity of the unskilled labour in time will rise, justifying higher real wages for the majority of unskilled Australians who will become winners also in the intermediate run from the lower top tax rates.

The foregoing argument for lowering the top tax rates is an application of the well-established theory of optimal taxation. That is, economic efficiency is enhanced by relatively low tax rates on factors with a high supply elasticity (to Australia), in this case the internationally mobile skilled labour and capital, and relatively higher tax rates on factors with a low supply elasticity (to Australia), in this case the internationally immobile unskilled labour. Further, the economic burden of the present high statutory income tax rates on the relatively higher elastic supplied factors will be passed on to the other factors as lower pre-tax returns than otherwise. To the extent that in Australia most internationally mobile and therefore high elasticity of supply factors face the higher income tax rates, and that the relatively internationally immobile are among the low- to middle-income earners, lowering the top tax rates is a crude application of optimum tax theory in which the majority of Australians will benefit.

Lower top tax rates and a flatter income tax rate schedule reduce the logic of claims for income tax averaging measures for most, on average, middle- and high-income earners.

CONCLUSION

There are good efficiency and simplicity arguments to remove a large number of special exemptions and deductions in the measurement of taxable income in Australia. Base broadening measures have been identified which would generate up to another $10 billion a year. While such measures would affect some taxpayers at all income levels, most of the revenue gains would come from extra tax paid by those on higher incomes. Arguably the measures would also improve most notions of horizontal equity.

A package of base broadening measures and lower tax rates, especially at the upper income levels, that would roughly be revenue-neutral and which contains the number of losers was suggested. For example, the $10 billion gained from base broadening could finance a reduction in the lower rates by up to two percentage points, and of rates in the top two tax brackets by five or more percentage points. The latter would work to bring the top personal rate and the capital gains tax rate closer to the 30 per cent corporate tax rate. The resulting more comparable effective tax rates on different choice options, as well as the lower rates, would reduce distortions to decisions about the structure and operation of businesses and about the composition of saving and investment. The ensuing more productive economy, together with the effect of lower tax rates making Australia a relatively more attractive location for internationally mobile skilled labour and capital, would in time generate dynamic economic growth gains which flowed to low-income as well as to high-income taxpayers.

REFERENCES

Australian Taxation Office (ATO) 2004, *Taxation Statistics 2001–02*, accessed from <www.ato.gov.au>.

Australian Treasury 2005, *Tax Expenditures Statement 2004*, accessed from <www.treasury.gov.au>.

13 STANDING STILL IS NOT AN OPTION

Mr Michael Chaney AO
*Managing Director and
Chief Executive Officer, Wesfarmers*

Can I start by congratulating *The Australian* newspaper and The Melbourne Institute on their ongoing initiative in organising this conference, which builds upon its successful predecessors in 2002 and 2003, and now constitutes a very important forum for debate on Australian public policy.

It is very easy to take for granted the prosperity that this country has enjoyed over the last dozen or so years, and to fool yourself into thinking that we can sustain that prosperity by marking time. Why should we talk about change when things are going so well?

That same question arises within any successful company. There's a natural human tendency for success to be followed by hubris—a general self-satisfaction and a belief that you've developed some superior wisdom and skill—emotions that are so often a harbinger of disaster.

There's a tendency within any company to believe that the profits you are making from a particular activity will be secure if you just keep applying what worked in the past, and that to grow all you have to do is try a few new things.

It occurred to me some time ago that that isn't the case at all. In fact every dollar of profit you make is under threat. Somebody is trying to take it away—competitors, suppliers, customers, governments, to name a few—

and they will succeed. The only way to grow is through innovation—by finding new ways, first to replace the profits you are certainly going to lose and then to add to them. Innovation means developing new processes, technologies and products, moving into new geographies and developing new businesses.

That, I think, has been the key to the success of Wesfarmers, which over the past twenty years has grown in market value by a factor of 500 and whose activities now span a range of mining, services and agricultural businesses around Australia.

It seems pretty clear to me that the same situation faces our country at the present time. We live in a very competitive and increasingly open, global economy. No one owes us a living and unless we innovate, unless we continually find ways to increase our productivity, we'll go backwards. Our prosperity will be diminished, rather than sustained. Hence the title of my address to you today, 'Standing still is not an option'.

In 1992 I had the pleasure of attending a three-month management program at the Harvard Business School—an experience that gave me the opportunity to stand back from the day-to-day demands of the workplace and think about some of the bigger issues facing Australia. Things often look a bit clearer when viewed from a distance.

As it happened, the Australian economy was actually the subject of some of our case studies or, to put it less politely, it was the subject of a 'basket case' study.

The message about Australia was clear. Here was a country that had squandered its riches, had grown fat and lazy in the 1950s, 1960s and 1970s, had become a profligate spender in the 1980s and was now one of the most heavily indebted nations on earth. It was a country hamstrung by rigid institutional structures and low labour productivity, and with a primary industry focus in a world where elaborate manufacturing and knowledge-based industries were generating real prosperity.

The Harvard criticisms of Australia at that time were, in my view, a little harsh. Under Prime Ministers Hawke and Keating economic deregulation had started to occur, for example, with the floating of the dollar and in industrial relations, but there was certainly some basis for the negative view.

Later that year the Business Council of Australia (BCA) held a national Debt Summit, at which those same concerns were expressed and which laid out a blueprint for the microeconomic reform that needed to take place if Australia were to recover. That blueprint included reforms to industrial relations, competition policy, import tariffs, taxation, public ownership of infrastructure assets and government spending.

As we all know, reform occurred across all of those areas during the decade of the 1990s and the results have been nothing less than extraordinary —thirteen years of sustained economic growth in the face of the Asian crisis and a worldwide recession, a current unemployment rate of around 5 per cent and some of the most impressive productivity growth rates among the OECD.

From January 1994 to December 2004, more than two million jobs were created in Australia and more than one million of those were full-time jobs.

In the ten years to December 2003, real wages grew by nearly 20 per cent compared with no growth in the decade to 1993.

It is instructive to look back now at some modelling carried out for the BCA by Access Economics at the time of the debt summit.

Figure 1 shows how Australia's Debt/GDP ratio had risen from almost nothing in the early 1980s to around 40 per cent by 1992.

Access estimated that if no changes were made to the way we operated as a nation, Australia's external indebtedness would have risen to the unacceptable levels illustrated in figure 2 (a debt/GDP ratio of around 60 per cent within five years).

If, on the other hand, Australia managed to achieve the reforms I listed earlier, Access's modelling suggested that the debt/GDP ratio could be stabilised at a little more than 50 per cent (Figure 3) and we could avoid the deep recession or depression which would have otherwise occurred as

Figure 1: Australia's Foreign Debt to GDP Ratio

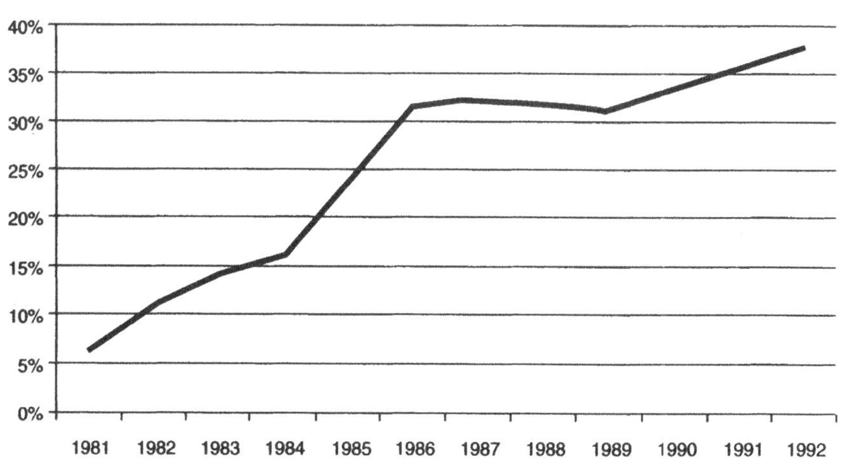

Source: Access Economics 1992

the rest of the world ran out of patience and withdrew our credit or hiked interest rates.

Well, what actually happened?

As you can see from figure 3, Australia's economic performance was much better than had been hoped. Our debt/GDP ratio stabilised earlier, and at a lower level, than forecast; the economy grew 40 per cent over the

Figure 2: Foreign Debt to GDP: If We Did Nothing

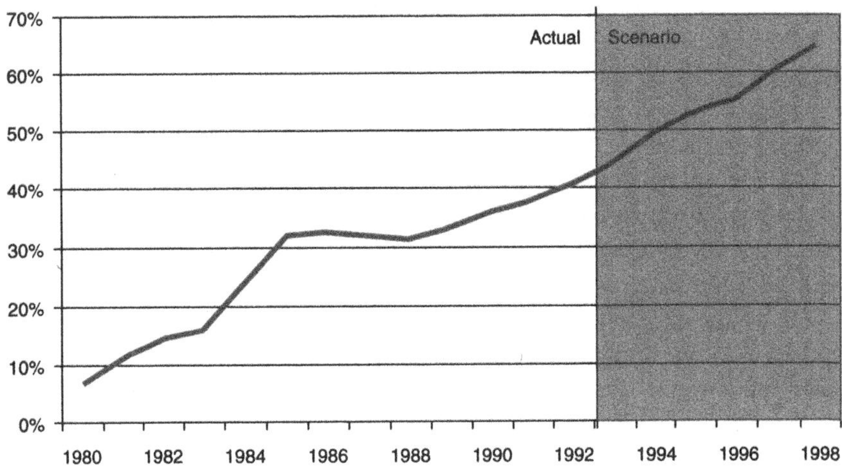

Source: Access Economics 1992

Figure 3: Foreign Debt to GDP

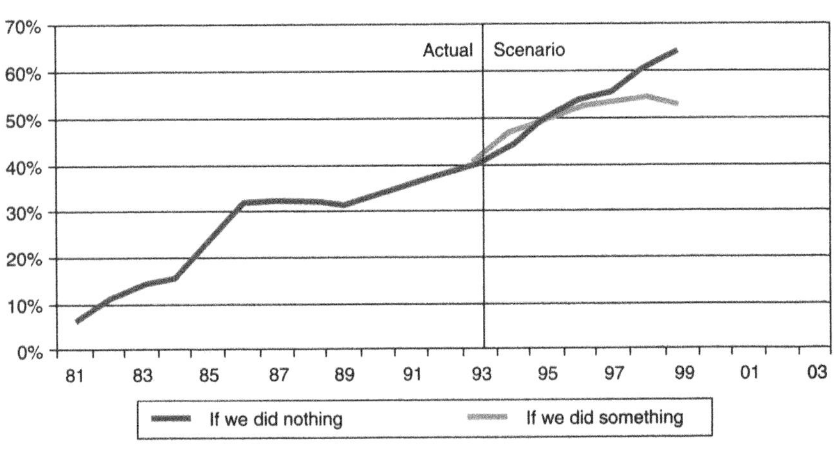

Source: Access Economics 1992

decade—higher than any other in the Western world—unemployment fell
and real wages grew, as I described earlier.

You will note that in recent years the debt/GDP level has kicked up
again and is currently around 47 per cent. That, amongst other things, highlights the need for renewed vigour in lifting our productivity.

I think there is a very simple reason for Australia's better-than-expected
performance during the last decade, and that is innovation.

When, in the early 1990s, we in our individual companies were looking
forward to a series of reforms (for example, in industrial relations with the
introduction of workplace agreements), we made estimates of the productivity improvements that we could expect to flow from them. It turned out,
in fact, that the productivity gains were much greater than we had assumed.

That was because of a wholesale change of attitude amongst the workforce. When they were freed from the institutional shackles that had
previously constrained them, employees allowed their creativity to flourish.
They became innovative, finding better, more efficient ways to do the job,
often motivated by the prospect of additional financial rewards.

I think that's what happened across the whole economy, and workplace
reform has been at the heart of it. Because of that, and also because I chair
the BCA's Workplace and Participation Task Force, I intend to focus my
comments today on that subject.

Well, how important have workplace reforms been in delivering
Australia's strong economic performance over the past decade?

The Business Council has asked Access Economics to undertake an
analysis of this issue and the results, while still preliminary, indicate that the

Figure 4: Foreign Debt to GDP

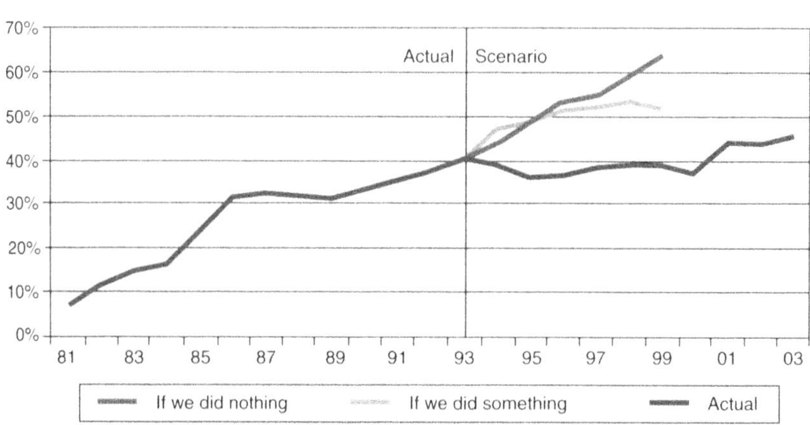

Source: Access Economics 1992

benefits have been substantial, namely that they have contributed around one-third of the reform dividend.

- That reform dividend itself is estimated by Access to be equivalent to $4200 in additional income per person per year in 2004, and the equivalent of more than $80,000 in wealth per person.
- Access also estimates that had it not been for reforms to workplace relations, the average unemployment rate would have been 8.1 per cent in 2004 and not 5.8 per cent.
- In other words, there would have been more than one-quarter of a million people who would have been without jobs who are now employed.

Australia's mining sector has led the way in workforce reform and productivity improvement over that time and, so far, has made the greatest use of individual workplace agreements. Let me outline some of the benefits enjoyed by that sector:

- Productivity, at a healthy 6 per cent per annum, has outpaced the performance of all other sectors in the economy.
- The mining sector is one of few with higher productivity than the same sector in the US. In fact, the Australian mining sector is more than twice as productive as its US equivalent.
- Strong productivity growth has supported very strong investment growth in recent years.
- Strong productivity growth has also supported high levels of incomes for workers in the sector. Average wage levels for those employees are more than $500 per week higher than the economy-wide average.
- Perhaps more importantly, and as I described earlier, workplace relations reform has enabled enterprises and their employees to be more accountable for performance and outcomes. The result of this cultural change in relationships and in accepting responsibility has been more diverse improvements including, for example, substantially improved workplace safety and sharp reductions in time lost to injuries.

You would imagine that that performance would provide sufficient evidence of the benefits of further reform in the workplace. But labour market reform is, and has always been, an emotive issue.

I suspect workplace relations policies have become something of a touchstone for broader concerns about the pace of technological change and increased global competition and what these have meant for individuals and society. The rapid evolution of new technologies provides fantastic opportunities, but also new challenges. New technologies are a key driver of change, including at the workplace, but they challenge traditional ways of doing things and often more traditional relationships.

Some are resistant to such change, but Australian business cannot be if it is to remain competitive and continue to seek opportunities for job creation, income growth and higher standards of living.

So where does this discussion leave us?

Australian business and the economy more broadly are facing two key challenges over the coming decade and beyond:

- how to sustain productivity growth, which in turn determines our competitiveness and ultimately living standards; and
- how to respond effectively to demographic trends which will see growth in our labour supply shrink dramatically.

Workplace relations reform has an important role in enabling us to respond to these challenges. Productivity improvements will increasingly be driven by the application and evolution of skills, new ideas and innovation.

Businesses must be able to respond quickly and flexibly in such an environment, reflecting their competitive circumstances and the requirements of a more diverse workforce. They must also be able to flexibly reward those contributing to productivity and competitiveness.

Demographic trends—low birth rates and population ageing—mean that business is going to have to work harder to attract and retain staff, including women and mature-aged workers who might otherwise not participate in the labour force. Again, this requires greater scope for flexibility in terms and conditions and working arrangements.

The BCA, as part of a broader reform agenda, released a Workplace Relations Action Plan in February. The focus of that plan is on:

- sustaining strong productivity growth;
- sustaining high levels of employment through job creation and higher workforce participation; and
- creating an environment where people can work to their potential and are rewarded for capacity and effort.

The policy priorities articulated by the BCA can be summarised under three broad headings:

- greater flexibility in agreement making;
- reduced barriers to job creation and participation; and
- more efficient workplace regulation.

Let me comment briefly on each of those.

FLEXIBILITY IN AGREEMENT MAKING

The BCA considers further award simplification, changes to the no-disadvantage test and processes around agreement making can enhance flexibility in agreement making.

In short, it should be easier to make agreements.

In advocating award simplification, there needs to be a substantial reduction in the number of allowable matters. Some have taken issue with the BCA's suggested pared-back list, but few have challenged the underlying argument that awards remain overly prescriptive and continue to underpin and limit the scope for more flexible agreement making.

The issue therefore seems to be one of scope and not one of fundamental disagreement with the thrust of these recommendations.

REDUCED BARRIERS AND INCREASED PARTICIPATION

The second area of reform is the need to reduce barriers to job creation and workforce participation.

The focus here is largely on reforming safety net wages—that is the way in which minimum wages are set in Australia and addressing the issue of high effective marginal tax rates.

Let me start with the issue of safety net wages.

The key point here is that higher minimum wages result in higher unemployment. This is clearly backed up by research done by Access Economics, which underpins the BCA's Action Plan.

In other words, where we choose to set minimum wages reflects the level of unemployment we are happy to sustain.

At close to 5 per cent unemployment many might argue that this is a moot point. However, the point is not where unemployment is this month or last, but more how we can sustain employment levels over the long run, including when growth is a bit weaker.

Also, focusing only on unemployment ignores the many thousands of people who have become discouraged from seeking employment or who would work more if the work was available.

What the BCA has called for is a change to the way in which safety net wages are determined.

We would like to see a board or committee established to make such determinations, taking into account the prospects of the unemployed, with a recommendation made to government for their approval. This is in line with the system that operates in the UK.

The BCA has not specifically called for a cut in minimum wages, but we have been frank in recognising that higher minimum wages means fewer jobs for low skilled workers.

The BCA has also called on the government to address the issue of high effective marginal tax rates. This refers to the situation in which additional income earned is eaten away by increased tax and/or through the impact of lost benefit payments—the so-called tax-welfare trade off. Ken Henry, Secretary of the Treasury, who is speaking at this conference, has in the past been a vocal critic of this situation and its effect on workplace participation.

High effective marginal tax rates discourage workforce participation at a time when we need to be doing all that we can to support it.

MORE EFFICIENT REGULATION

Let me turn finally to the third element of the BCA's recommendations—more efficient workplace regulation. The focus here is on the establishment of a national system of industrial relations.

The benefits of a national workplace relations system were recognised a long time ago in the Hancock report of the mid-1980s, but we have made little progress.

The duplication of regulation across six jurisdictions is costly and time consuming for enterprises operating around Australia. It also undermines clarity about roles, responsibilities and accountabilities.

The dual system is not ideal for the state governments; it is not ideal for the federal government.

The BCA has called for a voluntary resolution to this problem based around a referral of state powers. On the basis of the dialogue we have seen, this is pretty unlikely, and to be honest we thought that would be the case. Nonetheless, it would produce the best outcome.

In the absence of a referral of powers, we called upon the government to use the corporations' power to achieve as universal a system as possible. It looks as if this is where we are headed.

Frankly, I think the opposition to a single national system of industrial relations is short sighted and parochial. It reminds me very much of the loud protests about uniform corporations law that we heard in the 1980s.

As you might recall, prior to 1991 Australia had separate and different state laws regulating corporations and in 1989 the states successfully challenged the Commonwealth's attempts to achieve uniformity in the High Court. I well remember the howls of protest in Western Australia about how we would lose our independence to regulate *our* companies and how we'd potentially be subject to bad Commonwealth laws in the future.

By 1991 the states had come to their senses, accepted the benefits of one system and enacted uniform corporations law. It's hard now to believe that anyone could have argued otherwise.

Similarly, having six separate sets of industrial relations laws and regulations makes no sense at all in a country whose economy is smaller than California's. To those who support the status quo, I'd ask: Why stop there? Why not have separate IR legislation for employers north and south of Sydney harbour? Why not have a separate system in each local government area? Surely we're mature enough as a nation to have a uniform system nationally.

And, of course, we have a precedent. Victoria referred most of its IR powers to the Commonwealth in the early 1990s and the sky didn't fall in. You'll note that there's no move by Victoria now to get those powers back.

Well, those are the main issues of workplace relations where we believe reform is required now. They involve, in summary:

- giving employees and employers more flexibility to make agreements;
- making job creation easier and giving more opportunities to those who would otherwise find it difficult to gain employment; and
- creating a simpler, more understandable workplace system.

The BCA's proposal does make some additional recommendations for change but these are not as significant, so I shan't go into them here.

In closing, let me say that workplace relations is only one area in which further reform is needed at this time—others include infrastructure, tax and regulation—but it is in my view an absolutely critical one because of the clear link between workplace relations settings and employee attitudes. It is only through a positive workplace culture—in an environment where all employees consider themselves part of the same team where their interests are aligned with their employer's—that we will achieve the productivity improvements we need in order to sustain our national prosperity.

Given what has been achieved in this country through reforms over the past decade, I think further workplace relations reform is both a feasible and an exciting challenge.

14 MINIMUM WAGES: INDUSTRIAL RELATIONS REFORMS AND ECONOMIC ISSUES

MR GREG COMBET

Secretary, Australian Council of Trade Unions

The Howard government has been content to rely on economic growth driven by domestic consumption and household debt, and it has failed to address capacity constraints in the economy which have been evident for a considerable period of time.

The government has not sought to build personal savings or reduce dependence on overseas financing. It has instead fuelled consumption, especially whenever election time rolls around. It has also failed to address skills shortages which have been emerging for a long time, a deficit in infrastructure investment which has been obvious for even longer, falling growth rates in research and development investment, and a deteriorating trade performance.

Instead of starting the hard yards on these critical economic challenges, the government is touting its favourite old hobby horse—industrial relations reform—as the highest economic priority. My argument is that this government always prioritises politics over policy. Despite all the good intentions expressed at forums like this, and the fulminating editorials penned for *The Australian*, the government's record suggests that the next major piece of fiscal reform will come in the 2007 election year Budget in the form of a cash bonus attached to a Liberal Party How-to-Vote card.

MINIMUM WAGES

In the discussion of industrial relations reforms, minimum wages are receiving a lot of attention. About 1.6 million Australians and their families rely on minimum award wages. Proposals to freeze or enable a decline in the real value of their wages, therefore, could impact significantly on their living standards.

The ACTU is the organisation which each year seeks an increase in minimum wages. We do so out of our conviction that such increases are needed to maintain the living standards of Australians who work hard, who contribute to productivity and profitability, but who cannot bargain for higher wages and who have largely missed out on a fair share of the past decade's prosperity.

In 2005 the ACTU has lodged an application to increase minimum wages by $26.40 a week—taking the minimum wage rate to $13 per hour. This year as usual our claim is opposed by employers, the federal government and various commentators. Those who oppose increases in minimum wages usually argue a number of things:

- that any increase is unrelated to productivity;
- that an increase will cost jobs; and
- that the increase does not help the low-paid because the value of minimum wage increases is wiped out when income tax and the withdrawal of government benefits are taken into account (i.e. that there are high effective marginal tax rates).

Lately there have also been arguments to the effect that the members of the Australian Industrial Relations Commission, and the advocates before it, are economically illiterate; that the wage case is an exercise in splitting the difference between ambit claims; that the economic material considered is only window dressing; that the skills-based scale of minimum wages should be abolished in favour of a single US-style basic rate; and finally that we should change the whole approach and get a bunch of expert economists to do the job.

Let me try to briefly address these issues. First, key minimum wage dependent industries in Australia have experienced higher than average productivity and employment growth in recent years. In 2003–04, productivity across all Australian industries averaged a little over 2 per cent. But in retail, Australia's most award dependent industry, productivity growth was close to 7 per cent, more than three times the industry average. Productivity in the retail industry has grown by more than 26 per cent since 1996, a period during which the ACTU has achieved a real increase in the value of minimum wages of about 13 per cent. In accommodation, cafes and restaurants, Australia's second most award dependent industry, productivity rose by 3.4 per cent last year, and has grown by more than 19 per cent since 1996.

Second, minimum wage dependent industries in Australia are also outperforming other industries in jobs growth. Overall employment in Australia has increased by 13 per cent since 1996. But in the award dependent industries of accommodation, cafe and restaurants and health and community services, employment rose by more than 30 per cent. Minimum award wages in these industries increased by $118 a week over the same period.

While these figures are only snapshots, the National Wage Case hearings do in fact every year devote the dominant proportion of time—over months of submissions, evidence and hearings—to the economic issues. I cannot speak for the employers, but I can clearly state that each and every advocate the ACTU has had since Bob Hawke in 1958 has been economically qualified, and that we do our work. And so does the AIRC.

No credible domestic or international evidence that decisively determines that reduced minimum wages delivers more jobs has yet been established in the proceedings. And bear in mind that the government and the employers are at liberty to call any evidence and witnesses they like. Treasury officials have been there along with economic experts.

Peter Hendy, from the ACCI, has had plenty to say in the media but his organisation has never been able to justify its argument when it has been put to the test in the proceedings. The ACCI along with other business groups therefore ridicule the institution and want to change the rules. The Business Council of Australia has had a chop at the issue too, and recently commissioned ACCESS Economics to do some work. ACCESS argues, on the basis of a snapshot of 1999 figures for a number of OECD countries, that by reducing by 10 per cent the ratio between the level of the minimum wage to the median wage, unemployment would reduce by 1 per cent.

The ACTU doesn't agree. If you look at the figures for 2004 you get a different result, and if you look at a time series over 1994 to 2004 it is apparent that no reliable correlation can be drawn between minimum wages, median wages and jobs growth. Minister Kevin Andrews has gone to London to look at minimum wage setting in the UK, undertaken by the Low Pay Commission. What I could have told him is that every year in the National Wage Case, if contemporary material is available, the Low Pay Commission's research and findings are closely examined.

Earlier this year the UK Commission found that there was 'no significant effect of the minimum wage on prices or overall productivity although we found some evidence of small positive effects on labour productivity in the service sector'. The Commission went on to say that minimum wage increases did not appear to have had any significant negative impact on the labour market. These findings were made notwithstanding that the minimum wage in the UK has increased by nearly 35 per cent since 1999, about 27 per cent in real terms, and employment has grown by 4.4 per cent. For the same period in Australia, the minimum wage has increased by 21 per cent, or around 5 per cent in real terms, and employment has grown 10.4 per cent.

But, in the US, the minimum wage has been frozen at $5.15 since 1997. Its real value has gone backwards by almost 12 per cent. Since 1999, employment in the US has grown by less than 3 per cent. Australia has done more than three times better than the US in jobs growth, and more than double the UK, but the US has had real minimum wage depreciation and the UK much greater real wage growth than us. As they say in the States, go figure.

For some time now the ACTU has also argued that the high effective marginal tax rates experienced by many low-income families need to be addressed. Too many people lose too much in tax and lost benefits when they earn extra income through overtime, promotion or a wage rise, or getting a job. This stifles incentive and punishes people who work hard.

It should be fixed, and an equitable system of tax credits in partnership with reasonable minimum wage increases should be examined. This is in fact what happens in the UK. But the government has never embraced these ideas and is not likely to. And fixing the effective marginal tax rate problem should not be a vehicle for freezing or cutting minimum wages. In fact it is important to keep some perspective about the extent of the problem.

As part of its 2005 National Wage Case submission, the ACTU has commissioned independent research from NATSEM examining the effects of effective marginal tax rates on all Australian wage and salary earners. NATSEM used December 2004 incomes data and current federal tax and benefit arrangements to calculate an estimated effective marginal tax rate for Australia's 8,113,500 wage and salary earners.

The study shows that the vast majority of low-wage workers derive a significant benefit from increases in minimum wages. For each additional dollar earned by Australian wage and salary earners:

- 63 per cent of individuals keep more than 60 cents in the dollar;
- 92 per cent keep more than 40 cents in the dollar; and
- 99 per cent keep more than 20 cents in the dollar.

On the basis of these calculations, only 0.25 per cent of wage and salary earners may be affected by effective marginal tax rates in excess of 100 per cent. And yet this is what is highlighted by employer advocates of minimum wage freezes.

No case has been made for destroying the system that we have. The attack on the AIRC and its processes for considering minimum wages represents appalling, ignorant cronyism by the government's cheer squad. If the government goes down the path of reducing the value of minimum wages, or abolishing the skills-based career structure of minimum wages, it will be tampering with the living standards of millions of people and it will be vigorously fought by the labour movement.

THE FEDERAL GOVERNMENT'S INDUSTRIAL RELATIONS REFORM AGENDA

The more general industrial relations changes advocated by the government will also meet with our resistance. Based upon what we know, this is what the changes will involve:

- reductions in the real value of minimum wages;
- the probable abolition of skill-based classifications and career structures in the safety net awards;
- the abolition of a range of minimum employment conditions;
- the removal of protection for half the workforce against unfair dismissal;
- the marginalisation and undermining of the independent industrial tribunals, federal and state;
- the imposition of significant restrictions on collective bargaining and industrial action;
- the imposition of individual employment contracts on large tracts of the workforce;
- stronger support for tax dodging and regulatory evasion through so-called 'protection' of independent contractors;
- constraints on the right of employees to be represented by a union; and
- a renewed attack on union organisation in the construction industry.

These changes are to be delivered via the imposition of a unitary system of industrial relations. That is, the federal system of industrial relations is to be expanded dramatically to override state jurisdictions through reliance on the corporations power of the Constitution. (It's worth noting that a genuinely unitary system cannot of course be achieved without the co-operation of the states. All that the Commonwealth can hope for is an expansion of federal coverage.) In support of these changes little more than mere assertion has been made: the assertion that more jobs will be created, that productivity will rise, that incentives to work will be generated, that a single system of industrial relations is more efficient.

No genuine attempt has been made to examine the strengths and weaknesses of the current industrial relations arrangements, or to assess how they can be improved. No consultation has been carried out, other than with big-business insiders and their lawyers. No attempt has been made to understand the aspirations and concerns of employees. There are no proposals for protecting employee entitlements, to stop companies restructuring and running off with assets to escape obligations à la James Hardie, no ideas about linking productivity to skills acquisition and workplace co-operation, nothing about work–family pressures or the creation of better quality jobs, nothing about work disincentives. It's the same old hackneyed attack on costs and job security—the only vision some in the business community seem capable of in the face of competitive pressure.

The anticipated industrial relations changes will harm the capacity of working people to protect and advance their interests, particularly those people with little workplace bargaining power—low-paid, casual, part-time workers. Living standards and job security will be under pressure. The changes will undermine the principles of fair treatment and collective representation, and promote a dog-eat-dog world in the workplace. They will diminish the propensity of people to acquire skills and contribute to productivity, rather than improve our workforce capacity. Casuals, people on individual contracts, and independent contractors might be easy to get rid of and to pay less money—but no one trains them and they result in less attention to workplace safety.

The government's changes are designed to swing the pendulum of workplace power even further in favour of employers. Employees will be in a weaker position, and will be denied effective access to the protection offered by unions, collective bargaining and industrial tribunals. As a leader of the labour movement I would enjoy nothing more than to concentrate on making a constructive contribution to the wellbeing of our country. But confronted with industrial relations changes which I know will adversely impact upon the people and organisations I represent, I have no alternative but to fight.

And fight we will. Unions are resilient institutions of very long standing in the Australian community. We are bound by our commitment to four underpinning principles:

- The right of working people to a decent safety net of minimum wages and employment conditions.
- The right of people to collectively bargain for pay and employment standards in excess of the minimum.
- The right to union membership and representation.

- The right to fair treatment and access to an independent tribunal for the resolution of disputes and grievances.

These principles are directly threatened by the industrial relations changes which have been foreshadowed. We will campaign to defend and advance these principles. And we will maintain a focus on the real issues facing employees and the country.

BROADER ECONOMIC ISSUES

In this forum in 2003 I made the point that there had been a complacent and dangerous over-reliance by the government on domestic consumption, fuelled by high levels of household debt and rising housing prices, to drive growth. With a doubling of household debt-to-income ratios over the last 10 years, it didn't take much insight to recognise that interest rates had the potential to become a highly sensitive political issue, or that growth was exceptionally vulnerable to interest rate increases.

Back in 2003 I made the obvious argument that Australia's economic policy priorities needed to be changed to address inherent weaknesses. In particular, the ACTU believed that the government needed to refocus on building national savings, and to increase investment in skills, and in social and economic infrastructure, and research and development.

None of this has been done. We now face significant capacity constraints which are causing economic growth to slow—and we are paying for it. GDP growth slowed to just 1.5 per cent for the year ended December 2004, and interest rates may have to increase further to contain the inflationary pressure created by supply side constraints. The argument that both the Treasurer and the Prime Minister have advanced—that industrial relations is the defining priority area for economic reform—is laughable. Industrial relations reform has become a priority for one reason and one reason only—the Senate majority which will be enjoyed by the government from 1 July this year.

It is the productivity revolution which will derive from skill development, investment in infrastructure, research and innovation, from building national savings, from better incentives for work, and from improving Australia's export performance that will make the real difference. These fundamental challenges will not be met by keeping union officials out of the workplace, by attacking the most vulnerable in the labour market, by trashing industrial tribunals, or by forcing people onto individual contracts.

Australians deserve much more from their government.

15 UNDERPINNING PROSPERITY: OUR AGENDA IN EDUCATION, SCIENCE AND TRAINING

THE HON. DR BRENDAN NELSON MP
Minister for Education, Science and Training

Education, science and training now, more than at any other time, are crucial to Australia's future economic growth and social wellbeing. The links between sound public policy in these areas and strong and sustainable economic growth have never been more apparent—nor of greater importance.

The government's policies provide a blueprint for continued improvement and change in education—this work is underpinned by the key themes of consistency, quality, equity, sustainability, diversity and choice. The programs and initiatives now being put in place will create an Australian education, research and innovation system that will be marked by an unprecedented degree of national consistency, diversity and quality across the entire education system.

Let's take a look into the future and imagine an 8-year-old boy being able to transfer easily from a school in Victoria to one in New South Wales, knowing that what he learns in the classroom will be consistent across state borders. Perhaps later he will choose a school-based apprenticeship, opting for a trade from which he might build a thriving business enhanced by world-class Australian technology. Years later he may decide to study commerce at university and find it is an easy transition to make. He will be typical of a new generation of lifelong learners looking for a system that doesn't differentiate between study pathways, but focuses on choices which enable a fulfilling and challenging working life.

This is a vision the Australian government hopes will be shared by all Australians, as we work to implement the government's fourth-term agenda in education, science and training. The vision for education has been very much influenced by the aspirations of the Australian community:

- Parents want to be confident that their children will be able to read when they leave primary school.
- Businesses want to see more young Australians with high-quality technical and vocational training, especially in the trades.
- Australians want greater flexibility in moving between vocational education and university.
- Universities want to be able to compete on a level playing field when it comes to engaging in commercial activities.
- University graduates want to know that they have attained a degree from a world-class higher education system, one that is thriving in a globally competitive economy.
- Members of our highly mobile defence forces need to be able to move interstate without impeding their children's primary and secondary schooling.
- Indigenous students want full participation in education and employment.
- All school educators and careers advisers want to be assured that every student at risk of dropping out of school is supported to stay engaged and on track to complete Year 12 or its vocational equivalent.
- Researchers want to deliver innovation in a system where the very best research can be easily identified and appropriately funded.

In these early years of the twenty-first century, where so much that lies ahead of us is unknown, it is absolutely critical that our education system becomes more responsive—to economic needs and to parents' and students' expectations. Our education system will need to be more diverse, and yet less divided between sectors. It will need to be more nationally consistent, and yet offer greater choice. If we cannot achieve this, we risk compromising our future prosperity.

SCHOOLS

Within my portfolio, the schools sector has the greatest reach and some of the most significant challenges. Schools enrol 3.3 million students, employ 250,000 teachers and consume $26 billion of taxpayers' money each year. Apart from parents, schools exert the greatest influence on our children's development.

The key priority in schools is to raise the quality, professionalism and status of our teachers. Quality teaching is by far the most important factor that influences the educational outcomes of our children, accounting for up to 60 per cent of the variation in learning outcomes. Despite this, however, there are structural problems with enhancing teaching quality. Teachers are poorly organised professionally, there are doubts over the quality and adequacy of university education faculties, and teacher salary structures are so outdated and lacking in flexibility that it is no wonder that many turn away from the profession in frustration. Any profession must have the ability to train, recognise and reward its best and brightest performers.

The government is determined to tackle these challenges. One of the most important initiatives that we are undertaking is the establishment of and initial $10 million investment into the National Institute for Quality Teaching and School Leadership. NIQTSL is an organisation managed by the teaching profession for the teaching profession. Its mandate is to promote the profession, to conduct professional learning and research, and to develop nationally consistent standards for teachers and principals. Through this Institute, teachers and school leaders will finally have some control over their professional agenda.

There are undoubtedly problems in the training of teachers in some universities. I have seen research indicating poor standards and I understand anecdotally that not all education faculties are up to scratch. In the future, NIQTSL will have a role in accrediting teacher training courses. However, I have also asked the House of Representatives Standing Committee on Education and Training to inquire into the quality and adequacy of teacher education faculties. If, as I suspect, there are issues in the way in which our teachers are trained, then this Inquiry will be equipped to identify them and propose solutions. Other initiatives to support teacher quality include an investment of $159 million in teacher professional development and an additional $110 million for teacher practicum.

Providing a nationally consistent schooling system is also one of our key priorities. Last year, 84,000 school-aged children moved interstate—they might as well have moved to a different country. Our goal is to ensure that standards are equally high, regardless of where a child resides. We have an ambitious agenda in this area. We are insisting, as a condition of funding, that school starting ages be the same across the country by 2010. We are introducing common testing standards in key subject areas; we are driving consistency in curriculum outcomes and a common information system for the transfer of student data when students move interstate. Most importantly, we are beginning the work to implement an Australian Certificate of Education as the key Year 12 certificate. Of course we are proud of our state origins, but we live in an increasingly mobile and globalised world and it is time that our schooling system caught up.

The government is also ensuring that quality information about their child's progress and about the performance of schools is made available to parents. I am determined to put an end to school report cards that are meaningless and full of jargon. Parents want to be told in plain language how their child is performing against objective measures and against others in their year. Additionally, it is time that schools became more transparent in how they are performing so that parents have objective data when selecting schools and specific information against which they can judge schools and hold them accountable. The Schools Assistance legislation implements these objectives.

Other priorities in the schools sector include ensuring that school principals have more power over the running of their schools. Of particular importance in this area is the power over staffing. Without more control over day-to-day operations principals cannot be expected to be accountable for their school's performance.

I also believe that it is crucial that Australian values are explicitly taught in schools, and that special programs to assist boys and to stamp out school bullying are implemented. Education is as much about building character as it is about transferring skills, knowledge and the thirst for learning. Our national values education project will commit almost $35 million over the next four years to support values education and civics and citizenship education programs in Australian schools.

Of course we will continue to work on the basic building blocks of schooling. Literacy and numeracy initiatives will receive a major funding boost. The new overarching Literacy, Numeracy and Special Learning Needs program, introduced this year, targets the most disadvantaged students, including those with disabilities. Over this quadrennium it will receive funding of $2.1 billion, representing an increase of $445 million or 28 per cent over the previous four-year funding period.

In addition, we are providing $700 tutorial vouchers to the parents of children who did not meet the Year 3 reading benchmark in 2003. All schools will continue to be funded at record levels: $33 billion will be provided to schools over the next four years, a massive $9.5 billion increase over the previous four-year period. This includes the extra $1 billion committed during the election campaign for school capital infrastructure.

INDIGENOUS EDUCATION

The Australian government is committed to closing the educational divide between Indigenous and non-Indigenous students. We are currently implementing a $2.1 billion Indigenous education package that provides targeted supplementary assistance for Indigenous students over the next four years. This funding represents an increase of $381 million or 22.3 per cent over the previous four-year period.

By focusing on 'what works', the government is building on a range of new and ongoing initiatives that have delivered genuine improvements. One example is the Scaffolding Literacy program, which utilises a structured approach to teaching and has proven to be especially effective in assisting students in remote areas. The Australian Council of Educational Research described the results of Scaffolding as 'little short of sensational'. This program is now being rolled out in the Northern Territory with some $9 million of Australian government assistance, targeting 10,000 Indigenous students (90 per cent of whom are in remote areas) in 100 Northern Territory schools; 700 teachers will be retrained to implement this approach.

Two election commitments, the Indigenous Youth Mobility and the Indigenous Youth Leadership programs, will provide additional targeted assistance. Under the Indigenous Youth Mobility program, $19 million will be provided over four years, to provide the opportunity for 600 young Indigenous people in remote areas to relocate to major provincial centres and capital cities to take up employment and training opportunities. The program will target apprenticeships and other occupations in particular areas of community needs, such as nursing, accountancy, business management and teaching. Under the Indigenous Youth Leadership program, $10 million will be provided over four years to identify and develop future Indigenous leaders. More than 250 school and university scholarships of two, three and four years' duration will focus on Indigenous young people in remote communities. School-based scholarships will be offered at the best Australian schools.

The Australian government's initiatives will make a considerable difference but they will not be the panacea to every Indigenous education problem. All levels of government need to be contributing, and, just as importantly, education providers and Indigenous communities themselves need to be placing the success of their children at school as the highest possible priority. We have no time to lose.

HIGHER EDUCATION, INNOVATION AND SCIENCE

The Australian government's ambition for higher education is that of a confident, strong, high-quality sector that plays a vital role in our economic, cultural and social development. An increased investment of $11 billion over the next 10 years has already been committed for higher education. A wide-ranging reform agenda to improve the quality of our higher education system and the choices available to students is now under way.

If Australia is to remain internationally competitive we must foster all aspects of our social and economic framework. Most vitally, we must build on our higher education system and ensure it is nationally consistent, of high quality and flexible. The challenge is also to make sure that our system not only stays internationally competitive, but that our best universities are in the top tier of world rankings. Universities must continue to diversify, and to foster creativity, great teaching and research. At the same time they must be responsive to the needs of their students and communities.

Higher education today is operating in a vastly more dynamic environment, one which presents a number of challenges to the current framework. For example, we need to consider the blurring of the public/private institution divide and the growth of private higher education provision globally, including through internet delivery, new higher education frameworks in other countries that impact on growth and diversity, and the increasing demands of a knowledge-based economy.

All of these challenges necessitate a broader debate around the governance and role of universities. Management in public universities has not always kept pace with changes in the operating environment over the past decade. While the federal and state and territory governments have put in place a number of reforms to university governance, the broader issue of who should be responsible for higher education remains.

The fact that the Australian government has significant financial and policy responsibility for higher education, while state and territory governments retain major legislative responsibilities, has created overly complex arrangements which lack transparency. Legislative differences mean that universities cannot always operate on a level playing field when engaging in commercial ventures. Variations between jurisdictions in the recognition and accreditation of universities and courses have also been costly for providers seeking to operate in more than one state or territory and is often confusing for students.

It is timely for us to consider these issues and debate the merits or otherwise of changing the current arrangements. This is not about the Commonwealth taking control of universities from the states and territories. It is about taking a serious look at how we can best achieve more consistent, efficient and effective higher education provision through co-operation at all levels. I believe we have a responsibility to carefully examine the regulatory framework within which Australian universities compete with the rest of the world. With many other countries now offering more varied and specialised types of institutions, it is clear that Australia's current one-size-fits-all approach may not be the best model to position us internationally, to cater to our regional communities and to offer our students a choice of excellence in teaching and research.

One of the key priorities of this government is to stimulate an informed debate about the role of our universities. It is the government's view that universities should be defined more by their quality and diversity and less by their form and structure, which is currently the case. We need to re-examine the requirement for all universities to undertake research as well as teaching. We know that our best research universities are not our best teaching universities. The stellar performers in the nationally administered Course Experience Questionnaire are not our 'Group of Eight' universities, which are our best research performers.

Some countries, in looking at different ways of providing higher education, are inviting reputable foreign universities to establish new campuses at home; while others are asking their institutions to be more active in seeking to operate offshore. This is part of a global trend. In Australia, for example, Carnegie-Mellon in the United States is seeking to establish a university presence in South Australia. In addition, a number of private higher education institutions, which have been operating successfully for many decades and offering a high-quality education to students, are aspiring to be authorised by government to accredit their own courses and to use the title of university.

At present our higher education approval framework does not cater for these developing trends. The current National Protocols for Higher Education Approval Processes outline only one model for an Australian university—one which is active in both teaching and research across a broad range of disciplines. The government is currently encouraging a debate about the way in which we should define universities into the future. For example, how much research should be undertaken in order for an institution to be approved as a university and what should the definition of research be? Should the National Protocols allow for the creation of 'specialist' institutions covering only a narrow field of study rather than a wide range of disciplines?

Another key priority is to make it easier for Australians to enter higher education from a diversity of backgrounds and experiences. There are many pathways to higher education. In building a strong skill base for tomorrow, it is important that we recognise the skills and competencies people gain in the workforce and through vocational education and training and facilitate their entry into university. While Australia has been active in recognising prior learning and granting different levels of credit and recognition for such learning for the purposes of university entry, we need to do more to ensure that we keep pace with international developments and that we have a consistent approach across all states/territories and all institutions. The Australian government is determined to continue working with the states and territories to improve credit transfer and articulation between the two sectors.

For too long emphasis in terms of funding and profile has been disproportionately placed upon research in universities, and not on teaching. Under this government, excellence in learning and teaching will be placed alongside the delivery of research excellence as a valued contribution to Australia's knowledge systems. An increased focus on learning and teaching will foster diversity and help to ensure the ongoing high quality of our higher education sector. The government has been encouraging universities to focus on quality in learning and teaching for some time, and will reward those universities that can demonstrate excellence in learning and teaching through its new Learning and Teaching Performance Fund. With more than $250 million in funding over the period 2006–08, the aim is to have universities and academics that excel in teaching being truly recognised for their efforts. This is, after all, one of the most visible of university activities and one where students' learning most directly benefits from quality performance.

The government is also determined to improve universities' ability to respond flexibly to the needs of their constituencies, including potential and existing students, staff, employers, industry, and local, regional and national communities. It is the government's long-held position that employees should have a choice about their preferred form of employment arrangements or agreements. Higher education should be no exception. Workplace reform in the higher education sector will focus on a number of key areas, including offering employees genuine choice regarding their employment.

Just as the Australian government is addressing these challenges in higher education, it is also matching gaps in our research sector and looking to fund the best researchers. It is our scientists and researchers, who address the big-picture issues of our time, whose legacy will be the world our grandchildren inherit. Successful resolution of issues such as population ageing, land degradation and climate change, just to name a few, is vital to Australia's prosperity. If we are to tackle these and other issues successfully, we must continue to build a world-class innovation system. This ambitious agenda depends on effective partnerships between governments at all levels, researchers and business, to share the substantial financial investment necessary to ensure that ideas move smoothly from generation to end use.

Research and development activities perform a crucial role in both science and innovation, covering a continuum from pure basic research to applied research and experimental development. Innovation is the key to prosperity. Nobel Prize–winning economic scientist Robert Solow has said that technological innovation is pivotal to greater than 50 per cent of a country's economic growth. A Productivity Commission study in 1995 found the rate of return on domestic research and development was in the range of 25–90 per cent.

Australia's economy and population are relatively small by world standards, with comparatively limited resources. Our publicly funded science and innovation investments must therefore be well-directed and provide excellent value for money. The Australian government is committed to ensuring taxpayers' investment in research actually produces results that are of world standard and which contribute to addressing the economic, social and environmental challenges that Australia faces.

The Australian government has already committed an additional $8.3 billion to science and innovation through the 2001 and 2004 'Backing Australia's Ability' packages. We are also moving forward with major initiatives, including the Research Quality Framework and the National Collaborative Research Infrastructure Strategy, and implementation of National Research Priorities to ensure we build a system based on excellence and with clear focus.

The National Research Priorities focus research effort squarely on the economic, environmental and social challenges that we face. The Backing Australia's Ability package also provides $542 million for major investments in research infrastructure, to be designed in a way which directly addresses research priorities while driving greater collaboration in the national research and innovation system. The government is also committed to developing an Accessibility Framework for publicly funded research to ensure that research that is produced can be easily found and accessed by other researchers and the wider community.

Improving collaboration between universities and publicly funded research agencies is also a priority in achieving better outcomes for the research dollar. In a global environment where Australia produces just 3 per cent of the world's research papers, it is imperative that we continue to strengthen our international collaboration in science, engineering and technology. Solid progress is being made through formal and informal national, international, institutional and individual linkages and more will be encouraged.

Research conducted in our universities and publicly funded research agencies provides commercial benefits directly and indirectly. The direct route—through the commercialisation of specific intellectual property in the form of patented inventions and ideas—is strongly encouraged by the government as a way of generating demonstrable benefits to industry and the wider community, and as a way of garnering income for our research institutions. The indirect commercial benefits of publicly funded research are also very important. Australia's innovative businesses draw on ideas emerging from universities and research agencies through a wide variety of means. These include recruiting high-quality researchers and scientists trained in the universities, commissioning specific research through consultancies and contracts, drawing on new research findings published in learned journals and elsewhere, and participating in industry conferences, seminars, workshops, and the like.

BACKING AUSTRALIA'S SKILLS

It is long past time that young people approaching Year 10 had a choice other than university, which is regarded by society as a pathway of excellence. This country's vision must be to see that every young Australian is encouraged to find and achieve their own potential, whatever that is. For too long, students have been pushed by parents, teachers, and society in general, to consider university the one and only acceptable option for achieving status and success after school.

The challenge for Australia is to maintain and further strengthen the vocational education and training sector by building an industry-led system that delivers what Australian businesses, communities and individuals need to build their own personal, and our collective, economic and social prosperity.

Seventy per cent of young Australians do not go directly to university when they leave school. And many of those who do will drop out in their first year. Every year more than 1.7 million Australians enrol in publicly funded vocational and technical training, an increase of 35 per cent since

1995. The national skills shortage is resulting in increased attention in, and greater salaries paid for, trades careers. This, in addition to a vigorous marketing campaign undertaken by the Australian government to promote such careers, has resulted in a 19 per cent increase in New Apprenticeship commencements in trades and related occupations in the last year.

But there is more to be done. Even though most apprentices in traditional trades can acquire their skills in two to three years, we cling to a time-based rather than competency-based system, demanding that young and mature-aged new apprentices 'serve their time'. Particularly in the case of older workers, we fail to recognise prior learning as much as we could. And despite rigorous attempts to achieve national consistency, the states and territories continue to apply different licensing requirements for the same trade, inhibiting portability of skills.

In response, the Australian government is undertaking a major reform of the vocational education and training system. The reform is driven by three objectives:

- training policies, priorities and delivery driven by industry and business needs;
- better quality training and outcomes for clients, through more flexible and accelerated pathways; and
- simplification and streamlining of all processes.

Above all is our commitment to national consistency across the whole system. In resuming the functions of the Australian National Training Authority in mid-2005, we will have a unique opportunity to build on its successes to date. Our goal is to ensure that our training system will be even more responsive in future to the ever-changing needs of industry and will continue to build its reputation with young Australians, broadening their options after school. It will attract mature-aged Australians back to study and provide them with specialised skills, and pathways to new careers.

Last year, the Australian government committed a record increase in funding for vocational education and training, almost entirely directed to addressing skill shortages through increased places for pre-vocational training in trades, school-based New Apprenticeships, New Apprenticeship Access program places and, for the first time, incentives targeted at individuals— through opening up eligibility for the Youth Allowance to apprentices, introducing a Commonwealth Trade Learning Scholarship and offering tool kits for New Apprentices in the traditional trades. Overall, an additional $1.06 billion for vocational education and training and professional careers advice was committed over three years. This is in addition to the $2.1 billion each year which is currently directed to vocational education and training.

But Australia needs more than dollars and programs. Above all we need a cultural shift—away from the view that trade occupations and vocational training are less attractive than university. Training must be recognised as a path of equal importance and value as going to university. In the last week of the 2004 federal election campaign, the Prime Minister nominated his most important initiative of the campaign to be the establishment of 24 technical trade colleges. These colleges will be established across Australia in areas of skill shortage and youth unemployment. Catering for Years 11 and 12 students, they will offer a basic academic program, business skills training and a major focus on one of four traditional trades.

Australia has made a few mistakes over the years. Abolishing the old 'tech schools' was one of them. Although there will be no turning back the clock to kids streaming into trades in Year 7, there is an enormous gap for senior secondary excellence in skills training. Critics claim the technical colleges will duplicate what TAFE already does. Others argue that school-based apprenticeships and vocational training already meet demand.

The colleges will be the product of consortia involving local industry, education and training facilities. Public and/or private schools are encouraged to link up with industry and trade training organisations. TAFE can and should be a part of any proposal to establish a technical college. One of four trades will be the focus of each college: automotive, electrical, construction, and metals. Each college will have its own board of management, hiring and firing the principal who in turn will determine staff appointments. Staff will be trades-focused, recruited and retained on a performance basis. The government will provide funds to either build the colleges onto an existing facility or on a green-field site.

It is time we created centres of unashamed industry-led excellence in trade training. It is time to build pride and commitment in getting a trade. The Australian Technical Colleges will provide a strong stepping stone to this important cultural change. Cultural change will also be forged through highlighting best practice in trade training. The Australian government is establishing an Institute for Trade Skill Excellence to improve the quality of trade training and elevate the status of the trades as first choice careers. The Institute will be directed by key stakeholders, including the Australian Chamber of Commerce and Industry, the Australian Industry Group, the Business Council of Australia, and the National Farmers Federation.

Much is also being done to shape the views of those who have the greatest influence over young people in making their career decisions, including parents, careers advisers and teachers. This year, for the first time, we will include a parents' tear-out pack in the Job Guide delivered to every Year 10 student. The pack will assist parents in talking to their teenage children about the range of career options (not just university) and in helping them to make an informed decision.

Last year, I announced a further \$4.5 million to improve the standard of careers advice in Australian schools. Key initiatives in this area include the establishment of standards for all careers advisers, annual scholarships for careers advisers to undertake either an industry placement or further professional training, and the recognition of 'career lighthouse schools' demonstrating best practice in careers education and sharing that practice with other local schools. In addition, we will host forums bringing together school principals, careers advisers and industry representatives to be co-located with national careers expos to ensure that principals and advisers are learning about the range of modern careers open to young Australians.

This year the Australian government will establish an Australian Network of Industry Careers Advisers. This network will for the first time provide a comprehensive national careers and transition support network for all young Australians from 13 to 19 years of age delivered through 216 Local Community Partnerships (LCPs), which currently bring together schools and industry in local areas to provide worthwhile structured work experience for school students.

Funding of \$103.9 million from 2005–06 to 2007–08 will improve the career choices of young people and increase levels of student engagement and school retention by adding professional careers advice to each LCP. Each partnership will join local industry to promote to young people and their parents opportunities that vocational education and training pathways offer, as well as university pathways. The development of strategic partnerships between the LCP network and key local industry bodies will support the government's efforts to address skills shortages, including through the establishment of the Institute for Trade Skill Excellence and the Australian Technical Colleges.

CONCLUSION

The benefits of an outstanding education system are not just seen in our domestic economy. Australia is already recognised as having an internationally competitive education and training system. In 2004, some 270,000 international students enrolled in 320,000 courses of study in Australia. Another 100,000 students are studying for Australian qualifications offshore and this provision is expanding. The challenge is to make sure our system continues to keep ahead of our competitors. The rest of the world is not standing still.

If we are to protect our successful education industry and ensure that Australia's education and training sectors remains well positioned to meet the requirements of a competitive global environment, we must engage in further reform designed to keep us at the forefront of international competition. The Australian government accepts the challenge of equipping all Australians with the skills necessary for the twenty-first century, of developing an education, training, research and innovation system that has as its hallmarks:

- eight autonomous, high-quality state and territory school systems that are tied by an unprecedented degree of national consistency;
- informed choice for parents about what is available in various schools for their children and advice on how well their children are progressing;
- a higher education system delivering excellent teaching and research that allows our universities to compete with the world's best and at the same time cater to regional communities;
- research and innovation to create opportunities for economic growth;
- flexible approaches to recruiting and training new entrants in industries facing skills shortages and assisting industry groups to explore better ways to keep a skilled, adaptable workforce;
- the needs of Indigenous Australians addressed through a whole-of-government approach to eliminating the unacceptable education and training divide between our nation's original inhabitants and non-Indigenous Australians;
- all Australian students encouraged to study abroad, to study internationally relevant curriculum and to learn other languages, so as to engage in a dynamic global workforce; and
- recognition for Australia's status as a world leader in science and education based on its reputation for quality education, research and training.

Three broad aspirations are critical to our future prosperity and social cohesion:

- High-quality education: access to a first-rate education for all. A literate, and numerate populace which possesses the values and self-esteem needed to contribute to society and achieve their full potential.
- Skills to meet Australia's needs: a skilled workforce, adaptable, flexible and responsive to industry needs.
- World-class innovation system: a system which harnesses the knowledge, ideas and research to keep us competitive and prosperous in the twenty-first century.

Our progress as a nation depends on our progress in these three key areas. We will face obstacles and roadblocks along the way. However, if we achieve what we set out to achieve there will be benefits for everyone, including a great sense of pride in how this nation has addressed the issues, with an eye on future generations.

16 AUSTRALIA'S ECONOMIC CHALLENGE

DR CRAIG EMERSON MP
House of Representatives

STRUCTURAL WEAKNESSES UNMASKED

Australia faces serious economic challenges that, until recently, had been masked by more than a decade of strong economic growth. A dramatic unmasking occurred last month when the Reserve Bank lifted interest rates. In explaining its decision the RBA pointed to inflationary pressures generated by rampant domestic spending smashing up against capacity constraints.

Why didn't the Howard government recognise these emerging capacity constraints, given that Australia had been in its longest economic expansion in history? And why did the government fuel consumer spending through a $66 billion pre-election spending spree? The answer is that this government is all geared up to govern for the political cycle but not for the economic cycle.

If Australia's economic challenges are not addressed, Australia by 2010 could experience a cut of almost one-third in the economic growth rate per person enjoyed in the 1990s. This would be the slowest rate of economic growth per person since the decade of the Great Depression. How do we know? Treasury's Intergenerational Report projects this dramatic slump in growth from 2010 onwards. And it is likely to get worse: by the mid 2020s Australia's per capita growth rate could be half the rate of the past decade (Productivity Commission 2005b, p. 126).

These alarming official projections are the product of two insidious forces at work in the Australian economy: an ageing population and faltering productivity growth.

AN AGEING POPULATION

Over the next 40 years the proportion of the population aged over 65 is projected to double from 13 per cent to 26 per cent, leaving only a little over half of our population in work to support the old and the young. The die was cast half a century ago. In the coming four decades ageing baby boomers born in the 1950s and 1960s will replace the small numbers of older Australians born in the 1930s and 1940s.

Official projections assume a slowing in the historic rate of increase in life expectancy over the next 40 years. Yet past Australian Bureau of Statistics (ABS) projections have systematically under-estimated the increases in life expectancy. Plausibly, faster increases in life expectancy would strongly compound the ageing of the population. This ageing is the dominant cause of the expected slowing in GDP growth per person over the next four decades (Henry 2004, p. 11).

FALTERING PRODUCTIVITY GROWTH

The Intergenerational Report projects that the strong productivity growth Australia has achieved since the early 1990s will slip back to its mediocre 30-year average from 2005 (Commonwealth Treasury 2002, Chart 15). These projections are fast becoming reality. The OECD (2004b, p. 83) warns that Australian productivity growth might be faltering:

> During the four years ending in the financial year 2002–03, capital deepening maintained its trend, but market sector MFP [multi-factor productivity growth] slowed down to an average rate of 0.5 per cent. This *could indicate the end of its strong trend increase in the 1990s* [emphasis added].

The national accounts for the December quarter 2004, released on the same day the Reserve Bank hiked interest rates, confirm that productivity growth has not just slowed, it has turned negative! Some of us were warning about the dangers of slowing productivity growth three years ago, before the Intergenerational Report was released.[1]

WEAK EXPORTS

Exacerbating these emerging economic problems has been a sharp deterioration in Australia's export performance since 2000. The record run of 39 successive monthly trade deficits cannot be explained, as the government has sought to do, by terrorism, SARS, bird flu virus and slow world economic growth (of 5 per cent in 2004!).[2] These factors affect all exporting countries. Yet Australia's *share* of world exports has fallen to its lowest level since World War II. And this has occurred despite Australia enjoying its best terms of trade since the early 1970s—a lucky coincidence of soaring mineral prices and inexpensive Chinese manufactured imports.

CONSUMPTION RATHER THAN INVESTMENT

Federal government policy has deliberately encouraged consumption over investment. From March 2000 to September 2004 almost 70 per cent of total domestic spending was consumption spending and only just over 30 per cent investment spending. Australian households have been spending more than they are earning, financing the shortfall from borrowings against the equity in their houses. As pointed out by the Treasury, these household borrowings have been overwhelmingly responsible for the current account deficit (Parkinson 2004), which has hit a record 7.1 per cent of GDP.

Whether an economy can successfully reduce large current account deficits without a serious economic slowdown depends on the conditions prevailing at the time. Current account adjustments can hurt growth where the economy is already overheated at the beginning of the adjustment and where the current account deficit is a symptom of domestic overheating (Goldman Sachs 2005). These are the conditions of the Australian economy right now.

Strong economic growth has generated an air of complacency within the Coalition government about the fundamental economic challenges confronting Australia. Of the government's $66 billion pre-election spending, at best $7.5 billion could be considered investment, the rest consumption spending. Where is the new reform agenda designed to secure ongoing increases in prosperity in the face of an ageing population and structural weaknesses in the Australian economy?

HOW DID AUSTRALIA'S ECONOMIC REVIVAL COME ABOUT?

In the late 19th and early 20th centuries, Australia had the highest standard of living in the world. More than a century later it had slipped to around 18th in the world. By the early 1980s our country had shifted from an open, competitive economy to a Fortress Australia. The Australian economy was inward-looking, uncompetitive, incapable of generating jobs and prosperity.

The incoming Hawke Labor government was well aware of the structural weaknesses in the Australian economy. They were showing up in poor productivity growth, double-digit inflation and unemployment, and an acute vulnerability to any downturn in primary commodity prices. Labor recognised that today's productivity growth is tomorrow's prosperity. With all the inefficiencies in the Australian economy there was ample scope to boost labour productivity.

The new Labor government embarked upon an economic reform program designed to lift productivity growth while diversifying Australia's export base by engaging with Asia and promoting non-commodity exports. Labor transformed Australia into an open, competitive economy and vigorously pursued the opening up of other countries' markets through a non-discriminatory multilateral and bilateral trade policy. This transformation unleashed more than a decade of record productivity growth and economic growth. Australia surged through the international field from productivity straggler to a leader of the pack.

Australia's strong productivity performance during the 1990s has boosted average household incomes by an estimated $7000 (Productivity Commission 2003, p. 3). For the 13 years to 2004, Australia's economic growth compared with other rich countries was our fastest ever. There is now a general consensus that the economic reform program begun by Labor in the mid 1980s, and extended by the Coalition, has been overwhelmingly responsible for Australia's strong productivity growth and the prosperity it has created.[3]

MEETING THE ECONOMIC CHALLENGE

Australia's economic challenge can be summarised by the three 'P's: population, participation, and productivity (Henry 2004, pp. 6–11). In principle, the adverse economic effects of an ageing population can be offset by a combination of immigration, rising labour force participation, and strong growth in productivity.[4]

For the first time since European settlement Australia is facing the prospect of declining *population*. Australia is expected to experience a natural decline in population sometime in the mid 2030s (ABS 2003, p. 35). Immigration will be needed just to prevent our overall population from shrinking. Acute labour shortages can be expected in the Australia of the 2030s. Population ageing is a phenomenon common to the developed world. Australia will need to compete strongly against other rich countries for the world's skilled and semi-skilled migrants.

Community attitudes towards migration will need to change; Australia's future prosperity will depend on a bigger immigration program contributing to a bigger population. But migration will need to be directed to Australia's dynamic regions through a set of strong regional migration incentives, to take the pressure off our congested major capitals. This will require an infrastructure investment program that anticipates population pressures rather than simply reacting to them—to achieve a better dispersal of Australia's population.

The smaller the share of the population that is engaged in the workforce (i.e. *participation*), the greater is the burden on them to produce the income and taxation revenue to pay for those who are too young and too old to work. As people get older they participate less in the workforce. The ageing of Australia's population will reduce the overall participation rate. From now on, even large increases in age-specific participation rates can have only modest impacts on the overall participation rate in the next 40 years and therefore on economic growth prospects over that period (Productivity Commission 2005b, p. 81):

> Policies that elicit participation increases for the old alone cannot, by themselves, realistically act as an antidote for the sluggish labour supply growth arising from ageing.

Australia's participation rate is above the OECD average, but there is scope to lift it to the levels of Scandinavian countries (OECD 2004b, p. 164). If Australia were to achieve Scandinavian rates, the aggregate participation rate would still only be around 60 per cent by the mid 2040s, mitigating the effects of ageing by around half (Gruen & Garbutt 2003; Productivity Commission 2005b, p. 82).

Though policies to lift workforce participation cannot be the dominant feature of any plan to cushion the economic impacts of population ageing, they can nevertheless play a valuable role. That is why Labor, especially through Shadow Treasurer Wayne Swan, has been arguing strenuously for reducing high effective marginal tax rates to encourage the transition from welfare to work.

Much of the heavy lifting in securing Australia's future will need to be done by *productivity* growth. Governments must do everything possible to prevent productivity growth from slipping back from the rates achieved during the 1990s. How realistic is this? Part of the answer lies in a comparison of Australia's level of productivity compared with those of other advanced countries. Although productivity *growth* since the early 1990s has been impressive by international standards, we have not attained the *levels* of other comparable countries.

Figure 1 shows that Australia ranks below 15 OECD countries in the productivity stakes. If Australia were to achieve, say, US productivity levels, which are still below those of seven other countries, household income would rise by an estimated 20 per cent or $22,000 a year (Productivity Commission 2005a, p. 166).

How can Australia maintain the 'miracle' productivity growth of the 1990s so essential in combating the ageing of the population? Having opened the door to global and local competition in the product and labour markets through the reform program initiated by previous Labor governments, the same door cannot be opened a second time. Keeping the door open is essential to Australia's future productivity growth and it should be pushed wider where possible. But the biggest returns can be expected from the new sources of productivity growth in 21st century Australia: skills, innovation, and infrastructure.

FURTHER LABOUR MARKET REFORM

When the Howard government speaks of maintaining strong productivity growth, it invariably asserts that further deregulation of the labour market is the biggest game in town.[5]

Figure 1: GDP per hour Worked in OECD Countries, 2003

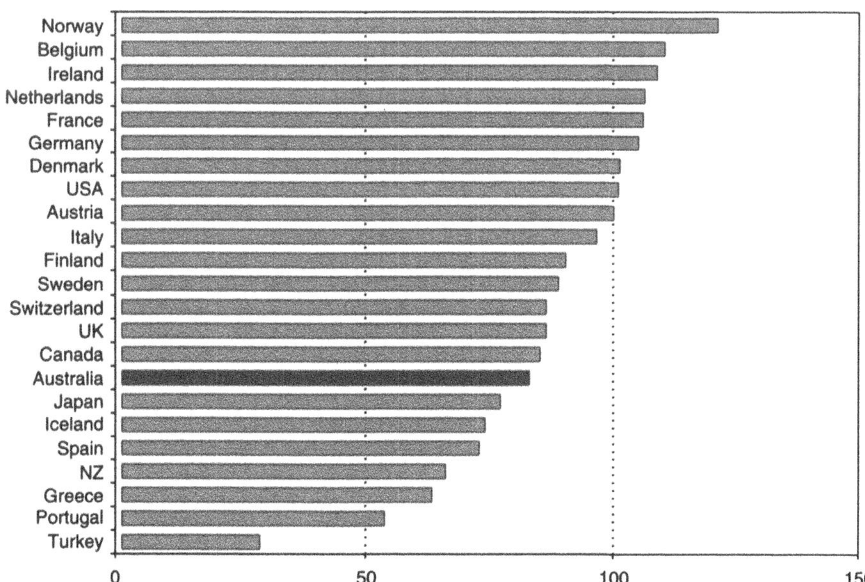

Note: Index calculated in 'purchasing power parity' terms; United States = 100.
Source: Productivity Commission (2005a, p. 167).

Most of the productivity-stifling restrictive work practices of the 1970s and 1980s have been removed through enterprise bargaining and award modernisation initiated by the previous Labor government and continued under the Coalition. Those who argue that further labour market deregulation is the key to the second round of productivity growth should identify the restrictive work practices that are retarding productivity growth.

No-one has been able to demonstrate beyond mere assertion that abolishing unfair dismissal laws for small business or expanding the use of Australian Workplace Agreements (AWAs) will unleash big productivity gains. The Treasurer refers to an OECD survey of Australia about possible employment impacts of unfair dismissal laws and asserts that it shows the abolition of unfair dismissal laws for small business would create 77,000 jobs.[6] In truth, the OECD (2003a, p. 100; 2005b, p. 44) finds that Australia's employment protection legislation is one of the least strict in the OECD. An OECD analysis concludes that: 'a reasonable degree of employment protection legislation could be welfare-improving' (OECD 2004a, p. 63). The OECD recommends reasonable employment protection legislation, in combination with a modest system of redundancy payments and effective re-employment services, as contributing to an efficient labour market (OECD 2004a, p. 99).

Since the OECD finds that Australia's employment protection legislation is one of the least strict among OECD countries, and concludes that there are net economic and social benefits from moderate employment protection legislation, the Howard government has not established a credible case for abolishing unfair dismissal laws for Australia's small businesses. Rather, a case exists for streamlining the unfair dismissal procedures for small business, including by removing unethical ambulance-chasing agents from the system. Labor, through Shadow Workplace Relations Minister Stephen Smith, continues to advocate a set of such reforms.[7]

A market exists for competing contractual arrangements covering workplace relations between Australia's employers and employees. More than 75 per cent have chosen collective agreements and common law contracts. Another 20 per cent have engaged in employment under the award system, leaving only 3 per cent on AWAs. If contemporary awards are as rigid and outmoded as the Howard government asserts, many more employers and employees would be opting for AWAs to boost workplace productivity and take-home pay.

In pursuing further labour market reform there will always be some scope for ongoing modernisation and simplification of awards. But if awards are to reflect the realities of modern workplaces, the modernisation and simplification process is best done by the relevant parties rather than by prescriptive government legislation. If sensible proposals for labour market reform are advanced, they should be assessed rigorously for their productivity-raising potential. But the rhetoric of further labour market deregulation is being used as a political diversion from the more challenging task of identifying and supporting the new sources of productivity growth.

FURTHER FOREIGN TRADE LIBERALISATION

Trade policy since the change of government in 1996 has been dominated by the negotiation of preferential trade deals. These deals discriminate in favour of the parties to an agreement and against countries excluded from it. In successfully opening up markets in East Asia, Labor in government did not seek preferential access, only an opportunity to compete; negotiations were conducted on a non-discriminatory basis.

Advocates of preferential trade deals, including the Howard government, argue that they are building blocks, not stumbling blocks, to global trade liberalisation. Yet progress in the Doha Round of (non-preferential) multilateral trade negotiations has been slow, as country negotiators concentrate on concluding preferential trade deals. According to the World Trade Organization, many developing countries, having secured preferential access to rich-country markets through discriminatory deals, are proving reluctant to give up their preferred access in the global negotiations towards genuine free trade (WTO 2004, p. 23). The OECD (2004b, p. 119) has warned against the Australian government's predilection for preferential trade deals:

> bilateral and regional trade agreements can have a trade distorting as well as a trade creating component. There is furthermore a danger that the coherence and predictability offered by multilateralism will be weakened if governments increasingly turn to regional agreements to manage their trade interests. A maze of conflicting regional regulations, standards and rules of origin risk becoming the new 'walls' between blocks.
>
> Against this background, the recently negotiated FTAs with Singapore, Thailand and the US merit close scrutiny as they run counter to Australia's general unilateral/multilateral approach.

The proliferation of preferential trade deals, with complex, restrictive rules of origin, will impose ever-increasing compliance costs on exporters. Different sets of records will need to be maintained, varying from country to country and even from one export product to another. A 'spaghetti bowl effect' of criss-crossing rules of origin hardly seems a recipe for free trade.

An opportunity exists to convert bad, trade-diverting policy into good, trade-creating policy. Australia could begin multilateralising the preferential trade deals it has negotiated. Recognising that a political climate has been allowed to develop in Australia against unilateral trade liberalisation, a conditional approach has been mooted (Garnaut 2004, pp. 9–13; 2005, p. 55). Under this approach Australia would allow, in each new preferential trade deal it negotiates, the most favourable terms of access it has already granted in any of its existing preferential trade deals—so long as the other party does the same for Australia.

Parties to preferential trade deals with Australia could have no valid basis for objecting to Australia extending preferred access arrangements to other countries. Australia would simply be fulfilling its obligations as set out in Article 1 of the GATT to extend to all member countries of the WTO any favoured treatment given to a country with which it has reached a preferential trade deal. It is possible that preferential agreements that also liberalise investment between the parties can create trade by promoting investment. But why should investment liberalisation be restricted to the parties to the agreement? If foreign investment is good, why liberalise only for particular countries?

In negotiations for the US–Australia free trade agreement, the two countries decided to relax Australian controls on US foreign investment by raising the threshold for Foreign Investment Review Board approval of non-sensitive investment proposals, from $50 million to $800 million. A report commissioned by the federal government estimates that this liberalisation will increase Australian living standards by more than $30 billion in net present value terms (Centre for International Economics 2004). No-one seriously believes this estimate, but if it were anywhere near the mark the policy implications would be clear—extend this liberalisation to all countries and treble the benefits! This proposition enjoyed strong business support at the time and was supported by the CIE report, but the Howard government has failed to act. The government should immediately raise the threshold from $50 million to $800 million for all countries.

HEALTH AND AGED CARE REFORM

Government health spending as a share of GDP is projected to almost double over the next 40 years, from just under 6 per cent to nearly 11 per cent. And government spending on aged care is projected to more than double (Productivity Commission 2005b, pp. 183–4). The number of older

Australians in high-care residential aged care alone is projected to increase from less than 100,000 in 2003 to more than 300,000 in 40 years' time (Productivity Commission 2005b, Table 7.1, p. 184).

A decent society provides quality health and aged care to all its citizens regardless of their financial capacity to pay. A fee-for-service philosophy still guides the provision of most health and aged care services in Australia. A provider who receives a fee for each service provided will have an incentive to provide more services, and risk-averse medical practitioners will over-provide diagnostic and related services to minimise the risk of litigation. Where health and aged care resources are limited and demand exceeds supply, the services will have to be rationed through the non-price mechanism of queuing. That is why waiting lists for GPs, elective surgery, hospital emergency department treatment, and aged care facilities are so commonplace in Australia. Those queues are not occupied by the wealthy! What is fair about lengthy waiting lists for Australians on low incomes when Australians earning high incomes are relieved of obligations to make a financial contribution to their health or aged care?

Co-payments exist in the delivery of GP services, in hospital and medical services covered by private health insurance and in residential aged care. A GP who does not bulk bill a particular consultation is requiring a co-payment from the patient. A private health insurer who does not cover 100 per cent of the cost of a procedure is requiring a co-payment in the form of a gap payment. And an aged care provider requiring a payment out of the age pension or a nursing home bond is requiring a co-payment from the resident.

Medicare's guarantee of universal access to public hospitals without charge must be retained—Medicare must not be means tested. And neither should access to bulk billing be means tested. But in particular circumstances, co-payments by the wealthy, within a universal health and aged care system, will be required if health and aged care is to remain affordable and accessible to all Australians. If bulk billing in an affluent locality falls, it should not be a government funding priority to restore bulk billing in that locality.

Confronted with an ageing population, Australia must never accept a two-tiered system with a second-class health and aged care system for the poor. Though not the centrepiece of necessary reforms to health and aged care in Australia, co-payments from the wealthy should be used to help fund quality health care for the poor.

And co-payments should be extended in aged care for the wealthy. There can be no valid philosophical basis for supporting nursing home bonds for low-care places but opposing them for high-care places, so long as bonds are restricted to the wealthy. If families with the financial capacity to pay decide they want to accommodate an ageing parent in a high-quality nursing home facility, why should they be prevented from doing so? And if some of the proceeds of a nursing home bond from wealthy families can be used to cross-subsidise high-quality care for poorer residents, surely it should be done. Bonds should not be obligatory but nor should they be prohibited for willing, wealthy Australians. Some of the proceeds of bonds should be used to improve the availability and quality of aged care for disadvantaged older Australians.

More fundamentally, population ageing will necessitate a re-thinking of the role of residential aged care. It should become the care of last resort. The stress and trauma of moving into a high-care facility could be avoided by earlier movement into retirement villages that have all the necessary aged care facilities.

NEW SOURCES OF PRODUCTIVITY GROWTH

Extensive international research identifies skills development, innovation and infrastructure as key determinants of modern productivity growth.

Skills development

The nurturing of intellect and the acquisition of skills are by far the most potent sources of productivity growth in the modern world (OECD 2003b, pp. 17, 78–9). Investing in skills also lifts lifetime workforce participation rates and improves health outcomes, further helping to combat the adverse economic effects of population ageing.

The acceleration in human capital formation of the 1980s and early 1990s under the previous Labor government has slowed, such that skills formation has actually *detracted* from productivity growth in Australia (Banks 2003, p. 5). This conclusion is confirmed by the OECD's empirical work which indicates that skill upgrading has made no recent contribution to Australian productivity growth (OECD 2003b, pp. 37–8).

Australia ranks a lowly 20th out of 30 OECD countries in the share of 15–19-year-olds enrolled in post-compulsory secondary education (OECD 2004b, p. 171). A range of indicators of educational attainment have been used to draw comparisons between Australia and other OECD countries, leading to the conclusion that: 'These international comparisons suggest that Australia's educational report card should be marked: "Started well, but slackened off. Substantial room for improvement"' (Dowrick 2002, p. 17).

Total government spending on education fell from 4.3 per cent of GDP in the early 1990s to 3.5 per cent in 2003–04. A small increase in private spending on education was insufficient to prevent an overall reduction in national spending on education over the period.[8] Since 1995 the privately funded share of education spending has risen more quickly in Australia than in any other OECD country, and Australia has been unique in failing to increase public education spending commensurately with the increase in private spending (OECD 2005a, p. 238).

The Intergenerational Report projections are for a *fall* in Commonwealth spending on education from 1.8 per cent of GDP in 2001–02 to 1.6 per cent in 2041–42 (Commonwealth Treasury 2002, p. 47). In an ageing population and likely absolute reductions in the number of young Australians over the next 40 years, a new approach is needed that focuses not on education spending as a proportion of GDP but on real spending per student. More than two-thirds of students were enrolled in government schools in 2003 but virtually all of the enrolment growth in the 20-year period from 1984 has been in private schools. Government schools should be equipped to continue playing their indispensable role of offering a quality education to every student whose parents choose the government system. But as parents move their children out of government schools into private schools, the student populations remaining in many government schools are increasingly from disadvantaged backgrounds. Yet, after adjusting for the differences in student population, the overall performance of government and private schools is similar.

The observation that the performance of different schools is strongly influenced by the socioeconomic status of their students has very important implications for reform of Australia's school system. The exodus of higher-performing students from many government schools is leaving them vulnerable and poorly placed to lift their standards. Australia is headed for a period of squandered opportunity and much greater inequality unless a new needs-based school funding model is put in place.

While performing well in reading overall compared with students from other OECD countries, the Australian student population exhibits above-average disparities in reading performance (OECD 2004b, p. 171; OECD 2005a, p. 101). Australia's poor performance in educating disadvantaged children is a blight on our society and a huge lost opportunity for the nation. The reform proposals advanced here are designed to lift the educational performance of disadvantaged young people while maintaining a quality school education for all young Australians.

The Howard government has strongly favoured private schools over government schools. Let's declare an end to the class war and abandon distinctions between government and private schools for funding purposes. Schools should be funded according to the needs of the child. It is the children who are important, not whether they are attending a government or private school. Consistent with Labor's election policy, schools with large numbers of children from disadvantaged backgrounds should receive more government funding than those with children from more privileged backgrounds.

Commonwealth and state funding could be co-ordinated into a collaborative effort in moving to needs-based funding. A standard amount per student could notionally be allocated, regardless of whether the student is attending a government or private school. In accordance with the principle of needs-based funding, the amount would then be adjusted to take account of the private income of the school. Extra funding would be allocated for each student who is disadvantaged—whether because of socioeconomic status or physical disability. Extra funding for each disadvantaged student in government and private schools would be spent on programs such as remedial learning, nutrition, school nurses and securing the best teachers for the most disadvantaged schools.

Skilled Australians living abroad

At a time when Australia is facing acute skill shortages, at least 750,000 mostly skilled Australians are living overseas on a long-term or permanent basis. Over the five-year period to 2003 Australia appears to have lost about 5 per cent of its total stock of employed professionals (Birrell et al. 2004, p. 50).

While it is true that Australia numerically has a net brain gain—with inflows of skilled migrants exceeding outflows of skilled Australians moving overseas—this is not an argument against attracting expatriates home and encouraging them not to leave in the first place. Of course, Australia can benefit from its best and brightest gaining experience overseas. But in the coming decades there will be fierce international competition for the world's pool of creative talent and it will not be good enough for Australia to accept 70,000 departures a year so long as overall there is a net numerical brain gain.

Very little research has been done on policies that could attract talented expatriates back to Australia. Is Australia's relatively high top marginal tax rate cutting in at moderate income levels the key constraint? Or is it a lack of synergies among researchers that are available in major research institutes in Europe and the United States? Does avoidance of HECS debts play any role?

Australia needs a better understanding of the reasons for the loss of such large numbers of skilled Australians before we can develop appropriate policy responses. But the need for that better understanding is urgent if Australia is to maximise its share of the pool of creative talent that will be so fundamental to determining the prosperity of nations in the coming decades.

Encouraging new ideas

It is clear from the experience of total returns to extra research and development in the order of 60 per cent that Australia is under-investing in R&D (Dowrick 2002, p. 23). Business expenditure on R&D as a share of GDP peaked in 1996 (Figure 2). The gap between Australia and the OECD narrowed consistently from the mid 1980s through the early 1990s. But following the incoming Howard government's cut in the R&D tax concession from 150 per cent to 125 per cent, the gap between Australia's business R&D spending and that of the OECD has widened.

A broader measure of Australia's R&D effort—a measure of investment in knowledge—aggregates public and private spending on R&D, higher education and computer software. On this measure Australia ranks a poor 14th out of 26 OECD countries surveyed (OECD 2003c, p. 17).

Australia's system of encouraging R&D needs a total overhaul. Following the cut in the R&D tax concession and the lowering of the company tax rate, the subsidy value of the tax concession has been reduced to such an extent that it appears to be eliciting little or no extra private R&D.[9] This is not to say that there is no private R&D in Australia; but it is to say that the concession, costing $400 million a year, is mostly a gift from taxpayers to companies that would have undertaken the R&D anyway.

Figure 2: Business Spending on Research and Development, 1982–2003

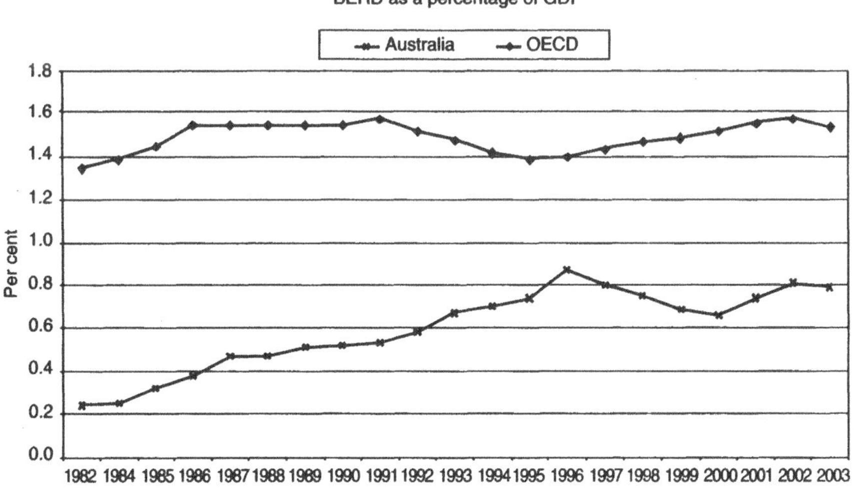

Sources: OECD, *Main Science and Technology Indicators 2003–2*; ABS, *Research and Experimental Development*, ABS Cat. No. 8104.0. Year to June for Australia. Year to December for OECD.

One option is to increase the rate of the R&D tax concession so that it again provides a genuine incentive for R&D spending by businesses. Another option is to convert the tax concession into government grants. The concession could be cashed out to create a pool of public funds for encouraging private sector R&D. It could be combined with other, smaller R&D programs to create a large Australian Innovation Fund (AIF) of around $3 billion. In determining the merit of applications for AIF funding, regard should be had for Australia's prospective comparative advantage. Australia's biological diversity is unique and the richest of all the continents. Biotechnology might therefore be an area of comparative advantage. So, too, might medical research, including research into cures for sun-induced melanoma cancer.

Investing in infrastructure

Critical parts of Australia's infrastructure have been allowed to run down over the last 20 years, but most strikingly in the last decade. Inadequate infrastructure is hampering Australian exports. Infrastructure investment has been too small and too reactive.

Extra investment in infrastructure in the right places can be an important source of the much-needed second round of Australian productivity growth. A national infrastructure plan should be developed that not only responds to existing infrastructure bottlenecks but also anticipates future needs and identifies future opportunities to support a bigger, more dispersed population settled in Australia's dynamic regions. Infrastructure proposals that complied with the plan could be subject to favourable financing and approval conditions. Non-complying infrastructure could still proceed with state and local government approval but would not be eligible for any favourable Commonwealth financial consideration.

ECOLOGICAL SUSTAINABILITY

An infrastructure plan for Australia supporting a bigger, more dispersed population would need to be ecologically sustainable. Water has rightly been identified as a constraint on future population growth. Yet three-quarters of the continent's water is used in the production of irrigated crops.

Why does Australia produce rice from its scarce water resources when rain tumbles from the sky during the monsoon season to irrigate the paddy fields of Asia? Crops like rice can be imported cheaply, allowing Australia's water resources to be put to higher uses such as ecological repair and consumption by a larger Australian population.

Proper price signals need to be applied to water consumption to ensure water is allocated to its highest uses, including restoring our rivers to health. Trading in water property rights would allow users producing low-value crops to sell their water to higher-value users, including governments seeking to improve river flows.

Some might claim that Australia's soil types do not have the carrying capacity needed to sustain a larger population. But the soil types of the Northern Territory's coastal plains replicate those of southern China which has a massively denser population and the soil around regional centres is generally of high quality.

FINANCING PRODUCTIVITY-IMPROVING INVESTMENTS

If Australia does not successfully meet the challenge of an ageing population, tax rates would need to rise sharply in the coming decades. Do we really want Australia's working-age population to go on strike, taxed out of any incentive to work? Wise early investment in productivity-raising education, R&D and infrastructure could avert the need for punitive tax increases later.

Federal and state governments have become debt-averse at a time when extra national investment is crucial. The Commonwealth should curtail its consumption spending in favour of investment spending. It should invest Budget surpluses in excess of those needed for macroeconomic stabilisation into an intergenerational fund to finance investments whose expected national returns are large and greatly exceed their private returns. Eligible investments would include education and skills development, R&D incentives and support for infrastructure investment that complies with the proposed national infrastructure plan.

CONCLUSION

Sustaining Australia's prosperity in the face of an ageing population will require sacrifices now to fund productivity-enhancing investments for the future. Encouraging consumption today through pre-election Budget spending sprees is economically irresponsible and a betrayal of future generations of Australians.

To sustain prosperity Australia desperately needs a second round of productivity growth built on a new economic reform program. The way ahead is to abandon governing for electoral cycles and to invest in the modern sources of productivity growth—skills, ideas and infrastructure—to provide opportunity for all Australians.

[1] See, for example, *Hansard*, 6 March 2001, and 'Think Big, Labor: It's What We Do Best', Brisbane, 7 April 2002.

[2] Trade Minister Mark Vaile blamed 'the slow level of global growth over recent years', *Hansard*, 16 March 2005.

[3] See, for example, Productivity Commission (2003, p. 6); OECD (2003a, p. 90; 2004b, p. 82); International Monetary Fund (2003, p. 14); Henry (2004, pp. 2–3).

[4] I am setting out some personal views on appropriate policy responses. They are not presented as the views of the Federal Parliamentary Labor Party but as my own contribution to the policy debate.

[5] For example, Treasurer Costello, *Hansard*, 1 December 2004 and 8 February 2005.

[6] Treasurer Peter Costello, *Hansard*, 27 May 2004, p. 29384.

[7] See Stephen Smith, *Hansard*, 10 February 2005.

[8] ABS; *Australian System of National Accounts*, Catalogue 5204.0, Tables 8, 44, 51, 64, 65.

[9] Surveys conducted by the Australian Industry Group and the Business Council of Australia point to R&D spending decisions being only marginally related to R&D tax concessions.

REFERENCES

ABS (Australian Bureau of Statistics) 2003, *Population Projections Australia 2002 to 2101*, Cat. No. 3222.0, ABS, Canberra, 2 September.

Allen Consulting Group 2004, *Governments Working Together: A Better Future for All Australians*, Melbourne, May.

Banks, Gary (Chairman of the Productivity Commission) 2003, 'Australia's Economic Miracle', address to the Forum on Postgraduate Economics, National Institute of Economics and Business, Australian National University, Canberra, 1 August.

Birrell, B, V Rapson, IR Dobson and TF Smith 2004, *Skilled Movement in the New Century: Outcomes for Australia*, Centre for Population and Urban Research, Monash University, Melbourne.

Centre for International Economics 2004, 'Economic Analysis of AUSTFA', prepared for Department of Foreign Affairs and Trade, Canberra, April.

Commonwealth Treasury 2002, *Intergenerational Report 2002–03*, Budget Paper No. 5, Canberra, 14 May.

Dowrick, S 2002, 'Investing in the Knowledge Economy: Implications for Australian Economic Growth', Australian National University, Canberra, 16 April.

Garnaut, R 2004, 'Contemporary Challenges for Australia in the International Economy', background notes for presentation to Trade and Development Seminar, Division of Economics, Research School of Pacific and Asian Studies, Australian National University, Canberra, 24 August.

—— 2005, 'Blend Trade Talks into Bigger Picture', *Australian Financial Review*, 23 March.

Goldman Sachs 2005, 'Do Current Account Adjustments Have to be Painful?', *Global Economics Weekly*, No. 05/04, 2 February.

Gruen, David and Matthew Garbutt 2003, 'The Output Implications of Higher Labour Force Participation', Treasury Working Paper 2003/02, Canberra, October.

Henry, Ken 2004, 'Policy Strategies for Future Growth', Address to Australian Industry Group's National Industry Forum, Canberra, 9 August.

International Monetary Fund 2003, *Australia: 2003 Article IV Consultation*, IMF Country Report No. 03/337, Washington, October.

Keating, Michael 2004, *Who Rules? How Government Retains Control in a Privatised Economy*, The Federation Press, Leichhardt.

OECD (Organization for Economic Co-operation and Development) 2003a, *OECD Economic Surveys 2002–2003: Australia*, OECD, Paris.

—— 2003b, *The Sources of Economic Growth in OECD Countries*, OECD, Paris.

—— 2003c, *OECD Science, Technology and Industry Scoreboard*, OECD, Paris.

—— 2004a, *OECD Employment Outlook 2004*, OECD, Paris.

—— 2004b, *OECD Economic Surveys: Australia*, OECD, Paris.

—— 2005a, *Education at a Glance: OECD Indicators 2004*, OECD, Paris.

—— 2005b, *Economic Policy Reforms: Going for Growth*, OECD, Paris.

Parkinson, Martin 2004, 'Australia's Medium Term Challenges', address to ABE Forecasting Conference, Commonwealth Treasury, 14 December.

Productivity Commission 2003, *Annual Report 2002–03*, Canberra.

—— 2005a, *Review of National Competition Policy Reforms*, Report no. 33, Canberra.

—— 2005b, *Economic Implications of an Ageing Australia*, Research Report, Canberra.

WTO (World Trade Organization) 2004, *The Future of the WTO: Addressing Institutional Challenges in the New Millennium*, report by Consultative Board to Director-General Supachai Panitchpakdi, Geneva.

17 THE WAY AHEAD

MR MALCOLM TURNBULL MP
House of Representatives

The way ahead begins with where we are today. After two days of advice and constructive criticism we have inevitably magnified the challenges ahead and diminished, even ignored, our achievements. But we would be foolish to ignore our present circumstances, where we came from and how we got here.

Australia's economy is stronger today than it has ever been. Inflation is low; unemployment is the lowest it has been for 28 years; interest rates remain low; and perhaps most telling of all, in the years of the Howard government, we have seen real wages grow nearly seven times as fast as they did under Hawke and Keating.[1] We are even having more babies ... surely the most tangible vote of confidence in our nation's future![2]

The New Tax System was the most comprehensive single set of reforms to the tax system in our nation's history. Company tax has been cut twice to its lowest level ever. Capital gains tax for individuals has been halved. Personal income tax rate has been cut on four occasions. More than 80 per cent of Australian taxpayers face a top marginal rate of 30 per cent or less.

As practical people we should judge our leaders, in whatever field, on output, not rhetoric; on substance, not process. Now, I am not one of those people who imagine that the government's management of the economy means it is responsible for all our prosperity. But, unless you were to imagine that the economy has prospered *despite* the government, then the record of the last nine years is one John Howard and Peter Costello are right to be proud of.

Certainly Labor is in no position to criticise the government's economic record, not least because they have no policies of their own to put up as alternatives. Last night Greg Combet, Secretary of the ACTU, complained about the lack of investment in 'roads, ports, transport and other infrastructure'. Well he might, but given that the Labor Party is the political wing of the trade union movement, it is a great pity that he has not directed his considerable political influence towards the Labor premiers.

In New South Wales, where Bob Carr has perfected the concierge style of government, we have a government which is rolling in money as a result of the GST and the property boom. They have never had it so good and possibly never will again. Yet Sydney, a city which is running out of water, has no plan to recycle its waste water. Sydney Water, the monopoly water company, has a profit margin of more than 25 per cent and a massive dividend yield the envy of anyone in the private sector. It is being run for cash. There has been no significant addition to the city's water supply for 40 years, and, as the Business Council of Australia (BCA) points out, within 20 years demand will be nearly 40 per cent greater than sustainable yield.[3]

Sydney is choking with traffic congestion, but the government has neglected its public transport to the point where patrons are driven away. Their attitude of contemptuous indifference was well summed up a few years ago when the then NSW Minister for Transport mocked me for my well-known preference for travelling by public transport. 'Surely you must get trains all the time', I innocently replied. 'Oh, no', said the Minister, 'I've got a driver'.

Much has been said about the failure to invest in our ports in Queensland and New South Wales and how this has retarded our exports. But the way in which state governments have misapplied their revenue boom to supporting a bloated bureaucracy rather than investing in transport, water, schools and hospitals is surely the political scandal of our times.

Many would say it is a failure of federalism. Citizens are impatient of the niceties of federal jurisdiction. If John Howard dares to point out to a talk-back caller that the problems with public transport are a state matter, the rejoinder is 'You're the Prime Minister, fix it'. So it is no wonder that the federal government is being drawn into more and more areas of traditionally state responsibility. But this trend contains a dangerous moral hazard: is the consequence of state governments' neglect of their responsibilities to be simply that the federal government will intervene and pick up the tab?

In New South Wales, the state government's spending on its own schools barely keeps up with inflation. Children are leaving the state system in droves; every movement of a child from a state school to a private school shifts an expense from the state to the federal government. The neglect of school buildings has resulted in the federal government establishing a new program of capital grants for all schools, including state schools. During the last election I was repeatedly told that the deficiencies in state schools were the fault of John Howard.

The lack of accountability of state governments comes close to a failure of democracy and a failure of federalism. Why are the state governments so unaccountable? Is it because the electoral arithmetic on the East Coast is such that it is most unlikely the incumbent Labor governments can be removed at the next election? How can it be that vital elements of national infrastructure are so readily ignored?

The Treasurer's frustration with the states is very understandable. He is seeking to persuade them to stick to their bargain and remove some (not all) of the business taxes they promised to remove at the time of the Inter-Governmental Agreement over the GST. But they are not simply refusing to stick to their bargain, they are imposing new taxes (such as the vendor 'exit' stamp duty in NSW) and they are expanding existing taxes. Consider payroll tax, probably the most iniquitous tax of all: a tax on employment. New South Wales has expanded that tax in recent years to include:

- employer contributions to employee share schemes (from 1 July 2003);
- trust distributions made in lieu of wages (from 1 July 2003);
- eligible termination payments (from 1 July 2002);
- director termination payments (from 1 July 2003);
- all lump sum payments made on termination for long service, annual or sick leave (from 1 July 2003); and
- the grossed-up value of fringe benefits, as opposed to the taxable value of those benefits for FBT purposes (first, using the lower type 2 gross-up rate from 1 July 2002 and then, with a cost of more payroll tax for the employer, applying both the type 1 and 2 gross-up rates from 1 July 2003).

There are also *rumours* that the trend to broadening the payroll tax base is set to continue, with the abandonment of the otherwise deductible rule in determining the value of fringe benefits for payroll tax purposes.[4]

So serious is the neglect of the Labor state governments that the next conference should focus sharply on what is happening at the state level. Or perhaps there should be a series of similar conferences to shine the spotlight on what is happening in the states. But, as this is a national conference and Dr Emerson and I are both members of the federal parliament, I will return to the debate about tax and welfare reform which the media have been quick to characterise as being criticisms of the government, even criticisms of its record.

The truth is that the reason we have today such an exciting public debate about the possibilities for policy reform and in so many areas is because over the last nine years we have not only seen a government which is prepared to undertake serious and controversial economic reform, but we have also seen the real economic dividends that that reform has produced. It is the government's record of reform that gives all of us the confidence to discuss and promote reform in the future. It is the government's energy over nine years that causes us to demand, and indeed expect, energy in the future. By way of contrast, the reason there is so much less energetic debate about infrastructure in our big cities is, I suspect, because most people have no confidence the state governments have the will or the capacity to do anything about it.

The debate about economic reform, of which this conference is an important part, far from being a criticism of the government's record is, in truth, paying it the very highest compliment. As we consider 'the way ahead', let us first reflect on what we know lies ahead, the terrain over which we must travel. Then we can consider how we may best tackle the social and political ridges and gullies of the decades before us.

The single biggest change to our society, and to the world, is demographic. The dimensions of this change were well described several years ago by the Treasurer in the Intergenerational Report. Because of a decline in fertility and an increase in longevity the percentage of our population which is 'aged' is going to dramatically increase. According to projections reported by the Productivity Commission (2005), those over 65 today make up 13 per cent of the population. In 40 years they will number a quarter of the population. More significantly, perhaps, those over 85 who today represent 1.5 per cent of the population (about 300,000 in number) will increase to 5 per cent of the population (or around 1.4 million). Between now and 2045 about 3.3 million will be added to the working-age population (defined as those aged 15–64), but there will be 4.3 million added to the 65s and over of whom more than half a million will be over 90.

Instead of there being more than five people of working age for every person over 65, by mid-century there were will be only two. This demographic change will add considerably to expenditure on health (especially the Pharmaceutical Benefits Scheme), aged care and age pensions. After taking into account some modest savings on education (fewer kids), there will be by mid century additional fiscal pressure of 6.5 per cent of GDP, amounting over 40 years to $4.2 trillion. If this were to be met by increased taxation, far from reducing tax we would need to increase it by 21 per cent.[5]

These momentous changes are upon us. They cannot be averted in the medium term. They make further substantial economic reform a vital necessity. As the Treasurer has warned, the last 'golden era' for Australia's economy was the 1960s, which ended in the chaos of Whitlam. This golden era could end as badly if we do not pursue continued economic reform.[6] As Michael Chaney said yesterday, standing still is not an option. Nor is running up and down in the one spot.

The consequences of ageing will be somewhat more severe if life expectancy continues to improve (and who among us would object to that?) or if fertility starts to decline again. However, there are no realistic increases in either fertility or immigration that will make much material difference.

The importance of increasing fertility to closer to the replacement rate of 2.1 is not to avoid the ageing crisis of which I am speaking. That is a function of the decline from a birth rate in the baby boomer years of 3.5 down to where it is today. But whether it had declined from 3.5 to 1.75 as it has or instead down to 2.1, we would still have a problem. The importance of maintaining a replacement-level birth rate is so that we do not have a perpetual cycle of ageing which, as I have said elsewhere, is for many countries just a euphemism for dying. On that point, I would observe that a stable population with a birth rate of 1.3 (which is higher than in Italy, Spain, Greece, Japan, Korea, most of Eastern Europe) reduces by 75 per cent over the course of a century. To put that in context, it means that if in a century Italy has the same population as it does today, not much more than 20 per cent of its population will be the descendants of today's Italians.

Without diminishing the scale of the challenges ahead of us, we must note that Australia is better positioned than any other developed country to deal with the consequences of ageing: we have little or no government debt, our retirement income system includes a growing element of personal savings and superannuation, and our birth rate while below replacement level is much higher than that in most other developed countries (apart from the USA).

Our prosperity, our 'national income', is a function of three factors: population, participation and productivity. It is clear we cannot, between now and mid-century, do a lot about population. Vital though a strong skills-based immigration program is, there is no practicable level of immigration which can materially offset the ageing phenomenon. I emphasise here that promoting a higher birth rate should be a national priority. Fertility is a critical element in our forward planning. For that and other reasons we should promote marriage and discourage divorce. But the results of those pro-natalist, pro-marriage policies will be seen many decades in the future.

In the foreseeable future, our own lifetimes, we know that the growth of our working-age population is going to slow; by mid-century it will represent 54 per cent of our population versus 63 per cent today. But at least it is growing in absolute terms. Japan, on the other hand, will by mid-century have seen its total population reduce in absolute terms by 14 per cent (17 million fewer Japanese) but its working-age population by 38 per cent (30 million fewer Japanese aged 15–64). However, there will be nearly 15 million more Japanese over 65.

The only factors we can work on, therefore, in that time-frame are participation and productivity. Our national goals, our compass markings as we chart our national journey through this century, must include greater levels of participation in the workforce and higher levels of productivity. Every aspect of government policy, be it tax, welfare, corporate regulation, workplace relations, should be tested at least by these questions:

- Is this policy making it easier and more attractive for people to go to work?
- Is this policy enabling Australian workers to be more productive?
- Is this policy promoting or assisting the formation of Australian families?

Any policy, any law, which does not receive a YES to all questions should require a very powerful countervailing argument to remain part of our national agenda. I will discuss here only the first two objectives; I have spoken at length about the third elsewhere.[7]

Greater participation and greater productivity are, of course, closely linked. If people are more productive they will be better paid; if they are better paid they will have a greater incentive to go out to work. Another objective, which should always be present in the mind of government, is to be frugal in the manner in which it spends public moneys. We all know, from our own experience in business, politics, even academia, that different people can in different ways achieve similar outcomes with significantly less (or indeed more) money.

As a Liberal, I believe a dollar is generally better situated in the citizen's pocket than in the Treasurer's coffers. Governments spend other people's money, extracted from them by force of law. Governments have an obligation to spend no more of the public's money than they need to, and when they spend it to do so to ensure the biggest bang for the smallest buck. Governments also have an obligation to ensure that the growth in labour productivity in the economy at large is reflected in the public service.

However, in addition to that commonsense view of matters fiscal, there is another consideration. A consequence of ageing which we can at best ameliorate but not avoid is that the legitimate claims on government for health care, pharmaceutical benefits, aged care and pensions and the like will increase and do so significantly. As the Intergenerational Report projects, we could be looking at a federal Budget deficit equal to 5 per cent of GDP by mid-century.

This adds to the urgency of promoting participation and productivity. But it also means that we must ensure that government dollars, and particularly welfare dollars, are spent where they are really needed. To put it in a business context: we cannot allow our national cost base to expand willy-nilly just because our revenues are strong. Because the reality is that the inescapable claims on government are going to grow and, with labour force growth slowing, one would be rash to project continued high growth in government revenues over the decades to come.

For the balance of these remarks, I will limit myself to only two important issues directly connected to the attainment of both these goals. They are tax and welfare. This is not to diminish the importance of other important issues, such as workplace reform and the development of infrastructure, especially in terms of transport and water. In that regard I would commend the recent BCA report by Port Jackson Partners (2005) as being particularly insightful.

In common with almost every other person or organisation who has made a considered comment or critique of the Australian tax system, I have made the following observations:

- Many people on low incomes who are in receipt of welfare benefits will, as they start to earn more income, lose in net dollars a considerable part (often much more than half) of each dollar earned by reason of the combination of the tax system and the loss of means tested benefits. This is known as an Effective Marginal Tax Rate (EMTR). For reasons I will come to, that is a very misleading term.
- The highest marginal rate (effectively 48.5 per cent) is high relative to that in comparable developed countries (especially the UK and the US, not to speak of Hong Kong and Singapore) and cuts in at a very low multiple of average weekly earnings (after 1 July, about 1.4 x average weekly earnings).
- This high tax rate is imposed on a tax base which has been eroded over the years by special deductions and concessions and can, quite legitimately, be avoided by those able to earn income through corporate entities (taxed at 30 per cent) and effectively split income between family members and corporations.

- While tax avoidance of the artificial or highly structured kind is, thanks to a concentrated effort by the government, harder to effect successfully than ever before, there remains ample opportunity for businesses to defer and thereby reduce income.
- PAYE and other 'unincorporated' taxpayers, however, have limited scope for tax avoidance, even of the most elementary kind, other than negative gearing where investments (more often residential real estate) are acquired with borrowed money and the excess of interest over rental income can be offset against other earned income.

In the light of this I have observed, in common with many others (e.g. BCA, CPA Australia, ACCI, AIG), that our tax system would be a better one if rates were lower and the base broader. To that end a worthy objective is to aim, over time, to have a top marginal rate of tax equal to or at least not materially greater than the corporate rate of 30 per cent.

Ever since the introduction of the GST and the new tax system, subsequent changes to our tax system have been incremental. The system has become more complex and compliance more of a burden. So much is obvious. There is an appetite in the community for a second round of substantial tax reform. As I've said before, I believe the direction of that reform should be towards lower rates and a broader base. I believe that it is important for all of us to engage in that discussion. There is no need to be defensive. Reform should be debated and modelled. It may be that in the final analysis the conclusion is that the only reforms practically available are incremental ones; but we will never know unless we have an open and lively debate and I congratulate the Melbourne Institute and *The Australian* newspaper in particular for contributing to that debate.

It is important to note here that while there is always scope for increased efficiencies in the delivery of government services and therefore cost savings, given the demographic challenges we face, it would be rash to assume that overall the expenditures of the federal government can be materially reduced. As a consequence, tax reform proposals need to be at least revenue-neutral.

There are numerous models proposed; most of them revolve around a lower rate approximate to the company tax rate[8] and the removal of many deductions and allowances so as to broaden the tax base. But every tax deduction once created develops a constituency which will fight to defend it. As a consequence, in my view, the only way in which a major simplification of the tax system can be practically effected is if there is a very significant reduction in the top marginal rate.

I am not sure whether it is necessary to waste many words in justifying taxation reform. I would simply observe that, apart from the obvious principle that citizens' wealth is better off in their pockets than that of the government, there is little doubt that our productivity would be enhanced if our tax regime were more competitive and if enterprise were therefore better rewarded. That, after all, was in large measure the rationale for the new tax system in 2000. We may be doing well with our natural resource sector today, but the real wealth of Australia is not under the ground but in the intellect and energy of Australians. We live in a borderless world. We cannot have a tax system which serves to encourage our brightest to seek to make their wealth somewhere else.

Yesterday Ross Garnaut proposed, in effect, a flat tax of 30 per cent. It appeared to constitute a traditional flat tax design with a twist: a low universal tax coupled with the removal of concessional deductions, and, instead of a generous tax-free 'personal allowance' to ensure that low-income earners are not prejudiced, Professor Garnaut proposed a substantial cash payment to all those in the workforce ('negative income tax') which would be around the level of the unemployment benefit.

Attractive though they appear, I remain very sceptical about flat taxes. In particular, I cannot see how Professor Garnaut's proposal could possibly be funded. The combination of the negative income tax element *and* reducing rates to 30 per cent would constitute an enormous drain on Commonwealth revenue. However, flat taxes are no longer solely the province of academics and Steve Forbes. Some of the new members of the European Union have introduced flat taxes in the last 10 years: Estonia, Latvia, Lithuania, Russia, Serbia, the Ukraine, and Slovakia. Poland will shortly follow suit. The average rate is around 20 per cent. *Their experience will be observed with great interest. Perhaps the sceptics, like myself, will be confounded.*

Another observation I would make is that substantial reductions in tax generally result in increased collections as a consequence of greater compliance and increased economic activity. Hence we have seen that as the top tax rate is cut, the top taxpayers account for more of the total income tax take. Reagan's tax cuts controversially slashed high marginal rates. Yet the bottom 50 per cent of taxpayers' share of tax collection was 8.3 per cent less in 1984 than it had been in 1981 before the cuts. Similarly, the top 5 per cent of taxpayers paid 35.3 per cent of tax in 1981, but in 1984 paid 38.9 per cent.[9] A similar experience was had in the UK when Mrs Thatcher cut the top rate of tax from 83 per cent to 40 per cent, where it remains today. In 1979 the top 10 per cent of earners paid 35 per cent of total revenues. In 1990, they were paying 42 per cent.[10]

I said earlier that the term EMTR was a misleading one. When we speak of high Effective Marginal Tax Rates we create the impression that this phenomenon, which undoubtedly does act as a disincentive for people to go to work and get off welfare, is a function of the tax system. The truth is that in almost all cases the contribution of the tax on additional income earned is by far the smaller part of the so-called EMTR, the bulk of which is the result of the welfare benefit being withdrawn by reason of income rising above the means test.

For example, ACOSS recently identified that an unemployed adult on Newstart Allowance would face an EMTR of 75 per cent as they start to earn income and lose their welfare payment. Given that tax is only 17 per cent (and that over $6000), it is obvious that the bulk of the EMTR is a function of the withdrawal of benefits. This insight is important, because it underlines the difficulties confronting government in dealing with this problem. It doesn't matter whether you call the benefit a transfer payment or a tax credit either. Any benefit which is means tested creates the same disincentives.

We will not eliminate high EMTRs simply by raising the tax-free threshold to, say, $13,000 as recommended by Peter Saunders in his excellent work for the CIS. The only way to completely eliminate high EMTRs would be to either remove the welfare payment completely or remove the means test. The other approach, of course, is to impose a more stringent work obligation so that the optionality (receive benefit versus work) is removed or at least heavily qualified. As Peter Costello said last night, it is inappropriate in a country with a labour shortage, facing the consequences of demographic change, to have people capable of work in the welfare system without those people having an obligation to seek work.

Neither approach is feasible (obviously) and so the avenues open to government are essentially limited to reducing the taper rate at which a benefit is lost as income increases. Over the last four years, Family Tax Benefit A, for example, has seen its taper rate reduce from 50 cents (i.e. 50 cents of benefit lost for every dollar over the means test limit) to 20 cents. However, the consequence of reducing the taper rate is to broaden the range of people who are in receipt of the benefit (a taper rate of 0 cents is equivalent to no means test, obviously). Another measure which governments can employ is to reduce 'stacking', which is to structure benefits so that their means tests cut in at different levels. However, even with different means test thresholds and lower taper rates, it is inevitable that those in receipt of multiple benefits will lose part of their benefits simultaneously.

There are real risks in reducing taper rates over and above the obvious additional cost to the Commonwealth. As Professor Dawkins recently observed, reduction in taper rates may lead some income support recipients, such as those on Newstart Allowance, to work part-time rather than full-time, representing a loss to the productive capacity of the labour market. The short point is this: high EMTRs are an inevitable consequence of means tested welfare payments. There is, therefore, no silver bullet.

But apart from continuing to tweak the interaction between tax and benefits to insure the loss of benefits tapers smoothly, we need to examine seriously the state of social welfare in Australia today. Let us consider a few facts about welfare:

- Australians have enjoyed enormous growth in their real incomes—more than 25 per cent over the last 10 years. They are now more than twice as high as they were in the 1960s.
- Australians are healthier now than we have ever been. Perils of obesity to one side, we are living longer and healthier than our parents and grandparents.

Yet the welfare state has never been larger:

- Forty years ago only 3 per cent of working-age adults relied mainly or wholly on welfare. Today 20 per cent of the working-age population are in receipt of income support; 70 per cent of those welfare recipients have no obligation to seek work, and almost of all that 70 per cent are made up of recipients of the Disability Support Pension or the Single Parenting Payment.
- Some parts of our welfare system are clearly anomalous. Recipients of the Disability Support Pension have more than doubled in the last 20 years to equal 5.5 per cent of the working-age population (16–64 years).
- The welfare system operates to redistribute income from the top 40 per cent of income earners to the bottom 40 per cent, with the 20 per cent in the middle getting not much more in welfare and other benefits than they pay in tax. It is also redistributive from the young and childless to the over 65s. Families with children on average are only modestly advantaged. Despite its significant redistributive effect, there is a great deal of churning in the system.
- The cost of managing the welfare system is enormous. The cost of administering the Family Tax Benefits system alone runs into hundreds of millions of dollars.
- For example, NATSEM has found that while younger people without children generally paid more in tax than they received back in welfare, and older people generally received more in welfare than they paid in tax, for people in their middle years earning and raising a family, the activities of the tax and welfare agencies tended to cancel each other out.[11] For

example, the average couple with school-age kids 5–14 received $507 a week in benefits but paid $393 in tax. A couple 55–64 with no kids received $264 in benefits but paid $223 in tax. On the other hand, a couple under 35 with no kids paid $426 in tax and received only $107 in benefits. The upshot is that singles and young childless couples are subsidising Australians over 65 to a considerable extent, and families with kids to a modest extent.

CONCLUSION

The circumstances of our times make continued economic reform a necessity—it is not an optional extra. It is vital to sustaining any prosperity, let alone the level we enjoy today. We have the opportunity, the chance, to ensure we are best positioned to deal with the challenges of demographic change. It is customary nowadays to say that demography is destiny. So it is, but the consequences of that destiny, the way in which it affects our lives and those of our children and grandchildren, will depend on the decisions we take today.

---

[1] Real full-time adult ordinary time earnings for males grew by 2 per cent per annum between March 1996 and August 2004 versus 0.3 per cent per annum between March 1983 and March 1995 (APH Library Research Note no. 10 2004–2005, Economic Indicators Whitlam to Howard).

[2] See *The Australian* 30 March 2005, 'Fertility Slump Ends in A Boom': 'For the past two consecutive quarters, about 67,000 babies were born in Australia, almost 10,000 more than for the March quarter, according to the Australian Bureau of Statistics. The surge has resulted in about 255,000 births over the past year—the largest 12-month total in nine years.'

[3] Port Jackson Partners 2005, *Reforming and Restoring Australia's Infrastructure*, Report prepared for the Business Council of Australia, March.

[4] When payroll tax on FBT was first imposed, the state government was at pains to point out that it would adopt the Commonwealth's definition of taxable benefits and would apply all ATO rulings on benefit valuation. This was done to reduce compliance costs for employers. The same rationale was applied by the NSW government when it moved from using the lower (and fairer) gross-up rate for all benefits, to applying both gross-up rates. Employers were meant to be pleased that it would be so convenient to identify the value of benefits subject to payroll tax, even though the change cost them more payroll tax. Given the speculation that the NSW government is considering eliminating the otherwise deductible rule, the previous concern to minimise the compliance costs faced by employers seems to have been moved firmly to the back seat. Very clearly, if this proposal is adopted, not only will it increase the payroll tax take in New South Wales, it will mean employers have to calculate the notional FBT taxable value of a benefit solely for the purpose of deciding what their payroll tax liability is (i.e. compliance costs will rise).

5   Productivity Commission 2005, *Economic Implications of an Ageing Australia*, Research Report, Canberra, p. 323.

6   Peter Costello, see chapter 1 of this book.

7   See, for example, my address to the Australian Population Conference in 2003. A copy can be found in the Speeches section of my website: <www.malcolmturnbull.com.au>.

8   A number of commentators, such as Peter McDonald and Rebecca Kippen, have observed that you do not need a precise equivalence between the top personal marginal rate and the corporate rate. They have recently argued that a top personal rate of 35 per cent would, in practical terms, remove the personal/corporate tax arbitrage which currently exists.

9   See Feldstein, 'Tax Avoidance and the Deadweight Loss of the Income Tax', National Bureau of Economic Research Working Papers 5055, cited in *A Flat Tax for the UK— A Practical Reality* by Richard Teather, Adam Smith Institute, 2004.

10 Teather, *A Flat Tax for the UK*, 2004.

11 Rachel Lloyd, Ann Harding and Neil Warren, 'Redistribution, the Welfare State and Lifetime Transitions', paper presented to Conference on Transitions and Risk, Melbourne, 24 February 2005.

PAPERS, PRESENTATIONS AND SPEECHES FROM THE SUSTAINING PROSPERITY CONFERENCE

Banks, Gary, Chairman, Productivity Commission
Reform Imperatives for an Ageing Australia (presentation)

Beazley, Kim, Leader of the Opposition
Sustaining Prosperity: New Reform Opportunities for Australia (speech)

Borland, Professor Jeff, Head, Department of Economics, University of Melbourne
Ten Things You Need to Know about Labour Market Programs (presentation)

Brumby MP, The Hon. John, Treasurer and Minister for Innovation, State and Regional Development
Commonwealth–State Relations: A New Co-operative Federalism (presentation)

Caldwell, Professor Brian, Managing Director, Educational Transformations Pty Ltd and **Professor Peter Dawkins**, Director and Ronald Henderson Professor, Melbourne Institute of Applied Economic and Social Research, University of Melbourne
Making Schools Better (paper)

Caldwell, Professor Brian, Managing Director, Educational Transformations Pty Ltd
Toward a New Enterprise Logic in Public Education (paper)

Chaney, Michael AO, Managing Director and Chief Executive Officer, Westfarmers
Standing Still is Not an Option (paper)

Chapman, Professor Bruce, Professor of Economics, Australian National University
A Commentary on HECS-HELP and FEE-HELP (presentation)

Combet, Greg, Secretary, Australian Council of Trade Unions
Minimum wages: Industrial Relations Reforms & Economic Issues (presentation)

Costello MP, The Hon. Peter, Treasurer and Deputy Leader of the Liberal Party
Sustaining Prosperity: New Reform Opportunities for Australia (speech)

Crawford, David, Acting President, National Competition Council
Federal–State Relations and the National Competition Policy (presentation)

Davis AC, Professor Glyn, Vice Chancellor, University of Melbourne
Regulating Universities: An Assumption and Three Propositions (paper)

Dawkins, Professor Peter, Director and Ronald Henderson Professor, Melbourne Institute of Applied Economic and Social Research, University of Melbourne and **Professor Ross Williams**, Professorial Fellow, Melbourne Institute of Applied Economic and Social Research, University of Melbourne
Towards a Level Playing Field for Australian Universities and Students (paper)

Dawkins, Professor Peter, Director and Ronald Henderson Professor, Melbourne Institute of Applied Economic and Social Research, University of Melbourne
Welfare to Work: Labour Supply Responses to Work Incentives, the MITTS Model: A Brief Description (paper)

Dutton MP, The Hon. Peter, Minister for Workforce Participation
Welfare Reform and Raising Workforce Participation (presentation)

Emerson MP, Dr Craig, House of Representatives
Sustaining Prosperity: The Way Ahead (presentation)

Freebairn, Professor John, Professor of Economics and Director, Melbourne Institute of Applied Economic and Social Research, University of Melbourne
Income Tax Reform: Base Broadening to Fund Lower Rates (paper)

Garnaut AO, Professor Ross, Professor of Economics, Australian National University
The Medium and Long Term Economic Outlook (presentation)

Gregory AO, Professor Bob, Research School of Social Science, Australian National University
Welfare Reform and Raising Workforce Participation: How Can We Move More People from Welfare to Work? (presentation)

Harding, Professor Ann, Director, NATSEM, The University of Canberra
Recent Trends in Income Inequality in Australia (presentation)

Harman, Professor Elizabeth, Vice Chancellor and President, Victoria University
The Teaching and Research Dichotomy—The Dangers of a Self-Fulfilling Prophecy (presentation)

Headey, Bruce and **Mark Wooden**, Principal Fellow and Professorial Fellow (respectively), Melbourne Institute of Applied Economic and Social Research, University of Melbourne
Income, Wealth and Joblessness: Insights from the HILDA Survey (paper)

Hendy, Peter, Chief Executive Officer, Australian Chamber of Commerce and Industry
Workforce Participation, Skill Shortages and Industrial Relations Reform (speech)

Henry, Dr Ken, Secretary, Department of the Treasury
Australia's International Engagement and Reform (paper)

Huggins AM, Jackie, Deputy Director, Aboriginal & Torres Strait Islander Studies Unit, University of Queensland
Sustaining Prosperity: New Reform Opportunities for Australia (presentation)

Kamener, Larry, Director and Vice President, Boston Consulting
Creating a Performance Development Culture (presentation)

Kelly, Paul, Editor-at-Large, *The Australian*
The Howard Surprise (paper)

Little, Ian, Secretary, Victorian Department of Treasury and Finance
Sustaining Prosperity: State Taxes (presentation)

McCallum, Andrew, President, Australian Council of Social Service
Signposts to Welfare Reform (paper)

Macklin MP, Jenny, Deputy Leader of the Opposition & Minister for Employment, Education and Training
Sustaining Prosperity: New Reform Opportunities for Australia (speech)

Madden, Dr Richard, Director, Australian Institute of Health and Welfare
Indigenous Health: Beyond Crisis Management (presentation)

Marginson, Professor Simon, Director, Centre for Research in International Education, Monash University
Universities: Potentials Created by the Nelson Reforms (paper)

Masters, Professor Geoff, Chief Executive Officer, Australian Council for Educational Research
Mathematics and Science Achievement in Australia's Schools (presentation)

Nelson MP, The Hon. Dr Brendan, Minister for Education, Science and Training
Underpinning Prosperity: Our Agenda in Education, Science and Training (speech)

Nicholson, Tony, Executive Director, Brotherhood of St Laurence
A New Social Policy For The New Economy (presentation)

O'Dea AO, Professor Kerin, Director, Menzies School of Health Research
Preventable Chronic Diseases Among Indigenous Australians: The Need for a Comprehensive National Approach (paper)

O'Loughlin, Mary Ann, Director, Allen Consulting Group
Against Unmanaged Care (presentation)

Owens, Helen, Commissioner, Productivity Commission
Technological Change in Medicine: An Opportunity or Threat for Australia's Health System? (presentation)

Pearse, Rod, CEO and Managing Director, Boral Limited and Chairman, Business Council of Australia Infrastructure Committee and **Rod Sims,** Director, Port Jackson Partners Limited
Restoring and Reforming Australia's Infrastructure (presentation)

Richardson, Chris, Director, Access Economics
IR, Welfare Reform and Participation (presentation)

Scott, Professor Tony, Health Economist, Melbourne Institute
For Love or Money? Alternative Methods of Paying Physicians (paper)

Shaw, Brendan, Senior Manager, Policy and Research, Medicines Australia
Take Your Medicine!: The PBS, Productivity and Future Prosperity (paper)

Swan MP, Wayne, Shadow Treasurer
Putting Incentive Back in the System: Tax Reform for Growth and Prosperity (presentation)

Trewin, Dennis, Australian Statistician, Australian Bureau of Statistics
Indigenous Health and Disability (presentation)

Turnbull MP, Malcolm, House of Representatives
The Way Ahead (presentation)

Printed and bound by CPI Group (UK) Ltd, Croydon, CR0 4YY

07/07/2026

14916223-0005